THE LITTLE BOOK OF

BIG
PROMOTIONS

by cheryl dangel cullen + lisa l. cyr + lisa hickey

BEVERLY MASSACHUSETTS

ROCKPORT PUBLISHERS

© 2007 by Quarry Books

First published in the United States of America by
Rockport Publishers, Inc., a member of
Quayside Publishing Group
100 Cummings Center
Suite 406-L
Beverly, Massachusetts 01915-6101
Telephone: (978) 282-9590
Fax: (978) 283-2742
www.rockpub.com

Library of Congress Cataloging-in-Publication data available

ISBN-13: 978-1-59253-355-8
ISBN-10: 1-59253-355-8

10 9 8 7 6 5 4 3 2

Cover Design: Dania Davey
Layout: Art & Anthropology
         Sussner Design Company
         Leeann Leftwich Zajas

Special thanks and acknowledgment is given to Cheryl Dangel Cullen for her work from *Promotion Design That Works* on pages 288–347; to Lisa L. Cyr for her work from *The Art of Promotion* on pages 6–149; and to Lisa Hickey for her work from *Designs That Stand Up, Speak Out, and Can't Be Ignored: Promotions* on pages 152–285.

Printed in China

contents

"I propose a toaster," she announced

Crisply.

"Just look what I bring to the table," she boosted

Saucily.

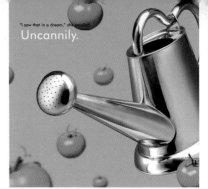

"I saw that in a dream," she recalled

Uncannily.

Introduction

positioning yourself in the creative marketplace

With the overall decline in the global economy, many creatives find themselves at a crossroad. Work is no longer abundant, and budgets have decreased significantly from years past. In the boom of the early 1990s, the biggest concern for most was simply coping with the workload and managing growth. In today's volatile marketplace, creatives now face many more challenges. To survive, they are reevaluating their approach to promotion and restructuring their position in the marketplace. They are beginning to take an honest look not only at how they work, what they have to uniquely offer, and the markets and clients they choose to work with but also introspectively at their creative interests and aspirations, belief system, and their definition of what it means to be successful. In these uncertain times, many are pausing to reshape their business so as to enrich their lives.

To combat the instability in the marketplace, many creatives are choosing to venture into entrepreneurial initiatives. They are transcending traditional nomenclature to discover new markets and diversify their offerings. Everything from direct-to-consumer merchandising, self-publishing, and licensing are being explored. To stay on top of future opportunities, many are adopting an ongoing research component as a part of their regular planning process.

When it comes to promotion, creating distinction is key. Because of the tremendous distractions going on in the world, promotions need to be truly unique and thought-provoking in order to capture the attention of any audience. To create distinction and call attention to their brand, creatives are producing memorable promotions that reveal something about their firm and its personality. These are not only highly innovative from a production standpoint but also keenly strategic where the overall messaging is mindful of a prospective client's needs. Many promotions serve secondary functions—as demonstrations of a firm's capabilities or as keepsakes that significantly increase longevity and effectiveness. Creatives are rethinking function and making strides into what is possible in form.

Many are realizing the importance of contact strategies in an age where electronic communication has become prevalent. To make their promotions more personalized, many firms are no longer producing mass mailings but instead creating smaller, more targeted promotions. They are also thinking in terms of a campaign, uniting all their messaging and correspondence to ensure clarity and consistency within the marketplace. Follow-up procedures are also becoming a regular part of the process. To maintain that vital connection with prospective and existing clients, creatives are finding almost any notable occasion worthy of a promotional message, from moving announcements, anniversary celebrations, and holiday greetings to the announcement of awards and achievements and the addition of new staff members. Personalized thank-you notes and expressions of gratitude are also going a long way in making lasting impressions with clients. Many firms are hiring personnel to cultivate new business, and more time is being given to other forms of promotion, like networking and public relations. After the events of September 11, 2001, people in general are seeing the need to work together—and creatives are also beginning to appreciate the benefits of collaboration. They are starting to focus their efforts on internal team-building as well as establishing relationships with sources outside their discipline.

Whether a company is new and embarking on a launch or a seasoned firm in the midst of a rebranding effort, market positioning can be challenging. It requires intensive thought and focus, evaluation, planning, and commitment in order to move forward. But for those who are willing to venture out with a unique voice and vision, it can be an enlightening and even empowering experience. Don't allow yourself to get caught up in the day-to-day so much that you lose sight of what is important. You have the power within you to design your own creative path and business future. Just remember to focus, plan, commit—and, most of all, believe in yourself.

PART I

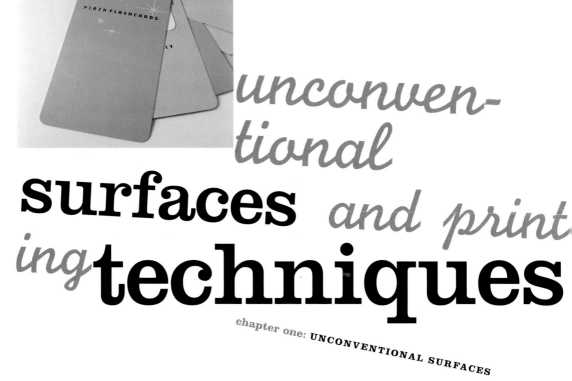

unconventional

surfaces _and print_

ing**techniques**

chapter one: UNCONVENTIONAL SURFACES

There is an ever-growing interest in exploring unconventional materials, surfaces, and techniques to create distinction. Creatives are looking to sources outside the communications industry, and they are finding interesting alternatives. They are experimenting with various techniques on a vast array of materials from metal, wood, and plastic to leather, handmade and custom paper, and laminated duplexes of every kind. Tactile processes like etching, laser cutting, sculpted embossing, and embroidery are becoming more widely used, and old techniques like wood type and letterpress are being revisited. Inks are glowing in the dark, glitter infused, heat sensitive, and scratching off to reveal an underlying message. Print is also becoming more animated with lenticular printing and three-dimensional with anaglyphic stereo usage. Technological innovations make the possibilities endless.

To keep abreast of what is out there, build relationships with suppliers from different disciplines and collect catalogs from myriad sources. Most importantly, don't be afraid to make mistakes when you are treading new ground. "The fear of making mistakes will always bring you to walk in the middle of the road," comments designer Mirko Ilić. "I always give myself the freedom to make mistakes in order for something unusual to happen." Finding new ways to combine different materials and techniques can give any project the edge that it needs to stand out in the marketplace.

marking
freedom

The construction that houses the calendar is heavy and blocklike to symbolize a wall. Throughout the solid structure is hand-lettering, a unique mixture of Latin and Cyrillic characters, giving the text an Eastern European flair. Specially mixed ink is used to imprint the letters, simulating the look of graphite. Glow-in-the-dark ink is also applied, illuminating the bricks of a wall. On the spine, two die-cut holes imply something interesting inside. The piece is written in both the English and Serbian language.

Every year since 1993, Publikum, a major printing company in Belgrade, produces a calendar of exceptional artistic merit that traditionally featured Yugoslavia's artistic heritage and rich pop culture. However, by 2001 many things had changed, and the calendar needed to reflect the new era. For Serbians, it was a new world without boundaries. "I started to work on the calendar in the year they brought down Milosevic," says designer Mirko Ilić. "I was in charge of developing the concept, and my first idea was to bring in something new, fresh ideas and new people, for an exchange of things to happen." With the concept of overcoming barriers at the forefront, Ilić entitled the calendar *ANTIWALL*. With the goal of opening doors to different perspectives, the imagery was selected to really push the envelope, be innovative, and, most importantly, take risks. Artists from all over the world were asked to submit work. Twelve were chosen, one for each month.

To communicate the weight and solidity of a wall, Ilić designed a construction that was almost blocklike to house the calendar of new life and contemporary art. "I wanted it to look like a part of the wall, like one of the bricks," he comments. Glow-in-the-dark ink was used throughout the piece to represent a beacon of light for those still trying to find a way out of the darkness. "One is a physical wall and the other is a wall that you create for yourself," explains Ilić. To protect the ink from being scratched, the front and back covers of the book were laminated. Two holes were die-cut from the spine as a device to entice the viewer to explore further.

From the left-hand side pocket, the square-shaped calendar unfolds. The stunning cover reveals a glow-in-the-dark wall with the names of the participating artists peering through. The images, thought-provoking and controversial, help illuminate each month, reveling in the vast opportunities that a new day brings. All the text is hand-lettered to give the project a human touch. To achieve this, Ilić designed a custom font, set the type in Quark, outputted at 150 percent, and had his staff laboriously trace each page in pencil onto translucent paper. Each sheet of tracing paper was then scanned into the computer and reduced to the appropriate size, giving the project a unique, handcrafted look.

Conceived with the idea that art has the power to promote change, the bilingual 2001 calendar serves not only as a reminder of the turmoil and destruction of the past but also as a source for inspiration and hope in the potential that a world without boundaries brings. At a televised celebration, the calendars were stacked like bricks in a wall. They were given to a select group of people, as were specifically designed shopping bags that also glowed in the dark. Exactly 2,001 calendars were produced.

TECHNICAL TIPS

Glow-in-the-dark ink is made by mixing translucent ink with a special powder. The surface can glow for long periods in the dark and has a shelf life of about two to five years, depending on where the printed piece is kept. To obtain the most luminosity from the specialty ink, make sure it is applied directly on a white surface. Use an overall varnish or lamination to seal and protect the surface.

When you are creating a unique construction, make several prototypes, analyzing the piece from the perspective of the recipient. If you want to avoid fold marks, try a heavy perforation that stops shy of the sides of the paper; this allows the calendar to fold away nicely without leaving a mark once it's hung on a wall. It also adds a nice decorative accent to the page.

DO IT FOR LESS

Many of the unique features of this piece were executed by hand. Using a standard font instead of hand-lettering would save tremendously in labor costs. To cut costs further, the calendar itself could be made smaller, eliminating the need for perforation.

When you open the piece, you see markings—2001, to be exact—that symbolize many years in captivity. The text, which begins in English and ends in Serbian, reads "The time is now." A perfect-bound book of new art and contemporary life is adhered to the right side. Inside the left-hand pocket lies a matching glow-in-the-dark calendar. To ensure that unwanted folds would not remain once the calendar is fully open, the designer utilizes a heavy perforation instead of a score. Loose cardboard is positioned in the back to keep the calendar erect; a wire rod is placed inside the spiral binding, allowing the piece to hang.

2

1

FIRM: MIRKO ILIĆ CORPORATION

CREATIVE DIRECTOR: STANISLAV SHARP, FIA ART GROUP

PROJECT COORDINATOR: NADA RAJIČIĆ FIA ART GROUP

DESIGNER/FONT DESIGNER: MIRKO ILIĆ

HAND LETTERING: MIRKO ILIĆ, RINGO TAKAHASHI, RYUTA NAKAZAWA, ASA HASIMOTO, AND JELENA ČAMBA DJORDJEVIĆ

ILLUSTRATION: SLAVIMIR STOJANOVIĆ

FEATURED ARTISTS: WIM WENDERS, VIK MUNIZ, BJORK, DRAGON ZIVADINOV, NATACHA MERRITT, MARINA ABRAMOVIĆ, BARBARA KRUGER, AES GROUP, TADANORI YOKOO, OLIVIERO TOSCANI, CHRISTO AND JEANNE-CLAUDE, AND DAVID BYRNE

PRINTING AND BINDERY: PUBLIKUM

wood type: redefined

A simple, yet elegant, brochure is used to promote a limited-edition series of typographic prints by designer Dennis Y. Ichiyama. Each brochure is housed in a three-panel, letterpress-printed wrap that piques curiosity, enticing the reader to investigate further. Inside, background information on the artist's experience at the museum and the work he created unfolds. Each four-color image was made with a Xerox technology.

After an artist-in-residence stay at the Hamilton Wood Type & Printing Museum, designer and educator Dennis Y. Ichiyama was hooked. Since 1999, he has been working with wood type, redefining its traditional nomenclature and reintroducing the almost extinct process back into the culture. "Its history and tradition are imbedded in stereotypical references that make for a great challenge," says Ichiyama.

With over a million pieces of wood type and ornaments to choose from, Ichiyama rolled up his sleeves and went to work. Free to determine his own design problem and approach, he seized the opportunity to play and experiment. "Rather than to letter a word, text, or paragraph, I decided that the letterforms themselves were interesting and unique enough just as shapes," he recalls. "They took me back to a period of my childhood when letters were combinations of curves, angles, horizontals, and verticals that did not create words but compositions of form and color."

Pure Type Forms, a series of typographic limited-edition prints, was the result of Ichiyama's efforts. Each print explores the elegance and beauty that wood type can bring to a surface. As a finishing touch, they are signed, dated, and imprinted in red with the artist's family seal. "I have always felt that as a designer I want to blend East and West," adds Ichiyama. "Whenever I sign my work, I sign it in both a Western calligraphic form and a geometric eastern form with my seal." The series of prints is housed in a custom presentation folder, adding elegance to the overall package.

To promote the work, a simple, yet elegant, brochure was created and presented within a three-panel, letterpress-printed wrap. Inside the accordion-folded brochure, the artist and his experience with wood type was revealed. To be cost effective, the four-color images within the brochure were photocopied and hand-tipped into each piece.

Ichiyama's most recent work, entitled *More Pure Type Forms*, evolved from typographic experimentation to the design of limited-edition keepsakes. To present these latest endeavors to the marketplace, the designer developed another promotional package. To maintain continuity, the overall design and format are consistent with the first promotion.

Because of Ichiyama's efforts, printing with wood type, once a vintage process, has now been rejuvenated and brought back to the masses for many to enjoy for years to come. "For me, it has been a low-tech activity that stirs the emotions and the soul," shares Ichiyama. "My course in typography [at Purdue University] has been enriched and my approach to graphic design has been expanded."

TECHNICAL TIPS

When working with wood type, do not expect perfection. Instead, embrace the wonderful irregularities and transparent overlays it creates. After several rounds of wiping and reinking, an interesting patina develops on the wood surface that gives an artistic quality to the resulting impression. If you are interested in knowing more about the history of wood type or obtaining access to a diverse collection, the Hamilton Wood Type & Printing Museum is a wonderful place to start.

The portfolio contains typographic artwork printed on superfine, soft white 80-lb. and ultrawhite, smooth 65-lb. cover using the museum's Vandercook SP 15 letterpress. Each print is housed inside a folder labeled with the appropriate number in silver. An introduction is also included to help explain the experimental endeavor. Everything is packaged in a three-panel, letter-folded wrap.

To present his most recent work, the designer developed a second promotional package. This brochure focuses on the development of limited-edition keepsakes created in conjunction with several events. Presented here are prints for the Society of Typographic Arts, the University of Reading's conference on printing history, and a remembrance piece from the tragedy of September 11, 2001 entitled *Tribute in Light*. For the sake of continuity, the design and format are consistent with that of the first promotion.

Because of the attention the typographic work has generated, the artist has been asked to work on several outside projects. This keepsake was created to celebrate the seventy-fifth anniversary of the Society of Typographic Arts.

1

FIRM: DENNIS Y. ICHIYAMA

CREATIVE DIRECTOR AND DESIGNER:
DENNIS Y. ICHIYAMA

ILLUSTRATION: DENNIS Y. ICHIYAMA

PRINTING: HAMILTON WOOD TYPE &
PRINTING MUSEUM

2

3

4

plainly
stated

The promotional ensemble is contained in a silk-screened, standard-size box. When you open the box, you are presented with an introduction card that is individually numbered with a letterpress printing process. The piece closes with a reply card that can be sent back to the design firm for follow-up purposes. An overview brochure provides insight to the history of the New England–based firm and the origins of the name Plainspoke. The piece is shipped in a corrugated material that wraps around and seals at the ends. Only one thousand pieces were produced.

"Plainspoke is a little different. As a name, it stands out, and we wanted to build upon that," shares art director and designer Matt Ralph. "With this promotion, I wanted to do something that was clever, well designed, and that would really make an impact. I did not want it to be hard sell, with a laundry list of capabilities. I wanted our greatness to come through in the quality of the piece." Because the firm was also looking to expand into new markets, the promotion had to be flexible enough for projects to be added or changed as necessary. Using various papers, bindery, and formats, the design firm developed an interesting promotional ensemble based on their distinctive name. "We thought it would be fun to create a kit of things where everything was built upon the whole idea of *plain*," Ralph adds.

To get the concept off the ground, the design team began with a brainstorming session, thinking of objects that could be associated with the word *plain*. Using the plain box as a point of departure, they chose an array of pieces that were interesting, different in shape and texture, and that fit inside a standard-size box. The resulting collection—a Plainspoke company brochure, a plain sight eye chart, a plain bag of notecards and envelopes, plain pencils, a plain pages notebook, and plain flashcards—all fit nicely inside a plain box. Each piece within the promotional package utilizes a different material and printing surface. The silk-screened bag provides a rugged texture while the flashcards bring a glossy finish to the overall matte presentation. The bindery ranges from the traditional saddle-stitching of the company brochure and the spiral-bound notebook to the less typical ring-bound flashcards and the drawstring bag. When you open the promotion, you are immediately presented with an introduction card that describes the contents as "a celebration of all things plain." The piece closes with a reply card that is user-friendly and quite entertaining, as it plays up on the *plain* concept one last time. "The piece is one big hit, and it really makes an impression," admits Ralph.

With this idea-driven collection, Plainspoke was not only able to make their name memorable through repetition of message but also to showcase to clients an array of reproductive possibilities. Because the piece was designed to be flexible, the *plain* concept can be extended to smaller promotions that can be sent more frequently. "With some clients, you just need to work on them overtime," Ralph points out.

3

2

The plain sight eye chart positions Plainspoke, as the solution to a prospective client's creative needs. The accordion-folded chart conveniently pulls out from a custom-designed sleeve. The grommet allows the piece to be hung if desired.

3

The silk-screened plain bag contains notecards, envelopes, and vellum sheets. The pencils are housed in a glassine envelope and sealed with a label. The plain pages notebook is spiral-bound; a wraparound label adorns the cover.

4

The retro-looking flashcards, printed on 18-point Chromolux 700 paper that is coated on one side, provides a fun and upbeat accent to the presentation. Printed in an array of soft tones, the flashcards continue the plain theme, cleverly utilizing word and image to deliver the message. Each card is drilled and bound with a ring.

1

FIRM: PLAINSPOKE

ART DIRECTOR: MATT RALPH

DESIGNERS: MATT RALPH AND NICOLE COMTOIS

PHOTOGRAPHY: BRIAN WILDER AND VARIOUS STOCK

PRINTING: PENMOR LITHOGRAPHERS (COMPANY BROCHURE, FLASHCARDS, LABEL, NOTECARDS, AND ENVELOPES), MARAN PRINTING SERVICE (EYE CHART, INTRODUCTION CARD, AND REPLY CARD), BLUE DOLPHIN SCREENPRINT (CLOTH BAG)

MANUFACTURERS: MASON BOX COMPANY (KRAFT BOX), SHIP-IT (CLOTH BAG), AMERICAN PRINTING AND ENVELOPE COMPANY (GLASSINE ENVELOPE), ROBBINS CONTAINER CORP. (CORRUGATED MAILING WRAP), AND CYRK (BLACK PENCILS)

2

4

organized
for success

"Most of the time, our clients are looking for us to take charge of a project, so we looked for ways to facilitate that," admits creative director Dann Ilicic. To get their clients and their staff focused and organized for success, the branding firm decided that a notebook would be the perfect vehicle. "We want to communicate that the whole process of branding is really about getting things organized so everybody can understand what needs to be done," Ilicic explains. "The whole notion of the notebook is to get both sides to know what questions to ask."

With the desired format underway, the next challenge was deciding on just the right look and feel. As part of their identity, the company had already produced business cards made of stainless steel. These were such a hit with existing and prospective clientele that it seemed appropriate to produce the notebook in the same material. However, when they tried to use the metal surface as a notebook cover, they realized it was much too heavy a substrate and was crushing the binding coils. After further research, the design team identified a better alternative: lightweight aluminum. The new material had the desired metallic look and feel, but without excess weight—a perfect solution. The 7 $\frac{1}{2}$- by 9 $\frac{1}{2}$-inch (19 by 24 centimeter) metal notebook was laser-cut with the company's logo and polished with sandpaper for a brushed look. Rounded corners were carried throughout to avoid sharp edges and keep the notebook smooth to the touch. An indention on the cover allowed easy access to the inside pages. To save money, the back cover was made of a heavy black stock.

Inside the notebook lies the heart of the project. When it comes to making things happen, Wow! believes you have to be clear about your desired outcome, know your next action, and assign responsibility and deadlines to each task. "It has been our experience that if people can't answer those questions, chances are the desired outcome will not be achieved," claims Ilicic. With this principle in mind, the design team developed an easy-to-use process whereby the user merely plugs in responses to certain simplified questions. Each spread was not only visually interesting but also highly functional. "Our company is called Wow! and one of the things we promote is creating distinction," shares Ilicic. "The desired response is to have clients look at us and think, 'Wow! These people are really thinking.'" Always given out personally at client meetings and presentations, the notebook serves as an excellent vehicle for making any desired outcome a reality.

1

2

The metal notebook cover is laser-cut and polished for a brushed effect. The book is wire-o bound with two pieces, giving the cover added support to prevent it from warping. The notebook is given to new and existing clients and is also used internally by the staff.

The action-driven notebook helps the branding firm and its clients get mobilized by asking a series of questions. To maintain the highest level of detail, the inside is stochastic printed. The firm created a two-color effect on an essentially one-color job by using a stock with a preprinted grid pattern—70-lb. Strathmore Elements text.

1

FIRM: WOW! A BRANDING COMPANY

CREATIVE DIRECTOR: DANN ILICIC

DESIGNER: PERRY CHUA

PRINTING: GENERATION TING LTD. (NOTEBOOK TEXT PAGES)

BINDERY: WARD DIGITAL

SPECIAL TECHNIQUES AND MANUFACTURER:

INDUSTRIAL LASER CUTTING (METAL)

2

play on words

A clear foil stamp accents the 20-point matte Calendered vinyl cover. The pressure and heat used in the stamping process also created a nice debossed effect, an unexpected bonus.

Creative director and illustrator Bob Hambly wanted to create a highly imaginative self-promotion to show off his graphic signature style. "It all started with my sketchbook," he recalls. "I was fooling around with words and I came up with the idea of creating arranged marriages." Out of a list of about fifty potential ideas, the artist selected those with the most broadest-based appeal. Working on a light table with a big chiseled marker, Hambly brought to life his creative play on words. Once he was satisfied with the gesture and look of the line art, each image was then scanned into the computer, streamlined, and colored. Using a diverse range of subject matter, Hambly developed fifteen hybrid images that cleverly illustrate how two seemingly opposing objects can be put together. "It helps to have a theme or a storyline to show art directors that you can solve a problem as opposed to just showing pretty pictures," he adds.

With an interesting collection of words and images under his belt, Hambly's next challenge was to put them together in a package that enhanced the illustrative content. "Because I work in a design studio, I am surrounded by lots of materials and promotions. One in particular, a paper promotion, used plastic that was not only silk-screen-printed but also embossed and debossed. It intrigued me, and I told my printer about it," notes Hambly. Working collaboratively, the printer and illustrator experimented with several effects. The result features a clear foil stamp that gives dimension to the illustrated plastic cover.

To maintain the cover's velvety look and feel, the interior illustrated pages are laminated. "Knowing that the pages would be constantly turning and pivoting, we wanted to make sure we put a coating over the ink so it would not scratch," offers Hambly. The interior was printed on Utopia One dull cover using a metallic blue and dark brown palette. The overall piece was trimmed with a custom die and bound with Chicago screws. To ensure that each page lined up perfectly, the hole that helps bind the piece was punched out as part of the die; drilling would have left too much room for error in the final product. The circular die around the binding, the rounded corners, and the circular page numbers work together to highlight the illustrator's fluid line work and soften the overall graphic presentation. "People will always want to keep and remember something that is well done," concludes Hambly. "The idea, execution, materials, and all the little details and final touches are important because they speak indirectly about how much you care about your work."

TECHNICAL TIPS

When blind-embossing plastic, it is important to run tests on the material. If the pressure is too strong, the plastic will crack, ripple, and warp. If it is not strong enough, you will not be able to see what you are applying to the surface. Die-cutting windows or shapes into the interior of plastic is not a forgiving technique, as the cut marks can be quite evident.

DO IT FOR LESS

By eliminating the plastic cover, you could save quite a bit. Instead of laminating each page, a varnish could be applied to both sides. Getting rid of the rounded edges and the need for a custom die would also save money.

The illustrated promotion is printed on Utopia One dull cover in metallic blue and dark brown. To ensure solid coverage, the brown is double hit. Each page is coated with matte OPP laminate (1.5 millimeter) as a visual and tactile tie to the plastic cover. The coating also helps protect the pages from scratches and tears.

The simple graphic renderings challenge the viewer's perception in a smart, attractive fashion. On the back, the associated word-play is revealed.

1

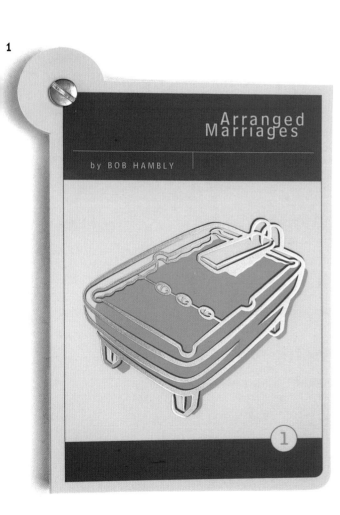

2

3

FIRM: HAMBLY & WOOLLEY, INC.

CREATIVE DIRECTOR: BOB HAMBLY

DESIGNERS: JASON ZALESKI AND ROB WILSON

ILLUSTRATION: BOB HAMBLY

PRINTING: SOMERSET GRAPHICS CO. LTD.

putting creativity to work

Over the last decade, Jason & Jason Visual Communications has experienced substantial and continuous growth not only in the staff they employ but also in the clients they serve. To more accurately reflect their global expansion and full-service capabilities, the communications firm set their sights on an extensive marketing campaign, including a highly impressive promotional kit to be used by the sales staff. "It is just one part of a highly focused and comprehensive sales and marketing program we embarked on three years ago when we launched our Web site," notes creative director Jonathan Jason. "Since that time, we have been engaged in direct marketing: e-mail campaigns, direct mail, promotional give-aways, print advertising, and personal tele-marketing."

After researching and analyzing their internal operations, existing client base, and the overall competitive landscape, the firm concluded that "we needed to communicate who we are and what we do, showing tangibles and backing up our claims with client case studies and projects," shares Jason. "This meant being able to present our value proposition in a way that would allow our customers to see and understand for themselves the added value of working with a company like ours." The firm also needed to reposition them-selves from a "passive supplier of commodity-like promotional items to an active provider of creative and customer-focused business solutions," Jason adds. "Great Ideas at Work" became the title and slogan of the project. When applied to secondary messaging like "Focus Your Vision, Build Your Brand, and Empower Your Company," the promotion really pinpointed the value that Jason & Jason Visual Communications could bring to any company.

With clearly defined objectives and a solid marketing strategy in place, the firm focused on the promotion's hierarchy and dissemination of information. To keep the content simple and organized, it was divided into three independently functioning pieces—a company overview brochure, a projects and supportive case studies brochure, and a new works booklet—that could also work together as a cohesive unit. "Breaking the material into sections helps the reader compartmentalize relevant information that may otherwise be lost," offers Jason. "In addition, we felt a project presentation made of multiple pieces was more interesting and gave the reader a feeling of being on a journey." The multipieced assemblage not only makes the presentation interactive but also gives maximum flexibility when material requires updating and revision, increasing the longevity of the promotion. In addition, an enclosed CD-ROM provides access to the company's multimedia presentation, a way to dissem-inate current information to interested parties.

The engaging, three-dimensional presentation folder, entitled *Great Ideas at Work,* houses a company overview brochure with an interactive demo on CD-ROM, a projects brochure, a new works biannual booklet, and a business card. Each piece fits nicely within the package in an almost Mondrian-like fashion. The folder is printed in five colors, process plus PMS 877 silver onto 450-gram Bristol semimatte coated stock. On the cover, the word *inspire* is highlighted through the application of UV lacquer. Inside, chartreuse complements the overall silver color scheme.

Entitled *Define, Develop, Deploy,* the projects brochure presents three case studies and the firm's portfolio of work from a targeted array of industries. Each case study not only includes an overview and strategic objectives but also out-lines how the firm solved the communications problem. This is enhanced by a double-page spread highlighting measurable results for the client. The matte-laminated and selective UV-lacquered wraparound cover employs a hidden spiral binding, protecting the pieces within the package from scratches and snags. The piece is organized in three sections separated by French-folded pages.

2

1

FIRM: JASON & JASON VISUAL COMMUNICATION

CREATIVE DIRECTOR: JONATHAN JASON

DESIGNERS: JONATHAN JASON AND TAMAR LOURIE

PHOTOGRAPHY: YORAM RESHEF

PRINTING: AR PRINTING LTD.

PRODUCTION: TOP IN (IMAGE SCANNING AND COLOR TESTS)

BINDERY: SABAG (SPIRAL BINDING)

SPECIAL TECHNIQUES: HI-TEC (DIE-CUT AND LAMINATION)

With the content divided into understandable parts, the designers next worked to develop the look and feel of the piece. A square grid design was chosen and the company's existing corporate color scheme and visual brand identity was applied. Throughout the promotional package, design elements repeat from piece to piece, giving the overall presentation a unified look. The messaging, design, and innovation in production were a tribute to the communications firm's keen attention to both strategic and creative detail. The marketing ensemble, a source of pride for the agency, was personally presented to prospective clients—mostly multinational business-to-business companies in the technology, biotechnology, pharmaceuticals, finance, and real estate industries.

DO IT FOR LESS

With a project of this magnitude, look to your suppliers for professional discounts. Increased work for you also results in a surge in work for them—a win-win situation all around. Other ways to reduce costs include maximizing your press sheet, eliminating the film stage of the process by going direct to plate, and utilizing digital photography wherever possible.

3

The corporate overview brochure, designed to function as a stand-alone piece as well, provides prospective clients with insight into the firm's corporate culture, value offerings, international staff, and working methodologies. The booklet employs foldover flaps for both the front and back cover; these not only add structural strength to the piece but also function as bookmarks and convenient places to hold the agency's multimedia presentation CD-ROM and a business card. On the cover, a tinted UV gloss lacquer draws attention to the brochure's theme, entitled *Focus, Build, Empower*. For protection, a matte lamination is applied inside and out.

A minibrochure, entitled *New Work*, is designed to be a cost-effective way to highlight recent work. On the cover, matte lamination is added for durability while a UV lacquer highlights key text and graphic elements on both the front and back. The flaps that extend the cover repeat a design element that echoes through the entire project. This is the first in a series that will be distributed every six months.

4

defining your niche

To survive in today's marketplace, you need to establish what makes you different from the competition. The best way to get in tune with your unique voice and vision is to take an honest look at not only your working process and approach, experience and capabilities, and client relations and market preferences but also your core beliefs and values, creative interests, and aspirations. These are, collectively, what make your offerings distinctive. If you present the marketplace with nothing unique, you open yourself up to becoming a sophisticated order taker, leaving the opportunity for buyers to price-shop alternatives. "You have to closely define what your goals are and where you really want to go," says Lars Harmsen of MAGMA. "For us, it was very important to determine our identity before we began working for clients, so that in the first contact, we could communicate our spirit and our meaning of design." By defining your niche, you are setting a foundation on which to strategically position and build your brand.

With an identity clearly delineated, you have a working model to turn to when it comes to promotional messaging. The biggest mistake any firm or freelancer can make is to promote an identity that is not genuine. To project one image and live another will result only in a great lack of authenticity and major disconnections down the road. "The traditional view of branding is that it is the icing on the cake—the logo, colors, and the things that people see. But the branding of the inside—the people, process, and culture—is just as important because it is the repeat business side," observes Dann Ilicic of Wow! A Branding Company. "You must walk the walk as well as talk the talk to make your brand live." For the creative team at Red Canoe, establishing a clearly defined mission statement was essential to staying focused and on track. Partners Deb Koch and Caroline Kavanagh made the decision early on that it was important to them to break away from the fast-paced, stress-inducing hustle and bustle of the everyday work scene to create an environment that would energize their spirit and fill their soul. A cabin, situated among 350 acres of breathtaking panoramic views, became their tranquil place of business and source of inspiration. Since 1997, Red Canoe's philosophical mission and tagline, "As we live, so we work," has been the foundation that has shaped their business plan to fit and enrich their lives.

Being selective in your approach to new business is key. By developing relationships with clients who share your vision, you begin to build recognition and market value. "In the beginning, we purposely turned away a lot of work, and that was very difficult. But now it has come full circle and we are able to capitalize on being known for what we do," acknowledges Ilicic. "We built a dream list of clients we really wanted to work for, and we purposely pitched those businesses." By actively pursuing work they are sincerely passionate about, the relatively new company has been able to launch their practice into the limelight with numerous accolades. "Doing the work you love begets like-minded clients and projects, creating the opportunity to do more," says Koch. "Sticking to that seemingly simple rule isn't always simple, but it is always worth it."

During the day-to-day madness, with the phone ringing and e-mails piling up, it is easy to lose clarity of vision. To maintain focus, many creatives are thinking outside the box—trying everything from team-building exercises, group sketchbooks, and show-and-tell to group challenges, field trips, and mobilized meetings, where business is conducted during the course of a brisk walk. "Every quarter, we go away overnight as a group to examine our business practices, talk about future goals, and examine where we want to be," says Sheree Clark of Sayles Graphic Design. "The agenda changes every time. If we have a new staff person, we will do some team assimilation of that person into our corporate culture. If we have run into a lot of production snags, we will sit down and talk about our processes and see what we need to do to tighten them up. As a result, we are closer as a group." Ric Riordon of the Riordon Design Group adds, "We want to make sure our designers are continuing to look and to be inspired. So we use a sketchbook as a creative catalyst within the studio. Every day, somebody adds something to it—a sketch, poetry, or prose. They look during the week for something that inspires them. When that sketchbook lands on their desk, it gets fed."

In a highly competitive marketplace that speaks to reduced budgets, creatives must, more than ever, set themselves apart from the competition. Rethinking one's brand and identity from the inside out requires brutal honesty, intensive evaluation, and commitment. For those willing to embrace the challenges rather than being threatened by them, prosperity will yield growth and renewal.

creating distinction

Wow! A Branding Company specializes in developing innovative practices geared toward helping companies understand, implement, and manage their brand. When it came time to establish their own identity and business system, Wow! put their time-proven process to work. "A lot of people start with a logo and try to work everything around that," says creative director Dann Ilicic. "We call the logo the punctuation to the identity, not the identity."

For their business card, Wow! began by setting all existing assumptions aside to reexamine form, function, and its relevance in today's business world. "The things that we questioned were why business cards are made out of paper, why they are typically 2 by 3 ½ inches (5 by 9 centimeter), and why they need to fit inside a Rolodex when everyone uses some form of electronic organizer," details Ilicic. "The ultimate function of a business card is to create an impression, so we pushed the design team to start looking for alternatives." In search of something distinctive, they explored materials from rubber and plastic to metal. A stainless steel surface was the clear winner.

To transform the metallic surface into a functional card, the design team looked at a variety of techniques before deciding on laser cutting. "It was difficult in the beginning because we really didn't know what we were asking for," recalls Ilicic. "It took a few months to figure out just how to do it." The metallic cards were laser-cut from a 4- by 8-foot (1.2- by 2.4-meter) sheet of stainless steel, leaving a slight tab around each card for silk-screen

printing purposes. To smooth the rough edges, a process called tumbling was employed. This had a dulling effect on the surface, so a varnish was later sprayed on top to bring back luster and protect the silk-screen-printed type from scratching off.

To complete their stationery package, Wow! developed letterhead with an unconventional horizontal orientation—a reflection of today's digital letter-writing preference. Rather than standard #10 envelopes, the branding firm chose silver antistatic bags that were blind embossed with the company's logo. By questioning traditional practices and venturing outside the norm, Wow! was able to develop an identity system that stood out from the competition. "Whenever anyone asks for our card, it is hard not to smile because we know the reaction we are going to get," says Ilicic. "We find that when we go to net-working events and functions, the cards always end up traveling throughout the room."

If you present the marketplace with nothing unique, you open yourself up to becoming a sophisticated order taker, leaving the opportunity for buyers to price-shop alternatives.

FIRM: WOW! A BRANDING COMPANY

CREATIVE DIRECTOR: DANN ILICIC

DESIGNER: PERRY CHUA

PRINTING: SPECIAL SCREENCRAFT PRINTING (CARD)

SPECIAL TECHNIQUES AND MANUFACTURER:

INDUSTRIAL LASER CUTTING (METAL)

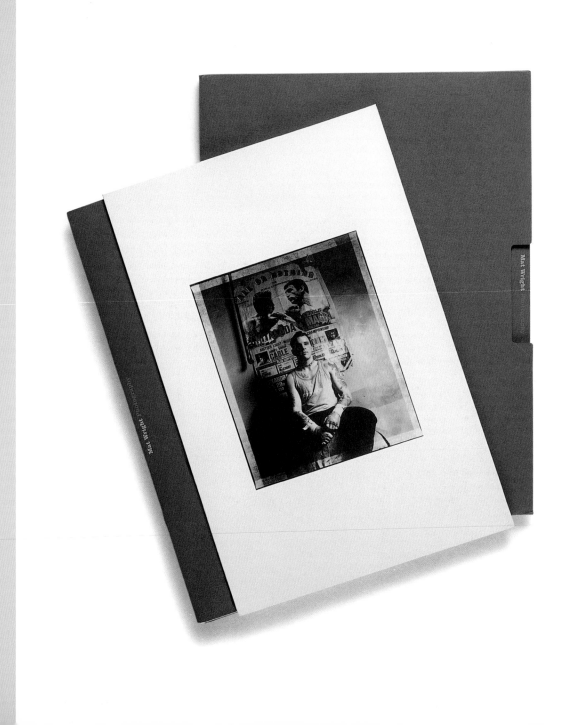

Being selective in your approach to new business is key. By developing relationships with clients who share your vision, you begin to build recognition and market value.

choosing the right projects

It is important to be selective about the projects you choose to work on, as they can dictate the type of work that will come in the future. Although this brochure was designed to raise awareness for Mat Wright as a photographer, it was also a great demonstration of Origin's capabilities as a design company. "We use this piece as a promotional item to reflect our philosophy, level of craft, and attention to detail," explains creative director and designer Mark Bottomley.

To drive the messaging of the piece, the designer came up with the theme of talking pictures. "Mat is a great portrait photographer and also a very no-nonsense person. He doesn't dress his work up with fancy words or explanations. He just takes great pictures," says Bottomley. "It's quite simple. The pictures just speak for themselves." Because the work didn't need any commentary for it to communicate to its audience, the piece became a picture book. To deliver just the right look and feel, the designer researched paper and bindery options for materials that would complement Wright's dramatic photographic style. To create the front and back covers, Curtis Malts Spirit 100-gram uncoated stock was adhered over 3-millimeter gray board. Both pieces were bound to a Curtis Malts Islay 300-gram inner cover, leaving a large silk-screen-printed spine showing on the left-hand side. Saddle stitching was used to bind the inside pages to the inner cover. Overall, the promotion boasted a distinctive and innovative presentation.

To protect and add the final finishing touch to the photographic picture book, a matching slipcase was created. "The activity of pulling the book out makes the viewer feel the paper and really appreciate the piece as a whole," adds the designer. "It also gives the book a much greater impact overall." By being selective in their approach to new business, Origin was able to add to their portfolio with work that really showcases their creative abilities.

CLIENT: MAT WRIGHT PHOTOGRAPHY
FIRM: ORIGIN
CREATIVE DIRECTOR AND DESIGNER:
MARK BOTTOMLEY
PHOTOGRAPHY: MAT WRIGHT
PRINTING AND BINDERY: APS GROUP

practicing what you preach

The fun, diverse, and eclectic group at Brown & Company Design has found creative and inventive ways in which to express their personality in almost everything they do, from the way they pitch clients to how they conduct day-to-day business. "Our marketing and new business area, a room with a big glass window that we call the fishbowl, has a funky leather couch, hanging bikes, a vintage barber chair, an Elvis jumpsuit for special occasions, and gumball machines filled with goodies for clients to snack on while they wait. Having all this in the entrance is purposeful, as it helps to set expectations," shares creative director and designer Chris Lamy. "We also have vintage days, cowboy days, and disco days where we all dress appropriately and carry on business as usual. We've even built a life-size robot suit once to deliver a proposal to a toy company. Our clients respect our thought process, and the work that comes in from them reflects that." When it came to providing visiting clientele with directions to their office, Brown & Company Design was not shy about flexing their creative muscle. Instead of merely giving details over the phone or sending a PDF map, the ingenious firm chose to build a three-dimensional virtual experience, making the trip to their firm memorable.

To serve as visual reference when a client was en route, members of the creative team cleverly photographed each other at various landmarks and highway exit signs. Each developed image was then placed in its appropriate position inside a View-Master reel. For the last image, the entire company was featured holding letters that spelled out the incoming client's name in 3-D. "It help set the tone for what the client could expect once they set foot inside the building," says Lamy. "It also let them know that we were a fun and creative firm." Because Brown & Company Design used their staff in all of the shots, clients saw familiar faces once they arrived.

To achieve the 3-D look, a Fisher-Price View-Master was used. The camera creates the illusion of three-dimensional space by taking two pictures simultaneously from a dual lens. "The patented View-Master cutter punches matching sets of slides out to a specific shape, allowing them to go into the reel in only one direction," Lamy explains. "All you need to do is ask the developer not to cut and mount the slides in frames." If you do not want to purchase the necessary equipment, companies like View-Master will not only rent out 3-D cameras but will also put your slides into reels.

To house the View-Master and reel, the team developed an engaging retro-style package. "We wanted the piece to stand out from the clutter on a prospect's desk," offers Lamy. "We also wanted it to look like a toy, something fun." Each box and insert was printed on heavy card stock and hand-cut, scored, and assembled in-house. The accent photography, taken during one of the firm's well-known theme days, featured the staff wearing 1950s-style vintage clothing. A small booklet, providing a hard copy of the directions and a phone number, was also included so the incoming client wouldn't have to keep looking through the View-Master while driving. The overall package and idea was entertaining and engaging, helping set a positive tone for incoming clients.

FIRM: BROWN & COMPANY DESIGN

CREATIVE DIRECTORS AND DESIGNERS:
MARY JO BROWN AND CHRIS LAMY

PRODUCTION AND ILLUSTRATION: CHRIS HAMER

PHOTOGRAPHY: CLAUDIA KAERNER AND MARY JO BROWN

PRINTING: ON DEMAND IMAGING

SPECIAL TECHNIQUES: HOVEYS (FILM OUTPUT)

MANUFACTURERS: FISHER-PRICE (VIEW-MASTER),
REEL 3-D ENTERPRISES (REEL MOUNTS)

To survive in today's marketplace, you need to establish what makes you different from the competition. By defining your niche, you are setting a foundation on which to strategically position and build your brand.

hidden
message

"We are trying to position ourselves not only as the design firm that offers high-quality services but also as the one that provides unexpected solutions and concepts," says creative director and designer Nedjeljko Spoljar. "We wanted to create a piece that would reflect our ability to explore and use new techniques and to put things in unusual contexts." While making freeform notations in a sketchbook, the designer made an interesting discovery. "I realized that the sentence 'We love you' could be expanded to 'We love your money' simply by adding one letter and another word," observes Spoljar. "The combination makes a funny, surprising, and unusual statement." The next step was to find an interesting and innovative way in which to present the concept. "I had been waiting for a chance to use the scratch technique on something for a long time, and it was a perfect solution for this particular problem," Spoljar adds.

Taking their inspiration from scratch-off game cards, the design firm took their idea to Printel, one of the best printing houses in their area. The biggest challenge for both the printer and design firm came in trying to find just the right combination of paper and scratch-off ink to make the concept work. The ink not only had to scratch off easily but also had to be opaque enough so the type did not show through. "Because I wanted to create a great contrast between the paper texture and the smooth scratch surface, I tried to use a beautiful uncoated paper called Conqueror CX22. It was a disastrous solution because the ink couldn't be scratched off at all," acknowledges Spoljar. "Then I tried again using Sappi Magnomatt paper. It has a very fine and smooth coating that kept the ink on the surface, enabling it to be scratched." The process turned out to be quite simple in the end. First the cards were offset-printed in one color: black. The scratch-off substance, silver metallic ink mixed with glue, was then silk-screened onto the printed sheets. "The glue keeps the ink elastic to enable scratching, and the silk-screen color makes the ink nontransparent," notes Spoljar. After the cards were thoroughly dried, they were trimmed to the designer's specifications.

The layout was kept simple in order to call attention to the overall concept. "From our friends and peers to the marketing directors and museum curators that we work with, the cards seem to be interesting to anyone who gets them," concludes Spoljar. "We're planning to produce more materials using the same technique." Sensus Design Factory was able to highlight their unconventional idea with a familiar but not widely used technique, giving life and interest to an otherwise traditional card. The resulting work attracted international attention not only from the design community but also from prospective and existing clients.

The studio name and contact information is offset-printed onto a coated white stock. The scratchable ink is then silk-screen printed in silver on top, leaving only the company name showing. The recipient has to actively scratch off the silver to see the contact information underneath.

The back of the card features a tricky play with words. At first glance, a sentence reads "We love you," but as the surface is scratched, an entirely different message is revealed.

1

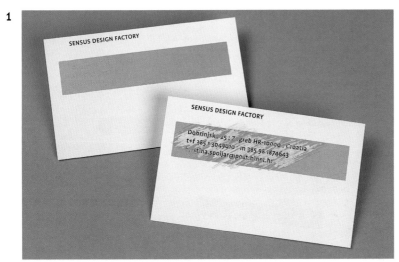

FIRM: SENSUS DESIGN FACTORY

CREATIVE DIRECTOR AND DESIGNER:
NEDJELJKO SPOLJAR

PRINTING: PRINTEL D.O.O.

SPECIAL TECHNIQUES:
PRINTEL D.O.O. (SCRATCH-OFF MATERIAL)

2

fun and stylish

The three-panel letter-folded invitation uses custom die-cut angles to simulate the walls and windows of the design studio. It is printed in four PMS colors and an overall matte varnish for a flat, solid look. It was sent in a semi-transparent envelope with a custom die-cut label to existing and prospective clients as well as vendors.

For Kolégramdesign's tenth anniversary, the creative team wanted to celebrate by having a happening cocktail party, retro style. "We think of ourselves as fun people, and we wanted to portray that in our promotion," admits designer Gontran Blais. "We also wanted to create something that people would remember, use, and relate to." The only challenge was developing an event that everyone in the studio was happy with. "We had a big brainstorming session, and almost everyone had a different concept," recalls Blais. "It is really hard when you are doing work for yourself and you have to please everyone." In the end, the team agreed that a fun and stylish yet classy promotion was the way to go.

The design team began with the invitation. "Because the party was to be held at our studio, we wanted the invitation to reflect the walls and windows of our space," says Blais. The invitation featured die-cut angles in a three-panel letter-fold format, thus conveying the sense of perspective and three-dimensional space the design team was looking for. They liked the angular architecture of the invitation so much they decided to carry the look through the entire promotion and event.

At the custom-decorated celebration, a barmaid served cocktails in martini glasses to guests ; a DJ played music throughout the night. As a parting gift, each guest was given a bar accessory kit. The package included a set of four tin coasters, a minibooklet of drink recipes, and a notebook for jotting down choice mixers. The coasters, which came standard in a tin box, were silk-screen-printed with an epoxy-based ink in five colors, including a double hit of white. Because of the beveled edge, the coasters could not be printed with a full bleed, as initially intended. The words *funky, groovy, wow,* and *cool* work hand-in-hand with the graphics to carry forward the retro theme that started with the invitation. The elongated shape of the booklet of drink recipes, the staff's personal mixers, was a nice addition to the overall square presentation. To ensure the tin box and notebook stayed together as a unit, a custom sleeve was designed to fit snugly around both items so neither would slide out. A secondary wrap was also created to completely seal the contents. "With the kit, there is one surprise after the other," concludes Blais. "People actually had a Christmas face when they opened it." Because the firm maintained a consistent look and theme, the resulting event and promotion were successful.

TECHNICAL TIPS

When you are working on an event, consider the whole package as a series of related parts. To maintain cohesion, begin with a theme and work on every aspect at once. Limit the ink coverage on tin surfaces and allow the color of the surface work for you. This will keep costs down and minimize noticeable surface scratches. Epoxy-based ink adheres best to metal surfaces.

2

The parting gift consisted of a set of silk-screen-printed tin coasters, a perfect-bound notebook, and a custom die-cut recipe book for drinks. A custom wrap holds them firmly together in a nice package. All of the pieces contain the same flat colors and angular retro theme that was initiated in the first point of contact—the invitation.

3

The Flash-animated screensaver, used on every screen at the party, reinforces the custom graphics and the overall retro theme.

1

3

2

FIRM: KOLÉGRAMDESIGN

CREATIVE DIRECTOR: ANNIE TANGUAY

ART DIRECTOR: MIKE TEIXEIRA

DESIGNER: GONTRAN BLAIS

PRINTING: IMPRIMERIE DU PROGRÈS (INVITATION)

AND SÉRIGRAPHIE ALBION (COASTERS)

BINDERY: IMPRIMERIE DU PROGRÈS (NOTEBOOK)

SPECIAL TECHNIQUES: CAPITAL BOX (DIE-CUTTING)

MANUFACTURER: BRYMARK PROMOTIONS (TIN BOX AND COASTERS)

simple but

meaningful

Hartpappe (1 millimeter), a bookmaking
material, was the stock of choice. Its black-
and-gray camouflage look, which came
standard, intrigued the design team because
of its military connotations. The piece is
entitled *Wahrnehmungsgerät*, which means
"perception tool." Typ 21/7-klein was added
at the end to give the piece a mechanical
context. A small tag with the MAGMA logo on
the back is attached to voice the firm's
political opinion about war.

"Every year we send out something from our office to friends and clients," says art director Lars Harmsen. "After September 11th, we really didn't feel like having something big, expensive, and obviously self-promotional to send out. It was a time to look at things from a different angle." Wanting to refocus people's attention, MAGMA developed an interesting tool they call Wahrnehmungsgerät typ 21/7-klein. In German, *Wahrnehmung* means "perception" and *Gerät* means "tool." "It is a perception tool to see the smaller things of this world, reducing things to what is really important," explains Harmsen. "It is a small piece that has a lot of political meaning for us." The 21/7-klein was added to the name for a mechanical touch, similar to how one refers to an engine of a car. This "engine to see things," as coined by Harmsen, is quite simple but very meaningful in a time when many people are feeling introspective.

  Designed to crop out distraction, the perception tool forces people to narrow their focus and look within their own communities to see how they can make a difference. The grommet hole and rounded edges of the device help highlight the firm's logo, an oil tower. "The idea behind our logo is to say that our research is done very deeply and our work is very rich—tearing out of the ground," offers Harmsen.

  The piece sits nicely inside an orange slip holder. The semicircle die-cuts that adorn each side make the piece easy to access. The text and graphics that provide operating instructions to the viewer are not offset printed but photocopied onto Colorit by Schneidersöhne. "To offset print was not necessary. It is not important to have things printed in fancy ways," says Harmsen. "It is the idea that counts." In a palette of orange, silver, and black, the ingenious device is an innovative way to communicate the firm's beliefs and philosophies.

  "There are two different categories of promotion," concludes Harmsen. "There is one that uses a brochure to show off past work. Then you have another approach where the dialog is much more intelligent. It is more of an idea or visualization of how your agency behaves or sees things. In my opinion, the latter is a more communicative approach." The promotion was delivered in the firm's corporate stationery.

TECHNICAL TIPS

To create an extraordinary, intelligent promotion, you have to make the idea your number-one priority. Spend time researching and develop an approach that is neither typical nor mainstream. Encourage vendors to keep you updated on new surfaces and techniques. If you can find custom-looking materials that come standard, you will save time and money by not having to print or produce them.

2

The company logo is stamped in silver foil on the back, providing an interesting contrast to the matte surface. The orange holder, photocopied in black, describes how to operate the perception tool.

3

The intriguing little device is sent to clients, vendors, friends, and colleagues using the design firm's stationery. MAGMA's corporate identity—graphic images of volcanoes and oil towers in a palette of orange, silver, and black—is carried through the distinctive series of business cards and letterhead.

2

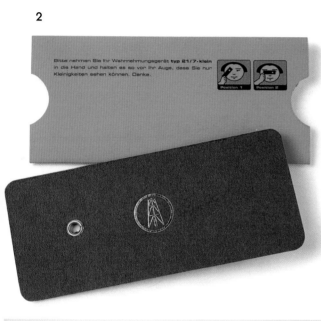

1

3

FIRM: MAGMA [BÜRO FÜR GESTALTUNG]

ART DIRECTORS: LARS HARMSEN AND ULRICH WEIß

DESIGNER: ULRICH WEIß

SPECIAL TECHNIQUES: BUCHBINDER MEISTER LUDWIG WEISS

the little engine that could

After completing a challenging series of high-profile full-color ads for the Pharmaceutical Researchers and Manufacturers of America (PhRMA), Grafik knew their heroic feat was worth tooting their whistle about. "In a very short period, we had designed fifteen ads for a single issue of *Newsweek*," recalls creative director and designer David Collins. "We were trying to break into the pharmaceutical market and felt our experience with PhRMA would help us in working with other pharmaceutical companies. The idea was to tell our story to the industry."

Grafik put on their thinking caps and thought of an interesting and captivating way to tell their story. "We bounced around a lot of ideas, knowing that we needed to grab the attention of the target audience—pharmaceutical marketing executives," Collins details. "Because we are a small company, compared to the much larger agencies that do most of the pharmaceutical advertising, we felt that the *Little Engine That Could* was an appropriate metaphor." To deliver the message, the design team chose a wooden train whistle. Its interesting shape and instant appeal made it the perfect vehicle. "The train whistle is a gimmick, but it relates to a very powerful story," reminds Collins.

To bring life to their concept, Grafik researched a variety of options, looking for the one that provided just the right look and feel. "We found a vendor that produced wooden train whistles in various sizes," notes Collins, "and would literally brand any message into the side within a limited space." To imprint type and graphics on both sides of the whistle, the firm had to provided the vendor with a digital file. They also made a prototype prior to final production to ensure the product was what they envisioned.

To complete the package, a brochure featuring the emotionally charged series of ads was wrapped around the whistle and the two were placed inside a box with packing material that simulated wood shavings. Grafik labeled the box with a visually arresting teaser, enticing the recipient to look inside. "Once the recipient gets into the mailer, all fifteen ads are clearly presented along with a brief case study," adds Collins. "Because there is no way to tell the complete story, we determined that the audience should have the option to see more. To accomplish this, our call to action was a Web page designed to give more detail about the ad campaign and provide access to the rest of the Grafik site." The story-driven mailer helped position Grafik as a small agency that generates big results for their clients.

TECHNICAL TIPS

To attract attention, don't give away the entire story; leave the audience wanting more—and always have a follow-up procedure in place to capitalize on your efforts. When imprinting into wood, make sure the level of detail and impact are what you want by having a prototype made first.

...hape and the intriguing ...t and curiosity. Inside, ...rapped with the tagline ...This red-hot engine ...ction between Grafik's ...ul childhood story.

The whistle is imprinted with the firm's identity on one side and their Web site on the other. The URL www.grafik.com/justwhistle provides information about the case study that could not be detailed in the direct mailer. It also introduces interested parties to the rest of Grafik's work and experience. The minibrochure that wraps the whistle includes all fifteen ads that ran in a single issue of *Newsweek*.

1

2

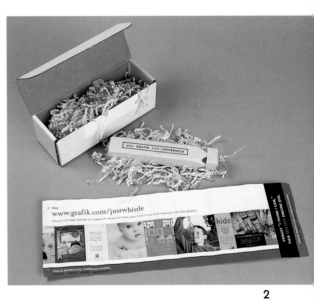

FIRM: GRAFIK

CREATIVE DIRECTOR: DAVID COLLINS

DESIGNERS: JONATHAN AMEN, DAVID COLLINS,
AND RON HARMON

PRINTING: COLORCRAFT OF VIRGINIA, INC.

SPECIAL TECHNIQUES: SPECIALTIES, INC. (WOOD BRANDING)

MANUFACTURERS: SPECIALTIES, INC. (TRAIN WHISTLE),
ULINE (BOX), AND PAPER MART (PACKING MATERIAL)

sporting
style

The 2002 fashion season was underway, and Reebok needed to draw attention to their new line. "We wanted to get into the minds of fashion and celebrity stylists to encourage them to use our products when styling a TV show, movie, or fashion layout," explains creative director and designer Eleni Chronopoulos. "Given that they are creative people, we thought a uniquely shaped sketchbook made of interesting materials would be appealing, something they would certainly want to hold onto."

With the desire to incorporate unconventional materials and techniques in her design, Chronopoulos consulted production experts for assistance. "I worked with our materials manager to explore material and branding options for the cover and a production expert to figure out how to put the whole thing together," she details. After exploring a variety of options, the designer chose embossed red synthetic leather as an exciting way to set the stage for the modish piece. The surface was not only highly tactile but also representative of Reebok's fashion sense. The biggest problem was that the material, produced by the roll in Asia, was available in a diagonal pattern only. "We needed it to run vertically," acknowledges Chronopoulos. "This meant each piece had to be carefully lined up before cutting. Not only did it produce a lot of waste, it also slowed down the process." Once the synthetic material was correctly cut to the designer's specifications, it was mounted onto an 80-lb. black cover stock to give it substance and support. As an accent, a two-color stamped-aluminum logo, an existing detail in Reebok's apparel, was adhered to the cover with rivets.

The inside pages included an attractive array of fun and fashionable footwear and apparel intermixed with open pages available for sketching and creative notation of potential ways in which to use the new line. To add further interest, the piece was bound with custom rivets. Using materials and detailing from key footwear and apparel pieces helped Reebok give the audience a tactile glimpse into what the product line had to offer. "We could have easily sent a postcard to anyone remotely related to the entertainment industry," shares Chronopoulos, "but we knew we would have more of an impact targeting the influencers, in this case stylists, with a more thoughtful piece." It was sent in a black rope-tie envelope accented with a custom label. The only point of contact was a nick die-cut Rolodex card.

1

2

The brochure's cover, made of red synthetic leather and accented by a two-color aluminum tag, is both fashionable and sporty. The piece is sent to stylists in a black rope-tie envelope.

Inside, Reebok's 2002 seasonal line is displayed. To make the piece useful to stylists, blank pages for sketching and notation are added. Each page is perforated, allowing it to be easily ripped out of the book and used. A nick die-cut Rolodex card is the only point of contact.

FIRM: REEBOK DESIGN SERVICES

CREATIVE DIRECTOR AND DESIGNER:
ELENI CHRONOPOULOS

PHOTOGRAPHY: GARY LAND

PRINTING AND BINDERY: ATLAS PRESS, INC.

MANUFACTURERS: PAPER ACCESS (ENVELOPES) AND REEBOK
INTERNATIONAL LTD. (SYNTHETIC LEATHER AND ALUMINUM TAG)

2

1

defining
the edge

The departments of landscape architecture and urban planning and design at Harvard Design School undertook a joint venture that focused on Hong Kong's waterfront. Twelve students and two professors traveled to the harborside city to examine issues of density, connectivity, and sustainability. Upon completion of the educational endeavor, the university wanted to document their findings in a unique way that would not only capture the essence of the city but also appeal to architectural and urban designers, policy makers, city officials and planners, and the general public at large. The creative team of Nassar Design was up for the challenge.

To get a solid understanding of the city, the studio experience, and the work that was generated, the design team attended both the midterm and final reviews in Hong Kong. "This enabled us to provide the client with an overall design strategy and production budget," adds creative director and designer Nelida Nassar. "From there, preliminary sketches were drawn and different book trim sizes were tested." Because of the monumental quality of the architectural structures involved, a vertical format was chosen. The perfect-bound book was divided into two main areas of interest: commencing with an analytical section and closing with a more visual presentation. "Several thumbnails utilizing different grids and page layouts were studied," notes Nassar. In the end, a simple two-column structure was chosen. Throughout the educational publication, striking imperial red-and-gold duotones are juxtaposed with informative essays and groundbreaking research.

To make the piece stand out and have the unique quality the university was looking for, the design team did considerable research, looking through their archives, consulting the Web, and searching specialty stores for new and innovative products. "We really wanted to use a new material to express the energy of the city of Hong Kong," shares Nassar. The search paid off when they located the perfect surface for the book's cover; a lenticular film, which gives a three-dimensional feel to a two-dimensional surface, was chosen for its highly reflective surface and grid pattern. "The design was influenced by both the fluctuating lights, typical of harbor cities, and the more down-to-earth urban grid and physical configuration of the city's form," details Nassar. To add stability and strength, the lenticular material was laminated to a coated cover stock.

As part of the book's title, the words *Defining the Edge* also offered an opportunity for innovation. As a finishing touch, the type was set along the outer trim using a striking yellow foil stamp that calls attention to the edge and frames the highly reflective grid pattern inside. The resulting publication was not only stunning and dramatic but also served as an invaluable resource for students, educators, and professionals.

TECHNICAL TIPS

Purchase lenticular paper in sheets rather than in rolls, as sheets allow better control and eliminate unwanted curling. Be sure to order the sheets without an adhesive backing if you plan to laminate them to another surface. To imprint a lenticular sheet, foil stamping seems to offer both an opaque look and strong adhesion. Other processes, like silk-screen and offset, can cause registration problems when printing onto the outer trim.

1

The highly reflective and geometric cover, made of a lenticular film mounted on to a 10-point Kromekote board, helps communicate Hong Kong's urban grid and the flickering lights of its illuminated harbor. The typographic treatment, imprinted using foil stamping with a special mix yellow, was set along the trim to call attention to the book's title, *Hong Kong: Defining the Edge*.

2

The interior begins with a synopsis by various historians and urban design specialists. This is followed by a visual presentation of the work produced by the student participants. The book is distributed to architectural and urban design students, professors, and professionals as well as to policy makers, city officials and planners, and the general public.

1

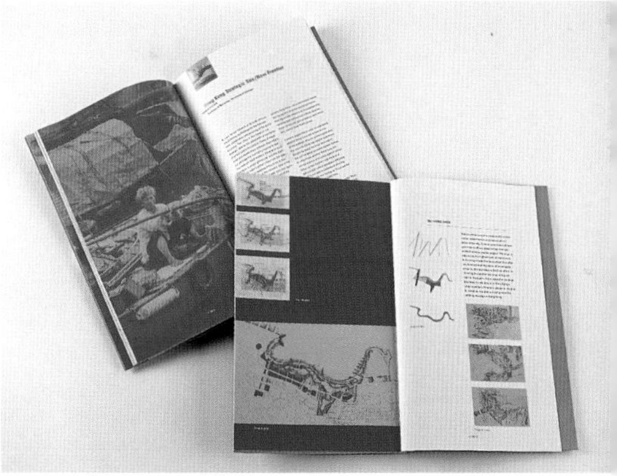

2

CLIENT: HARVARD DESIGN SCHOOL

FIRM: NASSAR DESIGN

CREATIVE DIRECTOR: NELIDA NASSAR

DESIGNERS: NELIDA NASSAR AND MARGARITA ENCOMIENDA

ILLUSTRATION AND PHOTOGRAPHY: HARVARD DESIGN SCHOOL

PRINTING: MERRILL/DANIELS

BINDERY: CREATIVE FINISHINGS, INC.

MANUFACTURER: COBURN CORPORATION (LENTICULAR PAPER)

unique

chapter two:

construc-

tions,

folds,

and die-

cuts

The architecture of the promotional brochure is evolving, and creatives are thinking outside the box when it comes to format and construction. From custom-molded containers and hand-made boxes to multipieced assemblages, pop-ups, and animated flipbooks, today's promotions are putting a new face on the once typical brochure. Unique constructions captivate an audience with their engaging folds, clever inserts, and interesting die-cut shapes. The interaction encourages active participation, and the overall messaging becomes memorable.

"When you encourage exploration, it starts to feed a lot of different venues," admits Dan Wheaton of the Riordon Design Group, Inc. "For instance, the engineering of a box to function in more than one capacity is not only innovative but also a way of exposing clients to different possibilities." To extend the life and effectiveness of any promotion, it is advantageous to consider creating a piece that can also be functional, acting as a keepsake or novelty item on someone's desk. That way, when it is time to assign a project, your firm comes to mind. If your promotion contains nothing for the recipients, they have no reason to hang on to it.

When developing promotions, don't be afraid to employ the assistance of professionals outside the communications industry. For instance, the assistance of an industrial designer helped to make DSM's watering container a beautiful interlacing of form and function, and an origami expert put an interesting twist on Weidlinger Associates' fiftieth anniversary promotion. Outside specialists have the knowledge and expertise that can raise any promotional endeavor to a high level of distinction.

shelter of
dreams

A miniature keepsake, built in the spirit of the Red Canoe cabin, is given as a heartfelt gift to clients, colleagues, and friends. It is sent along with a special note, encouraging recipients to use it as a source of inspiration and a shelter for their dreams. It is hand-signed by the Canoeists, a title that the partners at Red Canoe have come to love.

Four years ago, Caroline Kavanagh and Deb Koch forged into the woods to build a partnership in a place where they could live and work in harmony with nature. A cabin amid 350 acres of breathtaking wilderness became their safe haven and their muse. After celebrating yet another successful year in business, the partners at Red Canoe began to reflect, reexamining what started them on such a wondrous journey. In an attempt to share their shelter of dreams with others, the partners embarked on the construction of miniature cabins—representatives of the sanctuary that has brought the collaborators joy over the last four years. The individually hand-crafted labors of love serve as a home for inspirational notes, pictures, or the special cards one receives. The dimensions are 8 (wide) by 11 $\frac{1}{2}$ (long) by 10 $\frac{1}{2}$-inch (tall).

Many of the cabins' special details and accents originate from the breathtaking beauty of the great outdoors that surround the peaceful respite known as Red Canoe. Wood, sticks, and river rock that make the cabin come alive were collected as bits of tranquility to be shared. In building the keepsake pieces, the creative team looked toward the original construction of their Red Canoe cabin for guidance. "The interior walls of our cabin are made of rough-cut pine. The little cabins use squared logs of that same wood," details Kavanagh. "Here our ceilings and floors are birch, and the roofs and windows on the little cabins use that same birch." Because of the cabins' miniature scale, working tools had to be adapted to fit each task. For instance, a nail gun was vital, as the size and delicacy of the piece didn't allow for hammering. Clothespins worked perfectly as little clamps to assist in securely adhering the twigs with wood glue to the rooftops. The canoe that rests on the side of the cabin and the paddles that accent the door were both hand-whittled. To make the chimney, flat river stones were adhered with cedar-colored caulking. As a finishing treatment, each cabin was checked for sharp edges, which were filed down if necessary. The only point of contact was a subtle silk-screen printing of the company's contact information and original mission statement: *As we live, so we work.*

Each cabin was carefully wrapped and tied with twine. A poetic note, detailing the intent of the keepsake promotion, was attached. The piece was sent in a cardboard box wrapped with custom-designed packing paper created especially for the promotion. The care and love for one's craft expressed by the canoe workers featured on the outer wrapping resonated with the partners at Red Canoe, who felt compelled to preserve these ideas. Each of the 150 signed-and-numbered limited-edition pieces of art was sent to clients and special people who had become a part of the Red Canoe family over the years. The heartfelt gift was a way to show appreciation and gratitude for the wonderful experiences that have been shared.

TECHNICAL TIPS

With a project of this type, make a model to act as a guide. After establishing the final specifications from the prototype, it is helpful to have every item in sample form for sizing purposes. If you plan on doing the handwork yourself, make sure you will enjoy the process, as you will be a very unhappy camper otherwise. Producing a labor-intensive promotion such as this one involves much trial and error. You must be resourceful in choosing materials and processes. If you are up for the challenge, you must be mindful of the big picture, and don't get too focused on the minute details. Allow time for the complications that may arise. Note that wood must be very smooth to receive a silk-screen-printed message legibly.

DO IT FOR LESS

To save money, search for an off-the-shelf alternative and adapt it accordingly. This approach would, however, greatly diminish the piece's authenticity and uniqueness, which are such big parts of the concept.

2

One can enter the cabin's sanctuary by either lifting the roof or unlocking the door to the secret attic space upstairs—a place for little treasures, inspirational notes, and personal pictures. Once inside, one is presented with Red Canoe's contact information and philosophical tagline: *As we live, so we work*. Each cabin is a handcrafted, limited-edition piece of art.

The cabin is wrapped with twine and accented by a poetic note. Each signature piece is placed inside a box wrapped with custom packing paper created specifically for the promotion. The archival photography features early Canadian canoe factories and their dedicated workers.

As a follow-up, another promotion was sent four months later. Created as an April Fool's Day joke, the promotion alerts recipients to their cabin's flawed chimney flue. The notice—complete with illustrated diagrams, step-by-step instructions, and a recall form—seems quite legitimate and fooled many of its recipients. But after careful inspection and a trip to the dedicated Web site(www.redcanoe.com/flueproof), one came away with quite a chuckle. The clever promotion was sent in a box perfectly sized to fit the chimney, including protective bubble wrap. The piece became a reminder of how little time we take from our busy lives to really look at and appreciate the simplest things. The cabin and its follow-up were meant to give recipients renewed respect and appreciation for the God-given gifts we all share.

1

3

4

FIRM: RED CANOE

CREATIVE DIRECTORS AND DESIGNERS: DEB KOCH AND CAROLINE KAVANAGH

ILLUSTRATION: CAROLINE KAVANAGH

PHOTOGRAPHY: NATIONAL ARCHIVES OF CANADA AND PROVINCIAL ARCHIVES OF NEW BRUNSWICK (WRAPPING PAPER)

PRINTING: LITHOGRAPHICS, INC. (WRAPPING PAPER), STUDIO INK (SILK-SCREEN PRINTING), AND EPSON INKJET (NOTE AND TRIFOLD RECALL NOTICE)

SPECIAL TECHNIQUES: DEB KOCH, CAROLINE KAVANAGH, MARTHA AUTHEMENT, MORGAN AUTHEMENT, AND SONJA USRY (MASONRY)

MANUFACTURERS: NICK WARNER (CARPENTRY), TALLENT PLANNING & LUMBER (PINE WOOD), LOWES (HINGES, CAULKING, AND PAINT), ULINE (BOX, PACKING PAPER, AND TWINE), SHAKER WORKSHOPS (PAINT FOR CANOE), RED CANOE SITE (TWIGS FOR WINDOW AND ROOF TRIM AND STONES FOR CHIMNEY)

dreams for a better world

The custom-designed watering can is made out of polypropylene 5 (PP5). It houses a creativity book, inspirational video, and packet of seeds.

DSM was having their one-hundreth anniversary and wanted to do something monumental to celebrate. "They were looking for us to create a special gift for their employees," recalls creative director and designer Hans Wolbers. "The philosophy of the company is all about the word *unlimited*, which stands for unlimited possibilities in research. So we used their mission to implement and create this idea." Through the project, employees from around the world were invited to make a positive contribution to the planet by putting forth their dreams and talents. The project was delivered in the form of a contest where the best ideas would be realized.

To serve as mentors, the design team went in search of people that have put their dreams into action, making a difference in the world as a result. A diverse group of people with social and environmental pursuits was chosen. "We wanted to inspire all the employees and let them know that it is not so difficult to realize their personal dreams," says Wolbers. To get the employees' creative juices flowing, the design team employed the theories of Dr. Edward de Bono, "He is a famous professor who did research on how creativity works," offers Wolbers. "I went to a couple of his workshops and became really inspired. When this project came along, I decided to use his ideas." Throughout the promotional book, de Bono's theories are presented in an interactive fashion. Random stimulation, reuse, and opportunity seeking were chosen for their ability to change attitudes and fixed perceptions.

As a working tool for participating employees around the world to begin their journey, a spiral-bound creativity book was developed in several languages. "We wanted the book to be something you take out every day and read, draw in, and discover new details," adds Wolbers. The book and a companion video served as vehicles to inspire and enlighten the employees of DSM to participate in the once-in-a-lifetime opportunity. As a finishing touch, a packet of seeds was included in the ensemble as a symbol of growth and renewal. The book, video, and seeds were housed inside a custom-designed plastic watering can. The entire project, inspirational and uplifting, was a way for DSM to promote their friendly face to the world. It was launched at a worldwide breakfast for all the employees.

TECHNICAL TIPS

Lenticular printing, which creates the illusion of three-dimensional space and motion, comprises a flat image that is either mounted or printed directly on a lenticular lens material. If you are interested in utilizing this technique, consult a company that specializes in the process to see all of the animation options available.

To create innovative, multifunctional packaging, don't be afraid to employ the assistance of industrial designers, who understand how to manipulate materials and have readily available lists of necessary suppliers to make it happen.

With worldwide distribution, many organizational details must be attended to. First and foremost, the project must be translated in a way that is sensitive and knowledgeable about each language and culture. Outside experts are vital to assist in this process. If you are interested in distributing seeds internationally, geographic climates and custom importing regulations must be investigated thoroughly for each country. It would be counterproductive to send seeds for a tree that does not grow in a specific area or to have packages held up in customs. To ensure the right book, video, and seeds find their way to the appropriate country, an organizational plan must be put in place and a team assigned to the task.

DO IT FOR LESS

The custom-molded watering can could be replaced with a prefabricated outer packaging. You could also limit the inks and paper selection to one source for the booklet.

The spiral-bound book and video are tools used to inspire and enlighten the employees of DSM. The animation graphics that introduce the video also appear on the cover of the book as a three-dimensional lenticular sticker. The seeds, symbolizing growth, and the use of recycled and wood-free paper help spread a positive message about respecting and giving back to the environment. A hand-lettered card introduces the concept in a personalized and uplifting way. Both the book and video are produced in Dutch, English, French, German, Italian, Portuguese, and Spanish.

The book begins by introducing the employees to several people, who share their inspirational stories. The pursuits, mostly environment and social in nature, show how ordinary people can make a profound difference. To get the employees started on their path, a series of creative theories and exercises is put into practice. The inspiration wheel shown here acts as a random stimulation tool. It uses random words and images to create free associations, allowing one to break out of set patterns.

2

1

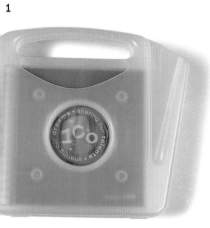

3

CLIENT: DSM N.V.

FIRMS: LAVA GRAPHIC DESIGNERS AND SIGNUM NIEHE EVENTS

CREATIVE DIRECTOR: HANS WOLBERS

DESIGNERS: YKE BARTELS, HEIKE DEHNING, HANS WOLBERS, AND HUGO ZWOLSMAN

GRAPHIC PRODUCTION: DEF. GRAPHIC PRODUCTIONS

THEORIES: EDWARD DE BONO

PHOTOGRAPHY: MARTIJN BEEKMAN, BILDERBERG FOCUS, BUDI, ROGER DOHMEN, DRIK, FLIP FRANSSEN, SAKE ELZINGA, FUTURE FORESTS, GRAMEEN BANK, PETER GRANT, PETER HILZ, HOLLANDSE HOOGTE, TIMOTHY HURSLEY, PETER HUYS, IMAGE STORE, JAN JORDAN, CHRIS KEULEN, KONINKLIJK INSTITUUT VOOR DE TROPEN, RENÉ NUIJENS, MARCUS PETERS, LAURENT PORDIÉ, STEYE RAVIEZ, SMITHSONIAN INSTITUTE, NIELS WESTRA, AND HANS WOLBERS

LITHOGRAPHY: PLUSWORKS

PRINTING: DRUKKERIJ KOENDERS & VAN STEIJN

BINDERY: HEPADRU (WIRE-O)

SPECIAL TECHNIQUES: HENK STALLINGA (WATERING CAN DESIGN)

MANUFACTURER: EDIS S.P.A (LENTICULAR STICKER)

going in with a bang!

Each custom-made silk-screen-printed box contains two small champagne bottles, a clear bag of six chocolates in red foil, a set of sparklers, a capabilities card, and a personalized notecard. Blue crinkle and silver foil add motion and excitement to the already festive package. The fonts used in the promotion, Tanek and Helvetica Condensed, are used on all of BBDI's identity and collateral. Only thirty pieces were made; each was hand-delivered.

With the opening of their affiliate office in Toronto, Bradbury Branding & Design, Inc. (BBDI), was eager to develop their presence and wanted a promotion that would enter this new market with a bang. "For Toronto, we wanted to create something that would serve as a fun and memorable follow-up after an initial presentation," says creative director and designer Catharine Bradbury. "We also wanted something that would be a nice thank-you to our existing clients for their previous business." Thinking about their desire to explode onto the Toronto market, the design firm came up with the idea of using fireworks to convey their message. However, because of the numerous complications associated with shipping explosives, they decided it was best to rework the concept. "Instead, we came up with the idea of using champagne as the big bang," shares Bradbury. "It was a fun item, something that people would certainly hang onto." Considering the events of September 11, just a few months later, the design firm was especially happy they had redirected their focus.

To house their big-bang package, a custom-built box made of ¼-inch (6.35-millimeter) MDF pressed fiberboard was employed. In a bold and dynamic palette of specially mixed colors, each box was silk-screen-printed on all sides, including the bottom. The lid, designed to sit flush on top of the box, has a center hole about ⅝ inch (2 centimeter) in diameter, allowing it to open in a unique way. Inside, a wonderful selection of treats is revealed. "Two bottles of sparkling wine, six chocolates, seven sparklers, and a card explaining the promotion and Bradbury's capabilities were included in each box," details the designer. "In addition, we included a simple notecard, handwritten with a silver pen, to each individual."

Because the bottles already came with a label, the design firm had to soak them in water, remove the existing label, and add a custom-designed silk-screen-printed label. White capsules were applied to the tops of the bottles and, as a finishing touch, a metallic red raffia bow was added. For the chocolates, the design firm approached a local supplier, who custom-wrapped each piece of candy in red foil. The package of six, three milk chocolate and three dark chocolate, were accented with a silver handwritten tag. The sparklers were simply wrapped in a bow. Everything was assembled in-house and hand-delivered to each client.

With a delicious array of sizzle and pop, the big bang promotion shows how BBDI is bursting with the ideas that can ignite any company's business. "All of our promotions have an element of uniqueness, and we always push ourselves to go just a little bit further each time," remarks Bradbury. "This promotion is an investment not only in gaining new clients but also in nurturing our existing client relationships."

TECHNICAL TIPS

When assembling a custom box of this material, carpenter's glue works well. Next, prime the natural brown surface with white latex paint to lessen the absorbency and to give the finishing colors a white surface to reflect off. When you are silkscreen-printing a custom box, you will need to build a jig in order to properly imprint the box on all sides. To remove labels from bottles quickly and easily, soak them in warm water for about an hour. If you plan to use food in your promotion, consider the eating habits of your audience and eliminate potential allergens like nuts. Last, be open to change; allow the piece to evolve. Try not to stay too attached to any one idea, especially if it ultimately does not serve your purpose in the end.

DO IT FOR LESS

Switching from a custom-built box to a cardboard box available in a standard size can save quite a bit of money.

2

The candy, an assortment of milk and dark chocolates, is wrapped in red foil and packaged in sets of six under the Harden & Huyse label. The hang tags that adorn the chocolates are actually key tags purchased at a local office supply store. The sparkers are wrapped in a raffia bow in sets of seven. Two bottles of champagne, adorned with custom silk-screen-printed labels, are also included in each box.

3

The capabilities cards are digitally printed on an inkjet printer, mounted on a heavy card stock, and hand-trimmed by the staff. Each notecard is hand-signed using a silver paint pen and fits nicely inside a matching envelope.

FIRM: BRADBURY BRANDING & DESIGN, INC.

CREATIVE DIRECTOR AND DESIGNER: CATHARINE BRADBURY

PRINTING: RSS SIGNS & GRAPHICS (SILK-SCREEN)

MANUFACTURERS: DARYL BASKERVILLE (BOX CREATION AND ASSEMBLY),

AND HARDEN & HUYSE (CHOCOLATES)

2

1

3

promotion redefined

Because of the technological advances of the last decade, an overabundance of communications in print, broadcast, and electronic media is being disseminated, and most of it is going by the wayside. Because the effectiveness of the familiar sources of promotion has diminished, creatives are beginning to explore new vehicles and initiatives. They are creating alternative ways for their work to enter and remain viable in the marketplace.

The hard-core sales approach of years past has become passé. To be effective, today's promotion must be engaging and thought-provoking, something that a prospective client will want to retain and utilize. Providing value for the recipient encourages active participation in the overall messaging, greatly increasing the chances for work down the road. "Things that are unabashedly promotional have a shorter life. The recipients will throw away the thing that has expiring value and will keep the thing that speaks to them," adds Sheree Clark of Sayles Graphic Design.

To break through the clutter and make an impact, creatives are finding innovative ways in which to deliver their message. No longer are firms putting out portfolio brochures with self-indulging copy. Promotions are now showing prospective clients what a firm can do in much more innovative ways. "The objects that you send out and give clients should be intelligent, creative, and extraordinary, showing off your firm's personality and thinking," offers Lars Harmsen of MAGMA. "To do that, you have to spend time on your ideas, researching things that are not mainstream." Don Chisholm of dossiercreative agrees. "We have to innovate and create things that did not

exist previously. By breaking the normal paradigms, we can challenge and change perceptions in the way things function, like rethinking the way a brochure works. Because of technology, that is where the industry is going to be pushed."

Designers are pushing themselves to think strategically and to experiment more with unconventional surfaces and printing techniques, interesting bindings and fasteners, and unique constructions and formats. Promotions are also being created as demonstrators, where strategy and creativity come together seamlessly. "The idea of any promotional piece is to go beyond the initial profile enhancement it does for your studio," explains Ric Riordon of the Riordon Design Group, Inc. "Providing examples that are interesting and innovative helps clients make the transition to using you for something similar. It's a springboard for new possibilities." Firms are also hiring consultants and full-time staff from other disciplines to help them conceptualize and think outside the box. "The competition is tough, and everyone is looking to work with the best. At that level, you need to be doing things that are different and stand out," comments Matt Ralph of Plainspoke. "To make a connection, you need to put out a promotion that really has an idea behind it and not just a portfolio of your past work." Creatives who continue to think in narrow terms and rely on the traditional sources for promotion may find themselves limited. Being a little more entrepreneurial in one's approach is key.

Rather than relying on any one venue to deliver their message, firms are thinking in terms of a campaign, penetrating an audience from many fronts. "Whether you are a one-person operation or an agency staffed by 150, an effective and comprehensive marketing and communications program is an absolutely essential business need in order to guarantee the long-term viability and growth of your business. It is the only effective way to target the clients you want, communicate the message you want, shape your market perception—and, ultimately, the direction your business will go in," acknowledges Jonathan Jason of Jason & Jason Visual Communication. "Otherwise, you are essentially assigning the development of your company to good fortune or fate alone."

To supplement their efforts, creatives are investing in public relations and networking opportunities more than ever. Whether a business is relatively new and implementing a pioneering campaign or is a well-established firm in the midst of a relaunch, courting industry trade magazines and book publishers by submitting press releases and feature ideas can attract attention to a particular niche or specialization. "I will contact an editor or writer whose work I admire to let them know that Red Canoe may be up to something of interest," offers cofounder Deb Koch. "I've even put forth a few ideas, offering to write opinion pieces. *HOW* magazine took me up on one idea and gave me the privilege of writing a piece for the 'DeSign Off' column. Everything has the power to lead to something else."

Once a story is picked up by the media, the promotional impact can be extended by announcing the publicity to prospective and existing clients through a newsletter, print or electronic, or an e-mail with a PDF posting. "We have been included in a number of prestigious international design magazines and annuals in the last few years. We have managed to promote our successes by articles and reviews in some of the major national newspapers," shares Nedjeljko Spoljar of Sensus Design Factory. "By increasing general awareness of our studio, this form of promotion has helped a lot in getting higher prices for our work."

Technology has made available new outlets that offer great promotional potential. Interactive Web sites, branded e-mails, online newsletters, and other such venues allow instant and up-to-date information to be cost-effectively delivered to a worldwide audience. "It's a new discipline and an area that is becoming a bigger part of our business," acknowledges Riordon. "Promotions can be custom-tailored with the added benefit of motion and sound, elements that you don't have with a print piece. So what you lose from the tactile side is nicely compensated for by the opportunity to animate and add life to a promotion, making it engaging on a whole different level."

For a more personal approach, event marketing, trade shows, and active involvement in business and professional associations, organizations, and conferences are other ways to connect and build relationships with a targeted audience. "I particularly enjoy trade shows because I can meet potential clients and talk to them about how I can address their communications goals," says Harvey Hirsch of Media Consultants. "Walk through a few trade shows and you will find many companies that are showing their products or services with poorly designed sell sheets, displays, premiums, and so on."

Many creatives are looking within and rethinking their own branding and identity. They are becoming more innovative and strategic—analyzing what they do that is unique and capitalizing on it. An entrepreneurial mindset is in the air, and creatives are just starting to unveil new approaches and possibilities.

repetition of message

A good way to drive home a message is to do it consistently, but with a bit of a twist each time. A pig for Hambly and a sheep for Woolley are repeatedly used in a variety of interesting ways to reinforce the design firm's namesake and ingenuity. "Each year our company sends out a different promotion, and people look forward to what they are going to receive next," adds creative director Bob Hambly. "We always try to create something that is first and foremost fun. It is also important that our promotions have general appeal, are nondenominational, for both sexes, and one-size-fits-all."

Featured here are three promotions from an ongoing series. With a pig embroidered on one and a sheep on the other, a pair of socks promotion travels with its recipient to work and play. It is wrapped in a custom-duplex box with beautifully illustrated winter imagery blind letterpress-printed inside. Baaa-Oink, a kitschy toylike promotion, contains a handmade paddleball with a graphic illustration of a pig on one side and a sheep on the other. The rubber ball attached to the paddle is silk-screen-printed with a pair of nostrils. The whimsical promotion is wrapped in plastic and staple-bound in a fun and entertaining package. The company's mouse pad, again featuring the signature pig and sheep, is sent out at Christmastime with a paper band around the middle that reads, "Not a creature was stirring, not even a mouse." By utilizing an ongoing theme, Hambly and Woolley have successfully built name recognition in the marketplace.

Providing value for the recipient encourages active participation in the overall messaging, greatly increasing the chances for work down the road.

FIRM: HAMBLY & WOOLLEY, INC.

CREATIVE DIRECTORS: BOB HAMBLY AND BARB WOOLLEY

DESIGNERS: DOMINIC AYRE (MOUSE PAD), BARB WOOLLEY (PADDLE), AND CHARLIE KIM (SOCKS)

ILLUSTRATION: BOB HAMBLY (PADDLE) AND ALISON LANG (SOCKS)

PHOTOGRAPHY: CSA ARCHIVES (MOUSE PAD)

PRINTING: RP GRAPHICS (MOUSE PAD), ANSTEY BOOKBINDING, INC. (PADDLE PACKAGING), AND LUNAR CAUSTIC PRESS (SOCKS PACKAGING)

MANUFACTURER: RP GRAPHICS (MOUSE PAD)

rounding up the flock

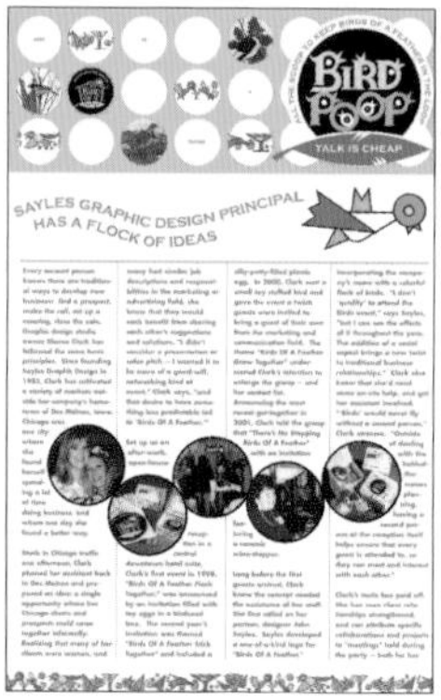

Sayles Graphic Design understands the effectiveness of networking. For the last five years, the firm has organized an event called Birds of a Feather. This annual gathering provides a way for the design firm to intermingle with existing and prospective clientele in a fun and relaxed atmosphere. In the spirit of collaboration, no guest is left unattended and partnership opportunities are encouraged. Photos are taken to document the event, making sure everyone is accounted for. The prints are later sent to each attendee along with the guest list to encourage further contact. After each event, invitees walk away with a special gift and, of course, a business card.

To uniquely kick off each Birds of a Feather function, an intriguing invitation is sent. A three-dimensional, self-mailing piece, decorated with the event's logo and signature graphics, always presents a unique surprise inside. For the theme entitled There's No Stopping Birds of a Feather, a wine cork was enclosed. The ceramic top is decorated with a clear decal printed and sealed with a ceramic glaze. To supplement the event's efforts and keep contacts active year-round, the firm's newsletter is cleverly entitled *Bird Poop*.

To bring in new marketing professionals, Sayles Graphic Design recently adopted a bring-a-guest program. This ingenious idea has significantly increased the number of prospective clients. "I've been able to work on many great design projects, build strong business relationships, and develop some lasting friendships as a result," says principal Sheree Clark.

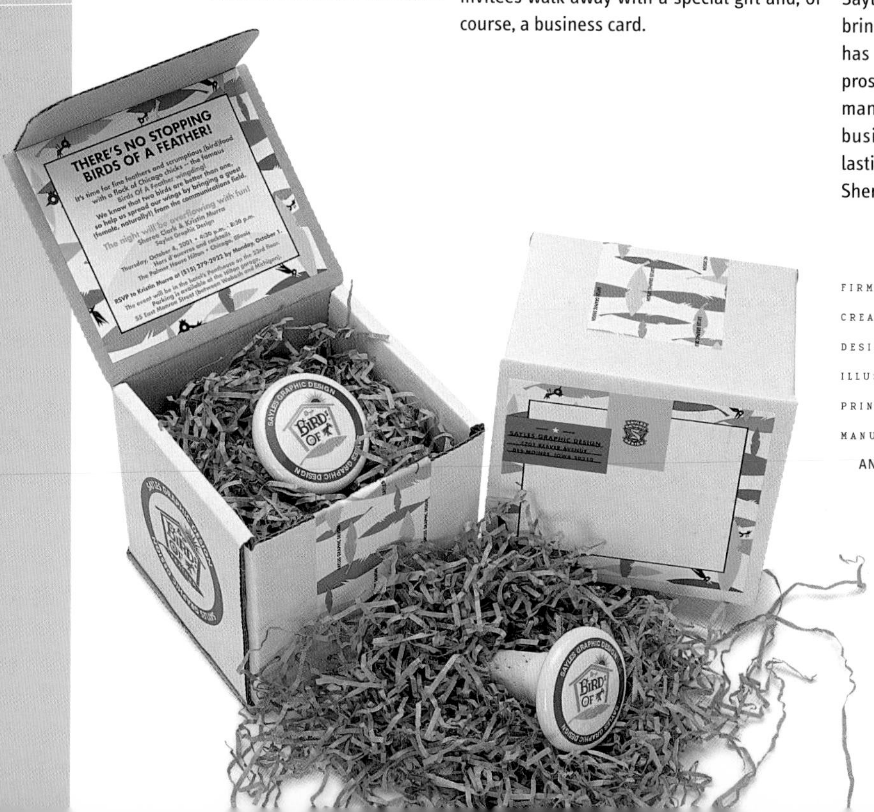

FIRM: SAYLES GRAPHIC DESIGN

CREATIVE DIRECTOR: JOHN SAYLES

DESIGNERS: JOHN SAYLES AND SOM INTHALANGSY

ILLUSTRATION: JOHN SAYLES

PRINTING: ARTCRAFT, INC.

MANUFACTURERS: ELWOOD PACKAGING, INC. (BOXES), AND GLAZED EXPRESSIONS (WINE STOPPERS)

tokens of appreciation

Personal messages and expressions of gratitude can go a long way toward building lasting relationships with clients. Designer and illustrator Mike Quon has been doing just that with his one-of-a-kind handmade tokens of appreciation. "Art directors are bombarded with e-mails and mass mailings, so I am always trying to do something a little bit more individual," he shares. "There are probably over five hundred art directors in the New York City area that have one of my customized pieces posted on their wall. They all love getting them." Such personal touches leave warm and lasting impressions in the minds of clients. "It is investing in yourself over a long campaign," adds Quon. "It's an ongoing light that says you are vital and active and that working with you will be a lot of fun."

Using a corrugated cardboard surface, Quon paints with acrylics to create a customized image. When he is done, the painted image is hand-cut with a razor blade into a unique shape. The artist individually signs each piece with a black marker, then sends them as postcards to thank clients for their business. In addition to the handmade postcards, Quon also creates one-of-a-kind books—personalized collages sealed with Elmer's glue—that he gives to special clients as gifts. Each token of appreciation he sends goes a long way in building strong clients relations for the future.

FIRM: DESIGNATION INC.

CREATIVE DIRECTOR AND DESIGNER:
  MIKE QUON

ILLUSTRATION: MIKE QUON

not your average press release

IE Design had just completed an identity assignment for fashion designer Jennifer Nicholson. The problem that the client posed was indeed challenging: something a bit rock-and-roll, bohemian yet vintage, that somehow included a seahorse. The design firm was so proud of their solution that they wanted to share it with the design community. To capture the attention of busy editors, the creative team knew they had to come up with an approach more engaging than a just a typical press release. "We tried to think of what we could do to get the recipient involved in the piece and not to throw it away," says creative director Marcie Carson. Their solution was an interesting three-dimensional media ensemble.

The design team began by adorning the outside package, a standard-size box, with intriguing text and visual accents. By presenting the design challenge posed by the client, the outside of the self-mailing box entices the viewer to open it. The inside not only unveils the firm's ingenious solution but also contains a sampling of the clever promotion. To make it easy for publications to feature their work, a CD-ROM was enclosed with an image of the complete Pearl identity, including stationery, felt jewelry pouches, garment bags, fabric bags for hats and shoes, gift boxes, hang tags, and a shopping bag.

To keep costs down, everything was produced in-house. The text was printed on blue metallic paper and adhered to the box flat with spray mount, except for the areas where the CD-ROM and business card insert, which were carefully masked. Styrofoam, covered with sandpaper to simulate beach sand, was placed on the bottom of the box to cut down on the movement of the elements within the box. The shells and the shimmering tulle netting laid freely in the box beautifully conveyed an ocean ambience for the Pearl identity to rest while the color scheme and patterns helped to make a connection to the whimsical and vintage clothing line. By creating an interesting spin on a press release, IE Design was able to highlight and call attention to their niche.

Whether a business is relatively new and implementing a pioneering campaign or is a well-established firm in the midst of a relaunch, courting industry trade magazines and book publishers by submitting press releases and feature ideas can attract attention to a particular niche or specialization

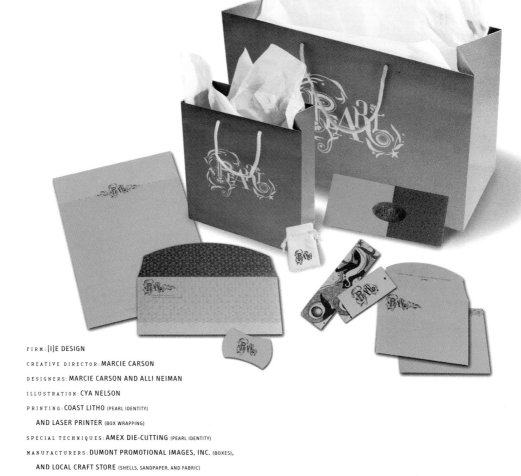

FIRM: [I]E DESIGN

CREATIVE DIRECTOR: MARCIE CARSON

DESIGNERS: MARCIE CARSON AND ALLI NEIMAN

ILLUSTRATION: CYA NELSON

PRINTING: COAST LITHO (PEARL IDENTITY)
AND LASER PRINTER (BOX WRAPPING)

SPECIAL TECHNIQUES: AMEX DIE-CUTTING (PEARL IDENTITY)

MANUFACTURERS: DUMONT PROMOTIONAL IMAGES, INC. (BOXES),
AND LOCAL CRAFT STORE (SHELLS, SANDPAPER, AND FABRIC)

a time for intro- spection

The dual-functioning package serves as an outer container as well as a desk stand. It is built using a custom duplex of Curious Metallic Ionized and Silktouch Rivercord from Fibermark. The outer surface features the calendar year, a line drawing of the company's building, their logo, and their Web address. Each piece is letterpress-printed with a special mix metallic ink to match the paper, giving it a subtle debossed effect. The iridescent bellyband, which provides assembly instructions, holds the calendar cards in place.

"Every year we try to do a promotion that is a bit of a keeper for our clients," shares art director Ric Riordon. "Given the sensitivity of September 11, we wanted to be a little more thoughtful about what we were communicating as a company—not just to our client base but to the world at large." The idea was to create a promotion that would be a source of inspiration and wisdom in a time where many people were pausing to think and reexamine their lives. With faith and philosophy as driving forces, the design team developed a memorable keepsake calendar. Meant to be a soft sell, the promotion's only point of contact is a Web site listing.

To kick-start the creative process, the design team looked toward the Bible for inspiration, particularly the Old Testament. "We went through a ream of scriptures to determine which were most easily embraced by the largest number of people," recalls Riordon. To ensure the imagery was as thought-provoking as the text, the design team chose a conceptual approach. The images, warm and mostly figurative, work harmoniously with the text to deliver each heartfelt message. Printed in four-color process plus silver, the calendar is calming, reassuring, and stable. An aqueous varnish, applied to both sides of the monthly pages, adds luster, while the rounded edges that appear throughout soften the presentation. A translucent bellyband keeps the cards from moving around within the package and provides a simple diagram to assist in assembly. "The level of excellence in the finishing and details comes together in one package. It is a statement in and of itself," admits creative director Dan Wheaton. "It says what we are capable of and aspire to." Riordon agrees. "We see it as a testimony to our thinking, our craftsmanship, and our creativity."

The biggest challenge was to develop an outer packaging that also served as a stand for the calendar. "Technically, the container was a bit of a twister," admits designer Amy Montgomery. "We wanted a container that was attractive but also functional. A disposable piece would have wasted our efforts." After playing with numerous options, the design team finally came up with the solution they were looking for. Die line in hand, they explored an array of fabrics and papers, producing a few mockups to ensure the proper weight, look, and feel of the piece. To add visual interest, the surface of the custom duplex was letter-press-printed with a special mix metallic. The closure mechanism, made from a purse clasp and a grommet, also serves as a hanging device for the cards. After receiving this promotion, several clients approached the firm about producing a similar project.

TECHNICAL TIPS

When using a custom duplex, always make a mockup before going into production so you can better determine how the materials will look, feel, and assemble. When printing on a colored stock, always run a few tests to make sure the resulting effect is what you want. Don't be afraid to try new materials and explore new ground in your promotions, as they will later serve as a way of exposing clients to other possibilities.

1

The closure mechanism, made from a purse clasp and a grommet, also serves as a hanging device for the calendar. Each month features thought-provoking text accompanied by conceptually driven imagery. The self-contained piece is designed to sit on a desk year-round as a source of strength and hope.

The calendar is displayed in a palette of six subtle tones that repeat to form a visual rhythm. Although they appear to be reproduced as rich duotones, each card is printed in four-color process accented by silver metallic ink. On the reverse side is a double hit of silver. A finishing aqueous varnish is applied to both sides for luster and elegance. The cards are drilled, allowing them to easily hang off the accompanying stand.

3

2

FIRM: THE RIORDON DESIGN GROUP, INC.

CREATIVE DIRECTOR: DAN WHEATON

ART DIRECTOR: RIC RIORDON

DESIGNERS: AMY MONTGOMERY, SHARON PECE,
AND SHIRLEY RIORDON

ILLUSTRATION: TIM WARNOCK

PHOTOGRAPHY: RIC RIORDON AND VARIOUS STOCK

PRINTER: CONTACT CREATIVE

BINDERY: CONTACT CREATIVE AND ANSTEY BOOKBINDING

SPECIAL TECHNIQUES: ANSTEY BOOKBINDING

from production to design

The custom die-cut folder is beautifully printed in three solid PMS colors on Mohawk Navajo 100-lb. cover stock with an overall matte varnish on both sides. A metallic sticker, silk-screen-printed with the company's logo, nicely accents the circular die-cut pattern on the cover. The bilingual package was sent in a silver bag sealed with a consumer product called InstaSealTM/DM.

When Kolégramdesign decided to redirect their company from a production house to a full-service design studio, they knew an image-building brochure was in order. After investigating the competitive landscape, the design firm decided to create a presentation that really stood out strategically as well as creatively. "We picked up profiles of design companies in the region and noticed that they were doing just typical brochures," says creative director and designer Mike Teixeira. "We needed to do something different."

With an artistic flair, the design firm put to work an attractive combination of materials and techniques to deliver their message. The presentation begins with an intricate pocket folder that is embossed, matte varnished, die-cut, and custom scored. A metallic sticker made of brightly brushed stainless polyester adorns the cover with the firm's logo, elegantly silk-screen-printed on top. The promotion's overall theme, Back to the Source, is conveyed through the glossy tint-varnished circular arrows that are framed by the die-cut pattern—handsome but technically challenging to produce—on the front.

Inside the kit, a bilingual introduction card unfolds to reveal a series of six cards. Each card features a softly silhouetted image printed on Mohawk Superfine 100-lb. cover stock, giving it the look and feel of a fine watercolor painting. On the back, eloquently composed text calls attention to key aspects of the firm's unique approach and process. The custom folder closes with an individually numbered business card that inserts into die-cut slots on the back. It is perforated, allowing it to be easily detached and slipped into a business card holder or Rolodex.

To make sure the kit worked the way it should, the design team tested the piece on several people outside their studio to observe different behaviors. They also made several mockups, making sure to analyze every last detail. According to Teixeira, "For the piece to come together, we really had to match up everything, and the die had to be right on." Throughout the entire package, the imagery, text, production techniques, and materials work hand in hand to position Kolégramdesign as a technically innovative design firm with a keen sense for detail. The final design was delivered to prospective clientele in a metallic silver envelope, heat-sealed with a consumer product commonly used for closing food storage bags. The investment the firm made in this brochure has paid off in spades, as business has tripled since its arrival. "It has also set a trend in the region," exclaims Teixeira.

TECHNICAL TIPS

To make sure a complex pocket folder with various folds, scores, and die-cuts works the way it is designed to, test it on people outside of the design community to see how they open and interact with what you have created. Don't be afraid to use ordinary consumer products in order to produce the piece in-house. They are usually a lot cheaper than their industrial counterparts and often work just as well.

1 The folder, which boasts an array of interesting folds and angles, is embossed and scored with a series of width options for expandability. A business card, conveniently attached to the back of the folder, is individually numbered and perforated for easy detachment.

The six die-cut cards are held together by a gate-folded wrapper that also serves as an introductory device for the package. Each card features a concept image and supportive text in both French and English; these work together to communicate the firm's process and design philosophy. The artistic look and feel appeals to Kolégramdesign's predominately cultural clientele.

1

2

3

FIRM: KOLÉGRAMDESIGN

CREATIVE DIRECTOR AND DESIGNER: MIKE TEIXEIRA

PHOTOGRAPHY: HEADLIGHT INNOVATIVE IMAGERY

PRINTING: IMPRIMERIE DU PROGRÈS (BROCHURE)
AND SÉRIGRAPHIE ALBION (LABEL)

SPECIAL TECHNIQUES: CAPITAL BOX (DIE-CUTTING)
AND STYLEX 3D (EMBOSSING)

MANUFACTURER: ASSOCIATED BAGS CO.

moving announcement

Douglas Joseph Partners had moved just a hop, skip, and a jump down the road from 11999 San Vicente Boulevard to 11812 San Vicente Boulevard and needed to let people know about it. "Our goal was to announce our move and to do it in such a way that it was memorable," recalls creative director and president Doug Joseph. Because the piece was a moving announcement, a flipbook format seemed the perfect way to convey the information.

The game plan was to animate a man walking across the page, starting at the old address and moving toward the new location—simple, right? Well, not exactly. The feat required the designer not only to plot various gestures that simulated the movements of a man walking but also to create a character interesting enough to look at. In addition, the figure had to remain consistent in shape and height throughout in order to make the animation believable and seamless. The designer had to do all this within a given size and number of pages that were predetermined based on maximizing the press sheet. To get the mechanics just right, several dummies were produced.

The next task was to identify the paper and bindery that would best carry the subtle message. Providing just the right opacity and ease of use, Fraser Papers Pegasus 100-lb. smooth text in brilliant white was found to be the best stock for the job. Double bronze rivets were the clear bindery winner. "For a book whose sole purpose is to be flipped through over and over again, perfect binding would have failed eventually," adds Joseph. "The rivets will never fail." The entire piece was printed on one side only in a palette indicative of the firm's new office space.

To ship the animated announcement, a custom die-cut fluted cardboard box was created. It was designed to protect the flipbook, make it stand out in the mail, and be cost-effective. The mailing labels that seal the outer package were also created specifically for the moving announcement. The simple and straightforward piece was sent to existing and prospective clients as well as vendors. "Most people kept the flipbook on their desks because it was fun to pick up every now and then," shares Joseph. "We knew we were successful based on the number of calls and comments we received afterwards. In past moves, we've done simple announcement cards and never heard a word from anybody."

TECHNICAL TIPS

The animation has to be just right for a flipbook to work. Make several dummies, checking the fluidity of movement and the overall graphic appeal. Before the book is bound, make a final dummy from the press sheets as a last-minute check. To save money, maximize your press sheet.

1

By using a flipbook, Douglas Joseph Partners made memorable their relocation from 11999 San Vicente Boulevard to 11812 San Vicente Boulevard. The color palette throughout, PMS 617, PMS 7531, and a custom-matched yellow-green, are all taken from the new office space.

2

The animated moving announcement is sent to clients and vendors in a custom die-cut package made of fluted cardboard, both attractive and functional. It is sealed with a label designed especially for the announcement.

1

2

FIRM: DOUGLAS JOSEPH PARTNERS

CREATIVE DIRECTORS: DOUG JOSEPH AND SCOTT LAMBERT

DESIGNER: MARK SCHWARTZ

ILLUSTRATION: MARK SCHWARTZ

PRINTING: ANDERSON LITHOGRAPH

BINDERY: JENCO

double the
impact

A miniportfolio, housed in a translucent, orange, plastic box, is the device used to introduce Platform Creative to prospective clients. The portfolio pages, printed internally using a Xerox 7700DN dual-sided color printer, highlight the quality and diversity of the firm's work. The package is labeled front and back, shrink-wrapped, and sent as a self-mailer.

Sometimes a single mailing is just not enough. Clients often must be reminded several times before a message yields a response. To pack a one-two punch, Platform Creative developed a series of mailings to introduce themselves and their work to prospective clients. The first mailing, a miniportfolio of sorts, helped establish credibility and show off Platform's breath and experience in the marketplace. "The goal was to legitimize our services with our previous successes," says creative director and designer Robert Dietz. "In most cases, designers send out promotions to get a portfolio review which will then lead to a relationship. Our thought was to get the portfolio review out of the way right up front." The firm could tailor the customizable piece to any prospective client's needs. "We can also take feedback from pervious recipients and refine the type of information included for future mailings," adds Dietz.

To house and accent their work, the design team explored an array of materials before they decided on a brilliant orange plastic. "The impact is immediate," shares Dietz. "The translucent plastic acts as a tease in that you can see something bright and substantial inside. The color demands notice when combined with other mail and materials on someone's desk." The plastic, chosen for its visual impact and relationship to the company's branded color scheme, was purchased in large sheets and trimmed to create miniboxes, wire-o bound covers, and presentation portfolios. Because of the plastic's translucency, type can be clearly read from the printed material underneath, eliminating the need to imprint the plastic itself. The biggest challenge was nailing down the mechanics of the box; numerous changes were made before a design with just the right look, strength, and locking mechanism was established. The completed package was labeled and shrink-wrapped to minimize damage in delivery.

The follow-up promotion was designed to mimic the look and feel of the first mailing yet still have its own identity. Thus, the second mailing was delivered in bright orange, translucent envelopes. "The goal of the cards was to expound our business philosophies and reinforce key attributes of how we think and solve problems," offers Dietz. "We wanted the cards to map back to the idea that strong messaging, marketing, and visual platforms are the basics for a successful brand." The cards, designed to be interactive, play on the firm's name and philosophy. Each card has a key word on one side and a business statement on the back. A bellyband, used to keep the message-driven cards in their proper order, provides simple instructions on how they can be used to build a structure or platform. As a continuation of the overall messaging, more cards can be created and sent to the same target audience at a later date.

TECHNICAL TIPS

Work closely with your vendors, utilizing them for technical assistance when determining mechanical feasibility. Whenever you use a new material, create prototypes and perform test mailings to make sure the chosen vehicle successfully delivers your message intact. When using plastics, budget time for adjustments and revisions before final manufacturing. Don't hesitate to solicit feedback from existing clients about your promotions. Their insight can be quite valuable.

The s|
secon|
The o|
is me|
fit ni|
is coa|

The set of die-cut cards, printed on 100-lb Topcoat cover gloss on two sides, is held in place by a bellyband. The orange, translucent envelope looks and feels like the first mailing. The address label, symbolic of a three-dimensional box or platform, is consistent with the firm's letterhead, business cards, envelopes, and Web site. The stackable cards provide interaction and make a connection to the firm's philosophy that strong messaging and visual platforms are the basics for a successful brand.

An 11- by 17-inch (28- by 43-centimeter) portfolio, used as a presentation device at meetings, utilizes the same translucent plastic to make a connection to the promotional campaign.

FIRM: PLATFORM CREATIVE GROUP, INC.

CREATIVE DIRECTOR: ROBERT DIETZ

DESIGNERS: ROBERT DIETZ,
KATHY THOMPSON, AND JIN KWON

ILLUSTRATION: JIN KWON
AND KATHY THOMPSON

PHOTOGRAPHY: IRIDIO (PORTFOLIOS)
AND PHOTODISC (CARDS)

PRINTING AND BINDERY: GAC ALLIED

MANUFACTURERS: ACTION ENVELOPE
AND GENERAL BINDERY COMPANY

1

3

2

1

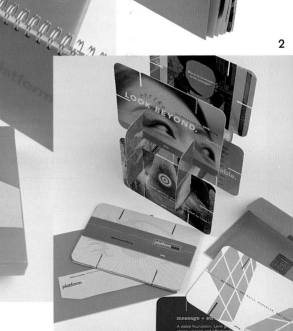

Gerald & Cullen Rapp, Inc., needed an elaborate, high-impact advertising piece to showcase their team of anaglyph, pop-up, and sound technology producers. They also wanted "to promote the illustrator, who did the background, as well as the design firm and printer I was representing at the time," adds creative director and agent Gerald Rapp. Working collaboratively, the team of experts developed a large-format, three-panel, letter-folded technology extravaganza.

For an element of surprise, the cover was designed as a standard black-and-white, two-dimensional brochure with the tagline "Say Goodbye to Flat Advertising." Once inside, a highly saturated color presentation complete with pop-ups, sound, and anaglyphic imagery unfolded. "Our brains are wired to expect something two-dimensional, especially when it arrives flat in the mail," comments paper engineer Phillip Fickling. "A pop-up adds huge emotional impact to your message, thereby increasing its retention. Pop-ups just have that wow factor." Throughout the excitement-filled promotion, each custom-designed pop-up was directly adhered to the surface with tabs. The overall use of paper pop-ups adds physical depth to the otherwise two-dimensional piece.

The recording that accents the technology-based piece utilized a small, battery-operated sound chip to carry its message. The inner workings were physically shown to demonstrate how the technology operates. In most cases, the sound chip is hidden within the constructs of a piece. "There are chips that will record almost any message, and they are typically used in small runs to a narrowly targeted audience," details Rapp. "If you are doing a larger quantity, you can use a prerecorded standard message that is already built into the chip." For this technology, there is a wide array of existing sounds at varying time intervals available.

The most intriguing aspect of the piece was its use of anaglyph technology. The 3-D glasses and stereoscopic viewers beckon the viewer to actively participate. "If someone receives a piece of direct mail or opens a magazine and sees a pair of 3-D glasses, there is something terrifically compelling about it," shares anaglyphic consultant Steve Aubrey. "The notice factor and the ability to rise above the general noise level are probably the greatest advantages of the medium in the competitive marketplace." With the use of anaglyph imagery, the subject matter is transformed from a flat reproduction to a spatially engaging and highly dimensional experience.

Acting as a demonstrative device, the high-impact, eye-catching brochure showed prospective clients the potential that dimension and sound could bring to their advertising. The effect is similar to when, in the *Wizard of Oz*, Dorothy breaks free from the confines of Kansas and enters into a magical, new world. As stated in the brochure, "Readers will experience your advertising in an entirely new way when they leave the overcrowded land of flat advertising and step into the new world of state-of-the-art printacular magic."

TECHNICAL TIPS

If you are interested in using anaglyphic, sound chip, or pop-up technologies, it is highly advisable to bring in experts to work with you as early as the concept stage. Engaging a good technical consultant allows you to effectively utilize each medium to its fullest. The Graphic Arts Technical Foundation (GATF) is a good place to start your search for specialists in anaglyphic technology.

When using pop-ups, produce an accurate mockup to ensure the art is where you want it to be and the paper is the right weight for the job. Also, pay attention to the paper's grain direction. As a general rule, creases should run parallel to the grain. To address durability concerns, remember that creases last longer than perforations and, over time, mechanical joins last longer than adhesives.

For anaglyphic usage, avoid using colors that approach saturated red and cyan, the two separation filters commonly used in 3-D eyewear. The closer you get to these colors the more your image will seem ultraneon and unnatural. However, if that is the effect you are looking for, you can exploit these colors by introducing them into the scene as accents.

There are two ways in which to show something in 3-D. One is by printing the left- and the right-eye images on top of each other using complementary colors. When you put on the red and cyan filtered glasses, you get the illusion of depth. Another way is by using stereo viewers, where the two images are physically segregated and do not require color separation filters. The advantage to this process is that it imposes no color limitations. The down side is that it is a bit more expensive per unit to produce.

The piece presents itself like a traditional two-dimensional brochure, creating an element of surprise once opened. It is sent in a custom-designed envelope with a cover letter to agency account executives, creative directors, and corporate communications people.

Inside the high-impact promotional brochure, three technologies—anaglyphic, sound chip recording, and pop-ups—are demonstrated. The piece is four-color offset-printed and laminated for durability.

DO IT FOR LESS

When using pop-ups, design your piece to minimize handwork, saving valuable time. It is also a good idea to stick to traditional paper, as more elaborate materials, like acetate windows and synthetics, increase the cost significantly.

If you know you want to employ anaglyphs in your promotion, remember that it is most cost-effective to photograph the piece in 3-D. If you are using illustration, a 3-D computer-generated image will also save in 2-D-to-3-D conversion time and money. Many 3-D software programs have stereo converters built in, making the process user-friendly.

1

FIRM: GERALD & CULLEN RAPP, INC.

CREATIVE DIRECTOR: GERALD RAPP

DESIGNER: BLUE BRICK DESIGN

ILLUSTRATION: SHARMEN LIAO

PHOTOGRAPHY: STEVE SPELMAN
AND KENNETH WILLARDT

PRINTING: FOX PRESS, INC.

SPECIAL TECHNIQUES: USA PRINT & POPS
AND ANAGLYPHIC IMAGING

2

the art of direct mail

In today's demanding marketplace, direct mail promotions need to be innovative from both a strategic and creative standpoint to leave a lasting impression on prospective buyers. They must instantly grab the recipients' attention, motivating them to look inside and participate in the overall messaging. A good direct mail promotion encourages interaction. To achieve this, firms are no longer doing mass mailings; instead, they are spending their time and money producing well-targeted promotions that speak to the audience in a very thought-provoking and personal way. "Your potential client comes across so many direct mail pieces all day long. You want to create something that your audience will want to hold onto and not something that ends up in the wastebasket," notes Charlotte Noruzi of Question Design. "The more personal and functional a promo is, the better." Harvey Hirsch of Media Consultants agrees. "Put yourself into the mind of the receiver and try to develop something that makes you smile, laugh, or gets you emotionally involved." The best promotions create an experience for the recipient.

To create distinction, mailers are increasingly incorporating alternative materials, formats, and techniques. The use of scented papers, three-dimensional packaging, add-ons, and textural accents all help engage the audience by appealing to the senses. "To make sure we are creating innovative and inspirational solutions, I try to keep everyone here refreshed and aware of what is going on in printing, production, and paper. I really utilize my vendor resources," offers Marcie Carson of IE Design. "Any time our printing reps get something

interesting in their shops or the paper manufacturers start a new line, they always call on us and let us know about them." Noruzi adds, "It is important to keep on top of the latest trends, equipment, mediums, and materials to come up with a different way to do something. Always innovate, experiment, doing whatever it takes to stand apart." The architecture of the, once typical brochure is evolving.

Copywriting, which once played second fiddle to design, has become an integral and vital part of the creative process. Most firms now see it as the foundation from which a promotion is built—and rightly so. Direct mail copy, a one-on-one form of communication, is strongest when targeted and motivational in nature. "We believe copy should always be crisp and succinct, because people don't want to have to read a lot of it. You must quickly address the recipient's needs, wants, and aspirations, and why they should consider your product or service," reminds David Collins of Grafik. "Whether the tone of the copy is light or somber, it must provide the information in a way that readers can appreciate and understand. In other words, it's not about you, it's about them." The whole package has to come together in a manner consistent with the overall concept, and every part of the promotion has to work hard doing its job: supporting and delivering a company's message. Strategies vary from single hits to a

series of mailings that function like a campaign. Direct mail is also being integrated with other promotional vehicles.

In a marketplace that speaks to reduced budgets and limited resources, creatives are doing all they can to make sure their promotions are as effective as they can be before they are delivered. A lot more time is spent doing mockups and analyzing just how recipients will read and use what is produced. Test mailings are conducted to ensure promotions arrive the way they should; deviations are corrected immediately. List maintenance is also important, and updates are made annually. Companies are developing coded systems to track their promotions, and follow-up procedures are becoming a permanent part of the overall process. "In today's competitive marketplace, it is critical that an aggressive program of telemarketing be employed if you want results," advises Hirsch. "I never wait for a prospect to get back to me." Business reply cards, toll-free numbers, telemarketing, and other such methods are all being explored.

Direct mail, one of the most responsive and effective forms of advertising, allows a message to be disseminated to a targeted audience in a personal and customized fashion. Because of technology, databases can be manipulated into solid mailing lists, which can target any market with pinpoint accuracy. With a captivating and engaging design, an accurate and well-targeted mailing list, and an incentive to respond, direct mail is a great way to go after new prospects as well as generate repeat business.

FIRM: QUESTION DESIGN

CREATIVE DIRECTOR AND DESIGNER: CHARLOTTE NORUZI

ILLUSTRATION: CHARLOTTE NORUZI

PRINTING: EPSON PRINTER (MASK)

MANUFACTURER: KATE'S PAPERIE (RIBBON)

seasonal message

"Each promotion is a chance to explore a new medium and a new way of doing something," offers designer and illustrator Charlotte Noruzi. "It is important to be as innovative as you can, making your piece memorable and personal. The more it feels like your audience is receiving a gift, the better." By using an unconventional vehicle—a handmade mask—the multifaceted artist was able to attract the attention of her publishing audience. The copy, reading "Kiss Someone this Halloween," helped tie in the season and, at the same time, highlight the artist's recently illustrated cover for a book entitled *Kissing Kate*. "The other intent of the promo was to actually have my audience wear the mask to a Halloween party and create a buzz," shares Noruzi.

The stylistically hand-painted mask was reproduced on heavyweight matte paper using an Epson printer. Each piece was hand-cut and assembled by the artist. A shimmering ribbon adorned the playful promotion, allowing it to be tied on or hung if so desired. The highly illustrative promotion was sent in a hand-lettered vellum envelope. The brilliant yellow color of the translucent outer package nicely complemented the whimsical purple mask inside. "I wanted my audience to be able to see through the envelope for their curiosity to be aroused as to what was inside," Noruzi adds. A limited run was created and mailed during October. "Targeting a small but specific audience is a much more successful and productive path," claims the artist. "It's better to know twenty-five prospective clients personally than one thousand impersonally or not at all." Targeted toward art directors and editors at publishing houses, the Halloween mask promotion was Noruzi's way of calling attention to her ingenuity, creativity, and vast array of skills. "I think uniqueness is important," she concludes. "In this age of computerization, a handmade promotion is a breath of fresh air."

FIRM: MEDIA CONSULTANTS

CREATIVE DIRECTOR AND DESIGNER:
HARVEY HIRSCH

ILLUSTRATION: ERIC ROSE

PRINTING: SHARP AR-C250 DIGITAL COLOR COPIER

SPECIAL TECHNIQUES: STEEL RULE DIES (FISH DIE)

AND HOLOGRAPHIC FINISHING (PRESSING)

making it pop

"I have been folding paper since I was a kid, and the finished piece always elicited a great response when I handed it to someone," recalls creative director and designer Harvey Hirsch. "When I started my own marketing graphics firm, I printed an illustrated fish on my black-and-white copier. It was a smiling fish that said 'Thanks for Swimming with Us.' I sent them to our clients, and the response was so positive that I had some printed in four color." After an assignment from Sharp Electronics to produce a dealer-directed campaign launching the company's digital color copier and printer, Hirsch made a breakthrough discovery. With this new technology he could decorate, personalize, and make dimensional his origami fish mailers with the press of a button.

Printed on a Sharp AR-C250 digital color copier using a metallic paper, each origami fish mailer can be adorned with any typeface and color, allowing modifications on the fly. The fish and custom envelope are scored and nicked to facilitate folding and removal.

To create distinction, promotions are incorporating alternative materials, formats, and techniques. The use of scented papers, three-dimensional packaging, add-ons, and textural accents all help engage the audience by appealing to the senses.

For alignment purposes, each sheet of paper has a hole that acts like a registration mark. "Adjusting the artwork on the computer so it fits precisely over the pattern when it prints requires only a few clicks and a few test sheets," notes Hirsch. Each fish is adhered to the promotional card with Velcro, making it removable.

The eye-catching, three-dimensional mailer was so successful that it opened new opportunities for the marketing and creative firm to explore. "I can now license my products and technology to selected clients by SIC and Zip codes," shares Hirsch. "This enabled me to spin off a whole new corporation, called Pop'N'Fold Papers, Inc., with a product line so innovative that I can offer almost thirty three-dimensional products that can all be personalized in short runs. This gives a user the opportunity to mail a high-response mailer and test offers, copy, prices, pitches, etc., without a plate change, and it can be in the mail in hours, not weeks. These little fish helped me build a business."

kinetic announcement

When it came time to relocate their offices, Levy Creative Management knew they had to send out an announcement that was far from ordinary. Working collaboratively with designer Mirko Ilić, they came up with an interesting and cost-effective solution: a moving announcement that moves! Each mailer, printed in fluorescent inks on Gilbert Gilclear 28-lb. vellum, was die-cut to reveal the firm's logo. The die-cut shape, printed with the new contact information, was put to work, moving around loosely within a clear plastic envelope. "As it travels through the mail, the Ls move and, no matter where the shapes fall, you can always read at least one or two words," explains Ilić. "The L also becomes almost like a business card that you can staple in your Rolodex." The logo, a strong graphic symbol for the creative firm, is highly visible in all of Levy Creative Management's collateral. "All of our materials create a cohesive and consistent image within our industry. Every marketing piece that leaves our office has our logo and our Web site, and they all coordinate," comments artist representative Sari Levy. "There's a consistency that clients acknowledge and appreciate."

When it comes to promotion, the youthful, eclectic, and happening group is not afraid to explore new and innovative ways to deliver their message. "You can promote yourself in a plethora of ways now, and it certainly doesn't need to be in a brochure format. There are endless opportunities to expand beyond what was once considered typical," says Levy. "We are extremely open-minded when it comes to direct mail and have thus come up with ideas such as games, flip cards, CD-ROMs, DVDs, videos, catalogs, brochures, and more." Levy Creative Management's internationally recognized artists cover a broad spectrum of markets, from movie sets, props, posters, and promotions to editorial, publishing, and advertising work.

In a marketplace that speaks to reduced budgets and limited resources, creatives are doing all they can to make sure that their promotions are as effective as they can be before they are delivered. A lot more time is spent on mock-ups and analyzing just how recipients will read and use what is produced.

FIRM: LEVY CREATIVE MANAGEMENT, LLC

CREATIVE DIRECTOR: MIRKO ILIĆ

DESIGNERS: MIRKO ILIĆ AND HEATH HINEGARDNER

ILLUSTRATION: DAVID COOPER, ALAN DINGMAN, SHANE EVANS, THOMAS FLUHARTY, MAX GRAFE, KRIS HARGIS, JENNY LADEN, TIM OKAMURA, ROBERTO PARADA, LAUREN REDNISS, OREN SHERMAN, DOUG STRUTHERS, AND JONATHAN WEINER

PRINTING: ROB-WIN PRESS, INC.

MANUFACTURER: IMPACT IMAGES (CLEAR BAGS)

BEST IF USED NO LATER THAN NOV 93

WE FOUND THIS ON YOUR ADVERTISING.
CALL US FOR A FRESH BATCH.

Eventually, every sales promotion becomes stale.
And every print campaign loses its fizz.
But don't let them get too outdated.
Call Grafik before it all goes sour.

For more than 20 years,
we've been restocking the region's
most notable marketing departments
with piping hot creative.

Call Lance Wain today at 703.299.4515.
Time is running out.

— WWW.GRAFIK.COM

DANGER! RISK OF SHOCK!

PREPARE YOURSELF.
OUR CREATIVE CAN BE SOMEWHAT JOLTING.

EXPERIENCE GRAFIK

EXPERIENCE GRAFIK

PREVENTS HAIR LOSS

DEVELOPING AN INTERACTIVE WEB SITE
DOESN'T HAVE TO BE STRESSFUL.

Believe it or not, you really can
create a robust web presence
without a lot of trauma.
Fact is, Grafik helps businesses
and organizations do it everyday.

Call Lance Wain at 703.299.4515.
Lose your troubles – not your hair.

— WWW.GRAFIK.COM

DON'T LET YOUR MARKETING FALL INTO
INEXPERIENCED HANDS.

You're busy. You're rushed.
You're under a lot of pressure.
In short, you have no time for whiny kids.

So why not talk to the
seasoned professionals at Grafik,
the marketing firm that's been providing
adult supervision for more than 20 years.

Call Lance Wain today at 703.299.4515.
It truly is the most mature thing you can do.

— WWW.GRAFIK.COM

KEEP AWAY FROM CHILDREN

Copywriting, which once played second fiddle to design, has become an integral and vital part of the creative process. Most firms now see it as the foundation from which a promotion is built—and rightly so.

just teasing

Looking for a creative way to develop new business, Grafik chose direct mail as the perfect medium to capture the attention of their audience: marketing VPs. "Our primary objective was to create a campaign of mailers that not only spoke directly to the clients' needs but also showed how we could help them solve their most difficult challenges," says creative director and designer David Collins. "We thought it would be fun to do a promotional series around the warning labels you find on products—the expiration date on food, prescription medication warnings, etc. They are common in everyday life, yet appealing as a short, straightforward means of communication." To keep the effort simple and cost-effective, the design team developed a series of two-paneled, wafer-sealed self-mailers to carry their message. Each piece was printed in three PMS colors plus black—a palette taken from Grafik's existing brand identity. To provide visual interest, attention-getting labels were hand-applied slightly askew to each self-mailer. Prospects received one piece every week for four weeks.

The first mailer that was sent shed light on the firm's experience. The teaser "Keep Away from Children" tapped into people's innate desire to protect their young. Hence, this mailer got opened. Inside, the piece warned prospective clients not to let their marketing fall into inexperienced hands and positioned Grafik as the seasoned choice. The second mailer, with the key line "Best If Used No Later Than Nov. 93," focused on the firm's advertising capabilities. Because the date was so old, the recipient was compelled to open the piece to find out what

was so outdated. Inside, they discovered it was their advertising. Grafik then boasted their ability to offer a fresh perspective. The third mailer got itself opened by claiming to prevent hair loss, a popular concern for many. Its slant was to focus on the firm's new media capabilities, stating that Web site development doesn't have to be stressful. The forth and final mailer, entitled "Danger! Risk of Shock!" was a three-paneled, letter-folded piece. It contained an interactive CD-ROM of the firm's visually arresting work.

With clearly defined objectives, a carefully crafted strategy that was mindful of the prospective client's needs, and a series of mailers that really captured the attention of its audience, Grafik was able to deliver their message and get the response they were looking for.

FIRM: GRAFIK

CREATIVE DIRECTORS: DAVID COLLINS AND JUDY KIRPICH

DESIGNERS: DAVID COLLINS AND HAL SWETNAM

PRINTING: McARDLE PRINTING COMPANY

interesting
bindings,
fasteners,
and wraps

Bindery has taken on a new look. Creatives are no longer locked into the traditional saddle-stitched, spiral, or perfect bound brochures. From elastics, stitching, and the tying of a cord to magnets, rivets, and screws of all shapes and sizes, new bindings and fasteners are being discovered. Wraps have also come a long way. Air packs, surgical swab pouches, antistatic bags, and injection-molded tubes are just a few ways creatives are packaging their work. Enclosures are being adapted from sources as diverse as the fashion, automotive, medical, and meatpacking industries. "Look at unexpected sources," advises Eleni Chronopoulos of Reebok International Ltd. "Items that are standard in one industry can appear custom-made in another." Marcie Carson of IE Design adds, "The fashion industry, in particular, is a great place to discover unique odds and ends. Grommets, stitching, button and string closures, ribbons, and wraps are all beautiful binding techniques that have a distinct apparel quality. Occasionally, when I am in need of inspiration, I walk through a fabric store or flip through a fashion magazine. I never know what I might find!" Exploring outside the traditional venues for unconventional bindings, fasteners, and wraps opens the door for new approaches and possibilities.

When searching for alternative solutions, allow yourself to be inspired and excited by even the most inconsequential things. Be sensually open and curious to what surrounds you every day, and you will discover new ways to solve old problems such as bindery. "It's just a matter of being observant," offers illustrator Barbara Lipp. "Someone I know described it as caressing the details of life."

creative
intelligence

The folder that packages all the materials is made of a durable substrate called Lexan. On the back, four rubber automotive joints are placed in die-cut holes to hold the piece together. Round magnets, adhered by hot glue, aid in closing the piece securely. Embossed circles act as guides to ensure proper positioning of the magnets. The business card is uniquely imprinted with the contact person's thumbprint on one side and a simulated magnetic strip on the other. The logo is derived from a 1950s filing cabinet that has steel label holders on the front of each drawer. When placed inside the holder, the label drops down slightly, cutting off the name a bit on the bottom. This look is graphically portrayed in the dossier logo.

Dossiercreative was looking to expand their market and services by repositioning themselves as a full-service branding company. They began their challenge by embarking on an extensive renaming project supplemented by a new identity package. "We started by changing our name to dossier, which means amassing information or intelligence on a subject or a person," says creative director Don Chisholm. "The concept was derived from thinking about how we have successfully worked with our clients. We use a process of collecting data that we call intelligence gathering." In developing their promotional material, dossiercreative wanted to play up on the intelligence concept by using an espionage-like twist.

To handle the task, the group was divided into several cross-functional teams. Once a comprehensive marketing strategy was in place, the design look-and-feel team took over, attacking the problem from both two-and three-dimensional perspectives. Once the idea was conceptualized, the project moved into the hands of the production and implementation team, which explored the feasibility of the desired design. The result was a well-thought-out, group-inspired, and fully integrated piece.

The Lexan folder, designed to simulate a secret report of sorts, holds the overview brochure, proposal brochure, cover letter, note cards, and a business card. Rubber automotive joints hold the piece together, and earth magnets, glued into position, lightly clamp it shut. The overview brochure and proposal, stochastic printed in four-color process plus PMS warm gray #9, features an artistically altered image of a briefcase on the inside French-folded covers. A satin spot varnish is used throughout. A semitranslucent Lexan sheet, silk-screened with a full coverage of warm gray #9, wraps each uniquely bound piece. Both brochures are visually accented with labels and number codes that also function as tracking devices for follow-up procedures. The letterhead and notecards are held together by grommets and a piece of Lexan—an interesting alternative to the paper clip. The business card is die-cut with a semicircle to tie in the grommets, magnets, and screws applied to the other components. Each card is individually marked with the contact person's unique thumbprint, further playing up the espionage concept. On the front of the card is a gray bar that will someday be replaced by a magnetic strip, allowing selective entrance into the firm. All the materials used in this piece add interest and texture to the industrial-looking package. The entire system was designed to be flexible, allowing for weekly or quarterly updates, as the firm requires.

TECHNICAL TIPS

With the Lexan, you cannot apply too much pressure when embossing or it will begin to stress the material, causing it to flare. Make sure you order enough material to test the stress points properly. If you are producing a brochure with both French-folded pages and standard pages, proper finishing work is integral to the success of a quality-looking piece. To avoid problems, each piece must be assembled before it is trimmed and drilled. The nameplates are a wonderful accent to this clever and engaging package. However, the acid-etching process is difficult to execute consistently. Many plates can be destroyed, leaving black and gray streaks on the metallic surface. It is best not to use this process when large quantities are required.

DO IT FOR LESS

Lexan, a washable and durable signage-based substrate, is expensive. There are other materials available that can deliver just as much or more for less money, such as PVC (0.10). Materialconnexion.com, a service that provides access to material specifications and supplier contact information for a nominal fee, is a great way to search for innovative materials and processes worldwide. Assembling the project internally can also save quite a bit of money. To tackle such a feat, you must develop a working plan—determining all of the necessary equipment, workspace, and storage required before the components are delivered. It is cost-prohibitive to produce a similar package using the same materials for large quantities; stick to a low run if budget is a concern.

The overview brochure, wrapped with a Lexan cover, highlights the firm's mission statement, operations, branding services, five-step working process, case studies, and diversified portfolio. It is bound with an acid-etched, stainless steel nameplate and a combination of stainless steel screws mixed with ⅜-inch (1-cm) aluminum Chicago screw backs—both special-ordered in the right depth. French-folded pages cover the brochure and divide the subject matter, giving weight to the overall piece. The letterhead is held together by grommets with a sampling of the Lexan material to make a connection to the rest of the package. The industrial-looking brochure is given to prospective clients. The proposal brochure, sent to existing clients, is bound with grommets, and the dossier logo is blind-embossed at the top and on the back of the Lexan wrap. It is used to hold proposals, case studies, and portfolio samples.

The notecards, which echo the graphics and key messaging from the overview brochure, are held together by grommets. A sampling of the Lexan material is brought in for visual continuity. The notecards are sent with the packet as a teaser or can be used as thank-you cards.

FIRM: DOSSIERCREATIVE

CREATIVE DIRECTOR: DON CHISHOLM

DESIGNER: MATTI CROSS

PHOTOGRAPHY: VERVE PHOTOGRAPHIC AND
   TONY HURLEY PHOTOGRAPHY

PRINTER AND BINDERY: HEMLOCK PRINTERS

SPECIAL TECHNIQUES: WESTERN NAMEPLATES

MANUFACTURER: PACIFIC FASTENERS

1

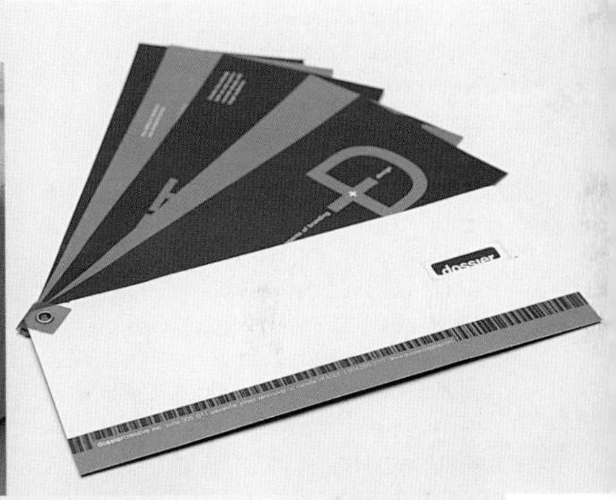

2

3

so you're getting married

The elegant keepsake promotion is presented inside a custom-designed box eloquently detailed with a silver foil–stamped logo. Inside the box, lies a side-sewn brochure accented by a silver grommet and hand-dyed ribbon. Candles are used as add-ons and serve as symbols of warmth and hope during this special time in one's life.

Good Gracious! Events, specialists in event planning and custom catering, wanted to have a signature piece to promote their wedding services. "When I sat down with the owner, it was clear that a typical white-and-gold bridal package would not suffice," remembers creative director and designer Marcie Carson. "Good Gracious's wedding events are magical, colorful, and romantic, and we really needed to convey that feeling in the piece."

To communicate just the right message, the promotion had to exhibit an artistic, almost signaturelike, quality with a keen attention for detail. It was important that the piece seem like a keepsake, something that signified the beginning of a beautiful experience to come. To make the piece more giftlike, both the designer and client agreed that candles, symbols of hope and life, were the perfect supportive elements. "We started with three candles—deep rust, magenta, and orange—avoiding the expected whites and creams," shares Carson. "We then began to look at box options and different coverings for the exterior, like bookcloth and handmade papers." The box had to be not only stunning but also durable enough to mail without looking bulky. To bring out the colors in the candles, the custom-manufactured box was wrapped with rust bookcloth and lined with handmade paper. A silver foil logo added detail to the exterior lid. Once the right look and feel of the box was in place, the designer began developing a brochure and identity system to bring the whole promotion together.

To showcase the company's extensive array of wedding services, a stunning brochure was created with many signature touches. The stitched binding, silver grommet, hand-dyed silk ribbon tie, and letterpress printing all contribute to the artistic quality of the piece. Throughout, key words like *promise*, *bond*, *savor*, *unity*, and *bliss* help position Good Gracious! Events as the company to make your wedding memorable from beginning to end. The warm and inviting wedding ensemble is sent as a self-mailer with a cover letter and business card. The entire package exudes the elegance and romance that most brides look for in their special day.

TECHNICAL TIPS

When creating a custom box such as this one, it is important to work closely with your vendors to be sure they clearly understand your vision. If you choose to use the box as a self-mailer, do a test mailing. The test mailing for this project showed that dividers were needed inside the box to prevent the candles from rolling around and chipping.

3

The promotional ensemble is designed as a self-mailer with the addition of a custom mailing label. The letterpress and offset-printed brochure juxtaposes beautiful floral patterns, which come to life with a tinted varnish, against copy that is warm, inviting, and reassuring.

Each package comes with a personalized note on custom-designed stationery. The letter-head, envelope, and business card make a connection with the rest of the promotion by incorporating the rust, silver, and tan color scheme and by picking up on the beautifully illustrated floral pattern.

1

CLIENT: GOOD GRACIOUS! EVENTS

FIRM: [I]E DESIGN

CREATIVE DIRECTOR AND DESIGNER: MARCIE CARSON

ILLUSTRATION: CYA NELSON

PRINTING: ROADRUNNER PRESS

(BROCHURE AND STATIONERY SYSTEM), AND AMES LETTERPRESS

BINDERY: C & S SALES (STITCHING AND GROMMET)

MANUFACTURER: C & S SALES (BOX)

2

team
players

To attract high-profile clients to their firm, Atom Design wanted to developed an image-building brochure with a strong business message that focused on creating partnerships, developing innovative solutions, and achieving results. "There is a lot of creative work out there, but it often doesn't meet the client's brief," observes creative director David Springford. "Our message is to convey that we are a young, approachable team who believe function is equal to form. Our creative and approachable nature is often appealing to large corporations, who can see the benefit in working with a smaller and more personal agency."

To ignite the process, a creative brief was formed, and the design team went to work. The result was an inviting brochure, an introduction of sorts. "We wouldn't expect you to want to work with a company you knew nothing about," the brochure copy details. "So, before you get involved with us, we'd like to tell you a bit about ourselves." The copy is warm, friendly, and flows from one page to the next to tell the company's story. Each spread delivers a brand-building message, whether for the design firm itself or for its clients. The dot patterns, symbolic of atoms, on the left-hand pages work in conjunction with the text and imagery to send a subtle message. "We wanted people to see that there is thought and depth behind the brochure," notes Springford. "Some clients pick up on it the first time and others the second or third."

On the cover, the firm's atom identity mark is interestingly portrayed. A small, centrally located die-cut hole reveals the logo through the brightly colored tissue-paper wrap underneath. The 28-page promotion is uniquely bound with an elastic band, which allows the piece to be expanded over time. The elastic is pulled taught, stitched, and wrapped over two half-circle cuts to keep it in place. The simple but elegant cover, unusual binding, use of vivid color, and the French-folded inside pages all add value and interest to the overall piece, leaving a lasting impression in the minds of many. "We wanted the brochure to be interesting, a little different, and precious," offers Springford. "Our aim was to provide prospective clients with an overall impression of our company and the varied work we produce." The piece is sent to prospective clients in a flat cardboard box that is folded and securely sealed with white cloth tape. "We are very proud of the result. We usually get a wow from people viewing it for the first time," concludes Springford. "It also allows us the opportunity to do something that clients fear. When they see the results, they may feel more comfortable pushing their boundaries."

1

The clean and understated cover is accented by the vivid color in the elastic binding and tissue-paper wrap, revealed through a small, centrally located die-cut hole. Throughout the brochure, each spread cleverly uses imagery, copy, and graphics to communicate key points to the audience.

2

The series of portfolio case studies helps show the range and diversity of work of which Atom Design is capable. Key words assist in highlighting how the design firm is able to work with clients to produce innovative solutions that achieve results. Each photograph is taken on client premises by the staff.

1

2

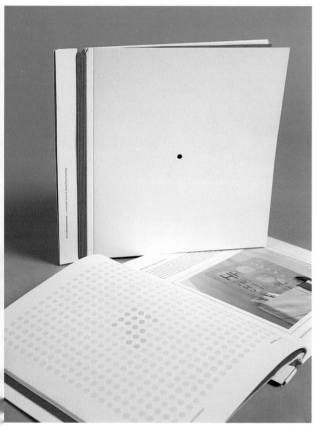

FIRM: ATOM DESIGN

CREATIVE DIRECTOR: DAVID SPRINGFORD

DESIGNERS: WILL PRICE, HELEN EVANS, AND DAVID SPRINGFORD

ILLUSTRATION: ATOM DESIGN TEAM

PHOTOGRAPHY: DAVID SPRINGFORD

PRINTING: ARC COLOURPRINT LTD.

SPECIAL TECHNIQUES: ARC COLOURPRINTER LTD. (DIE-CUTTING)

MANUFACTURERS: UK SEWING SERVICES (ELASTIC AND STITCHING), CITY LITHO LTD. (BOX), AND WRAPOLOGY LTD. (TISSUE)

committed
to work

The incriminating promotion comes in a black semigloss standard-size box adorned with an embossed metallic self-adhesive label that reveals the concept "Ten Years Hard Labour." Inside, a prison beanie, chocolate phone, and visitor's pass are added for visual support. All of the items sit securely inside a die-cut insert made of embossed Chequer-flute board that gives the appearance of prison cells. The promotion is sealed with a fluorescent orange sticker and hand-delivered to existing clients.

With ten years under their belt, the small New Zealand–based design firm wanted to celebrate. But what to do and how to do it was the question that creative director and designer Alexander Lloyd faced. To tackle the problem at hand, the creative firm immediately started brainstorming, looking for an unusual way to express their decade of hard work and business success. "I was trying to think of an angle and the phrase *Ten Years Hard Labour* seemed to pop out," says Lloyd. " To give the promotion a humorous twist, I came up with the idea of presenting myself as a convict."

The lead piece, a thirty-two-page, self-cover booklet and portfolio presentation, sheds insight into the mind and work of this ten-year graphic offender. "It begins so subtly, so insignificantly, you hardly realize you're getting involved in the world of graphic design. It might start with a logo here or a flyer there, maybe an advert or two, and before you know it, you're hooked," Lloyd cleverly writes. "And after a while you can't help yourself but spend countless hours studying the packaging at the supermarket or making covert brochure runs at visitor information centers—and fonts, don't get me started." Such confessions of a condemned lifer in the field of graphic design add an element of humor and interest to the portfolio display. The offset-printed piece closes with a section called The Casualties, which explores some of the ideas that have never seen the light of day—"forgotten designs in the minefield of graphic design," as Lloyd puts it.

The tongue-in-cheek promotion comes in a black box sealed with a fluorescent orange approval sticker from the pseudo Department of Graphic Design, Corrections, and Incarcerations. For the recipient, breaking the seal symbolizes acceptance of the enclosed graphic material, ten years in the making. An embossed metallic self-adhesive label mounted on the cover presents the concept. Inside lies the supporting cast of characters in this criminal escapade: a machine-embroidered black beanie, a visitor's tag, and a chocolate cell phone. The tag, printed in-house, is laminated with clear contact paper and trimmed to size. A clip completes the effect. The chocolate cell phone, bought at a local department store, was customized by replacing the backing and trimming the piece slightly. The biggest challenge, believe it or not, was removing the stubborn price tags.

By positioning himself as a graphic design junkie serving time for his serial offences, the designer was able to create a memorable and quite entertaining promotion to celebrate his first decade in business. With such dedication and creative ingenuity, it looks like Lloyd is in for another ten years. Parole denied!

TECHNICAL TIPS

If you are going to reproduce your portfolio in a booklet format, print more than you need so you can continue to hand them out throughout the year. The unit cost will be cheaper and you will avoid having to send out your limited supply of samples and tear sheets when clients request them. When creating a die-cut insert, make sure to account for the thickness of the paper. The insert must fit just right—not so tight that it buckles and not so loose that it slides out. When in doubt, make a mockup in the actual stock you want to use. Always contact your vendors for advice. When ordering custom-designed embroidery, you must supply camera-ready artwork rather than digital files.

DO IT FOR LESS

The die-cut insert is made with an expensive stock that comes embossed, but a simple, off-the-shelf paper can be used to save money. For further savings, a lot of printing, collating, bindery, and assembling can be done in-house.

The thirty-two-page, self-cover booklet, bound with an Acco 875 fastener, presents the design firm's criminal dedication to the field in a humorous and entertaining manner.

Within the promotional booklet, the design firm displays their best work. A range of projects is shown, including label and package design, business collateral, corporate identity, and branding, with a strong emphasis on logo development. At the end, four pages are dedicated to ideas that have never seen the light of day. The pages are conveniently scored so they turn easily within the tightly bound book.

1

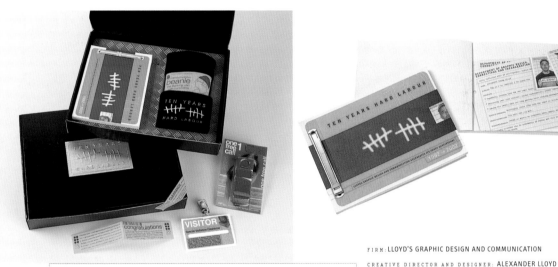

2

3

FIRM: LLOYD'S GRAPHIC DESIGN AND COMMUNICATION

CREATIVE DIRECTOR AND DESIGNER: ALEXANDER LLOYD

ILLUSTRATION: ALEXANDER LLOYD

PHOTOGRAPHY: ALEXANDER LLOYD AND JAAP VAN DER STOEL

PRINTING: BLENHEIM PRINTING COMPANY (BOOKLET) AND KNIGHT PRINT LTD. (BACKING FOR CHOCOLATE PHONE)

SPECIAL TECHNIQUES: NEWMAN GRAPHICS (HAT EMBROIDERY)

MANUFACTURERS: BERICA MARKETING (BOX AND BOX INSERT), ACCO NEW ZEALAND LTD. (BOOKLET BINDING), AND CORPORATE EXPRESS (TAG CLIP)

picturing words

Every year, Pentagram creates a little keepsake for clients, friends, and colleagues. The thought-provoking and intellectually stimulating gift is meant as a diversion during the crazy year-end months when everyone is overly bombarded with holiday messaging. To stand out from the crowd, Pentagram's signature booklets never refer to the season. This year was no different.

Inspired by the idea of wordplay, creative director and designer John McConnell chose to explore the game of crossword, giving it an innovative twist. Instead of using written clues to generate answers for the puzzle, he devised pictures or visual clues. Throughout the minibooklet, images—from Andy Warhol's Campbell's Soup Can to the bee from Paul Rand's famous reworking of the IBM logo—stimulate and challenge the viewer. Because of its universal appeal, the highly pictorial format was the perfect platform for Pentagram's international audience, as it utilizes a language that is not only familiar but also easy to understand despite cultural and language differences. As stated in the introduction, "Here's a crossword without any words for clues, just pictures instead. It's probably the biggest breakthrough in the history of making up crosswords since the cryptic crossword appeared in London's *Saturday Westminster* in 1925. It could even be as momentous as the very first crossword puzzle, which was created by Arthur Wynne from Liverpool and published in the *New York World* on December 21, 1913. With this acute sense of history, we draw a close to the twentieth century and the second millennium."

The ingenious idea had to be presented in a format that expressed its historical roots, so McConnell looked toward traditional bookmaking techniques. An exposed stitched bindery adheres an extended cover to three insert additions, making for an intimate twelve-page booklet. The highly textured black surface is accented, front and back, by white foil stamping that punctures the surface like an old letterpress. The simple but highly sophisticated piece was mailed in a white envelope to keep within the high-contrast color scheme. The only point of contact was a listing of Pentagram's worldwide offices on the back. It just goes to show how the simplest ideas can often be the most effective.

TECHNICAL TIPS

Small formats with interesting touches make a promotion more intimate and personal. Foil stamping can provide a nice, almost letterpress-like, effect. As an added bonus, an interesting graphic impression is created on the opposite side, something to incorporate into your overall design. Working with a colored stock is advantageous over printing a solid when you want even coverage that will not crack when folded.

DO IT FOR LESS

If you have more time than money to spend, read up on handmade books. Researching historical techniques and formats can add a vintage flair to your promotion. Reference sources also give step-by-step instructions on stitched bindery, ties, and wraps in an array of formats.

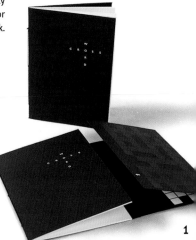

1

The white foil-stamped black cover sets the stage for a pictorial crossword game. The piece opens to a cleverly worded introduction that describes its historical significance.

2

Inside the stitch-bound booklet, well-known icons and universal imagery serve as visual clues to a white foil-stamped puzzle that unfolds in the back.

2

FIRM: PENTAGRAM

CREATIVE DIRECTOR: JOHN McCONNELL

DESIGNERS: JOHN McCONNELL AND HAZEL MacMILLAN

ILLUSTRATION: UK/BRIDGEMAN ART LIBRARY

PHOTOGRAPHY: TONY STONE IMAGES

PRINTING AND BINDERY: FERNEDGE PRINTERS LTD.

SPECIAL TECHNIQUES: FERNEDGE PRINTERS LTD. (FOIL SAMPING)

# of form
and
function

After a rebranding effort, ASK & Company made some interesting discoveries. The rebranding process sparked not only a name change but also a redirection for the company, now called Capsule. "Capsule is an environment where people and ideas come together around a process that results in understanding and insight," comments managing principal Aaron Keller. "We use the name to reference exploration, finding new ways of doing business as a design firm." To communicate their metamorphosis to the business community, the design firm needed a promotion that not only announced the name change but also expressed the new approach to design.

To develop just the right device to deliver their message, the design team did extensive exploratory research, analyzing the competitive landscape with respect to messaging, communications collateral, and overall brand development. They also sought secondary sources from the Internet, the local library, and a day trip to the space exhibit at the Art Institute of Chicago. Their efforts resulted in a promotion that helped communicate Capsule's process and approach to design—explore, discover, and evolve—in an interesting and intriguing way.

The tactile materials, bindery, and all of the accents offered an intriguing mix of contemporary and historical references. "We used the metallic paper to reflect a futuristic view of exploration," says Keller, "and the blotter paper and letterpress printing to reflect the historic craft of our business." To pique curiosity, the simple, yet effective, promotion was wrapped inside a beautifully embossed bellyband. "It requires someone to tear into the piece to find out what is inside," explains Keller. "That simple interaction starts the discovery process."

The piece is both aesthetically pleasing and multifunctional. Each page within the screw-bound brochure can be easily ripped out and converted into a coaster, giving the promotional endeavor an extended life. The die-cut accents are also structurally functional and visually interesting. The two indents on the top and bottom help secure the bellyband in place, while the curvilinear die-cut shapes serve as artistic detail that complements each page. "Combining functionality and aesthetics into one communications piece is a way of thinking beyond the message," adds Keller. "This promotion exemplifies the quality of our work without specifically providing a bullet point list of services. We used it to bring our firm to the next level of visibility."

Curious Galvanized 92-lb. cover, a metallic paper, gave the promotion's wraparound cover an intriguing space-age quality. The screwposts that bind the piece together are positioned to maintain overall stability when detaching each page from the base to create coasters. The embossed bellyband that surrounds the piece helps spark curiosity and interest, while the exterior packaging, a silver, heat-sealed, static-free bag, plays up the theme of exploration and discovery. Two die-cut marks on either side of the bag make it easy to open.

Inside the piece, thick, highly textured blotter paper is letterpress-printed, giving it a handcrafted quality. Silver ink creates a visual connection with the metallic paper and silver packaging. Each page within the piece can be transformed into a coaster by simply tearing at the perforated edge.

1

2

FIRM: CAPSULE

CREATIVE DIRECTOR: BRIAN ADDUCCI

DESIGNER: DAN BAGGENSTOSS

PHOTOGRAPHY: NASA

PRINTING AND BINDERY: DIVERSIFIED GRAPHICS, INC.

MANUFACTURER: ULINE (SILVER BAGS)

everyday
life:
abstracted

Nick Veasey, known for his abstract vision of everyday life, wanted a promotion that would attract the attention of both European and U.S. buyers. "Photography is a competitive business. You have to stand out somehow. Many promotions are thrown away or kept in some file that never gets looked at," admits Veasey. "I wanted something that people would keep and remember." To create a promotion that really deviated from the norm, Veasey employed the assistance of creative director and designer Zoe Scutts. "We talked things through over a period of weeks, showing each other found objects and looking through books," says Veasey. "Zoe wanted it to be small, while I wanted larger pictures. But she was right, because my clients get to see my pictures bigger when they call in for my portfolio or check the Web site. The piece works because of its size." Working collaboratively the two came up with a promotion that was as distinctive as the photography it highlighted.

To bring in an element of surprise, a commercial blister pack was chosen as the perfect packaging solution; it created the unexpected, yet still utilitarian, feel the team was looking for. "We both find beauty in the everyday," notes Veasey. "Actually, we got the blister pack idea from buying some screws in a store." Inside the transparent pack, selected works from the portfolio of photographer Nick Veasey are revealed. From page to page, abstractly interpreted slice-of-life shots were positioned against x-rayed still lives and figurative subject matter. Each custom die-cut page was matte laminated to tie in the look and feel of the outer plastic packaging as well as to protect the photographic promotion from wear and tear. (Originally, the team wanted to print on plastic, but research showed that the process was too expensive; in addition, it would not have served the promotion well because the printing quality is far inferior.) The piece was bound together by a chain, with a joining clasp applied over both ends to keep it shut. The chain not only provides easy access to the diverse array of images but also adds interest to the overall piece.

The pocket-sized promotion attracted attention on many fronts. "It is difficult to create something that will get noticed by the most visually aware people in the world," admits Veasey. "If you bring a bit of the other world into the offices of these people, it makes them stop and think for a second." The miniportfolio served as an introduction to new clients and a reminder to existing clients of the extraordinary work of photographer Nick Veasey.

TECHNICAL TIPS

When developing direct mail, you need to create something that is not only thought-provoking but also instantly grabs the recipient's attention, motivating them to look inside and further participate in the overall messaging. To create distinction, explore alternative materials, formats, and techniques. Suppliers can be found everywhere; the Internet is the best place to start your search.

The minipromotion is housed in a transparent plastic blister pack to create distinction and attract attention. Small address labels are affixed to the back, and the piece is mailed to prospective art buyers in Europe and the United States without any additional packaging.

Inside the blister pack is a chain-bound promotion featuring the work of photographer Nick Veasey. Each custom die-cut page varies from abstract imagery to interesting objects and figures that have been exposed in an x-rayed fashion. Each custom die-cut card is printed in four-color process on 350-gram Hello Silk stock.

FIRM: UNTITLED

CREATIVE DIRECTOR AND DESIGNER: ZOE SCUTTS

PHOTOGRAPHY: NICK VEASEY

PRINTING AND BINDERY: ONE EXCEPTION

MANUFACTURERS: MACPAC (BLISTER PACKS) AND ZINCO (CHAINS)

1

2

collaborative endeavor

Through collaborative endeavors, creatives are reexamining the fundamental methodology whereby they promote and do business, making a difference in their work, the industry, and the world at large. Under a group dynamic, each contributor brings his or her insight, creativity, and know-how to the table, offering a fresh perspective on problem solving. Their combined efforts, energy, and wisdom lift the group to a new level. "When collaborating, you give your ultimate best because there is a heightened responsibility to do so," shares Deb Koch of Red Canoe. "Working with someone new challenges me personally to rise to higher levels." Group-sponsored initiatives create an environment conducive to the pursuit of new ideas, encouraging participants to grow in ways they would not have individually.

When embarking on a group endeavor, it is important to be organized from the start. It is essential to set ground rules and to produce a detailed creative brief, outlining the project's intent, overall theme, and working specifications. A solid timeline, detailing individual responsibilities and due dates, will also prove helpful in keeping each participant on track. To ensure everything runs smoothly, it is beneficial to have someone in charge of project management, coordinating all of the many threads. "Collaboration among independent, passionate, and strong-willed people will naturally entail opposing opinions, so anticipate and expect some healthy conflict," Koch advises. "Establish up front precisely how problems will be handled and who will make the final decision for each aspect of the project. It might seem like a tedious process, but don't underestimate its necessity." Most important, it is essential for each participant to maintain an open mind and a clear channel of communications. Trust and mutual respect among all involved is vital as well.

By working collaboratively, the partners at Pentagram Design have been able to explore avenues far more outstanding than any one member would have had the budget, time, or resources for. Given their international network, each office can offer clients a broad range of services and expertise, from architecture, interior, and exhibition design to graphic and product design. Although they are a partnership, each of the highly recognized designers works independently as the head of his or her autonomous group. This infrastructure helps maintain administrative control among the group while allowing for a consistent, single point of contact for the client. "It also gives us the efficiency to take on very small jobs and permits each partner to stay fresh and involved with clients and projects," offers partner Michael Bierut. "When we collaborate, it is generally because two or more of the partners have skills or interests that can be brought to bear on a specific project." When shared skills are needed, various partners draw on the resources of the whole organization to realize the project, an incredible benefit that makes Pentagram unique in the marketplace. Through the experience, knowledge, and resources of the group, each partner has been able to expand on his or her own talents and abilities, reaching new heights as a result.

When you chose to collaborate, you begin to build relationships and connections to resources that can prove valuable down the road. Designer Milton Glaser, who has cultivated many contacts over the course of his career, can now use his talents and ingenuity to pursue causes he believes in, inspiring others to follow suit. "If you are in the communications business, you have a special opportunity to use your skills for some kind of public good. You can't only be involved with selling products, at least not in my view," he says.

"Every once in a while, you should take the opportunity to act." When you are pursuing a self-initiated project, certainly one that is not profit driven, it is difficult to create a point of entry into the marketplace. "Everything is driven by money. When there isn't sponsorship behind something, there is no effective means of distribution," Glaser adds. "You have to find some connective tissue to enter into the culture." Without an institutional contact or underlying support system, it is difficult to get the necessary visibility to make something effective enough to enter the public consciousness. "No matter how good the idea is, you are barking at the Moon without the personal connections that enable the idea to penetrate," comments Glaser. "You have to hook into the media, whether it is getting someone to sponsor a subway poster or getting radio or TV coverage. Also, the message has to be of sufficient interest intrinsically, so that you will get people to pay attention." By establishing relationships with people outside of your discipline, you gain access to the bloodstream of the market. Having media contacts, support from vendors, and established relationships with institutions can be invaluable when pursuing initiatives, especially those that are far more expansive than the mere selling of products or services.

It takes a lot of effort from dedicated people to launch a group-inspired endeavor. But for those willing to share their talent, cross existing boundaries, and try new ways of working, collaboration can be profoundly rewarding. Furthermore, once a group effort is successfully realized, it provides leverage for other endeavors, opening up new opportunities for all involved. Creatives choosing to work collaboratively are truly establishing new pathways in what is possible when it comes to promotion.

collaborations that educate

Since 1975, the partners at Pentagram have designed and produced a series of booklets, called *Pentagram Papers*, that cover a wide range of topics—sometimes controversial and other times quite entertaining. The educational emphasis is on exposing the masses to the extraordinary. To maintain consistency, each book utilizes a similar format, a wraparound jacket printed in solid black with a dull varnish on the outside and a gloss varnish on the inside. The books are distributed to clients, colleagues, friends, educational institutions, and libraries as a way to share ideas and inspiring subject matter with the industry. "Of all the things we publish to promote the partnership, the *Pentagram Papers* is the most enthusiastically received," shares partner Michael Bierut. "They never show examples of our work but, rather, examples of our interests and how we think." Through the efforts of the Pentagram partnership, an array of thought-provoking and intellectually stimulating books have entered the design community, sending the partnership into the limelight as innovators in a league all their own.

Many of the books reveal fascinating places and subject matter that would otherwise remain untouched. For instance, *Pentagram Papers 27: Nifty Places, The Australian Rural Mailbox*, is truly visual eye candy portraying the most bizarre adaptations to the mailbox, from old banged-up refrigerators to recycled milk churns and rusty oil drums. The audacity just screams for publication. "One of the most visible demonstrations of Aussie individuality and inventiveness, bordering on art on the one hand and environmental vandalism on the other, is the rural mailbox," says author Cal Swann. "They are all an expression of freedom and the rights of individuals to choose." Another good example is *Pentagram Papers 30: Neon-Lit, Kidney-Shaped, Low-Rent, Flat-Roofed, Doo-Wop Commercial Architecture, or, Learning from Wildwood, New Jersey*. The title is a long but accurate description of a series of photographs taken by Dorothy Kresz during her vacations to New Jersey's south shore. "Wildwood is an ossifying, urban, challenging place with a bad neighborhood or two, bars and nightclubs, drug problems, and a 26 percent unemployment rate," says author Jonathan van Meter. "It's a bit grubby and wonderfully tacky, lit with neon signs and dotted with big plastic palm trees in lieu of actual greenery." Many claim that the kitschy architecture and eye-catching urban signage is one of the strongest concentrations of midcentury commercial structures in the world. It is no wonder that partner Michael Bierut was so drawn to it.

Other books are inspired by an experience or unique project that comes along. Such was the case in 1995, when Pentagram partner John Rushworth was asked by the Savoy Group of Hotels and Restaurants to develop a new identity for its prestigious and historic luxury hotels. Awestruck by the architecture and the lighting, Rushworth and his design team created *Pentagram Papers 29: Savoy Lights*. The Savoy, located in London's West End, opened its doors in 1899. Creator Richard d'Oyly Carte, a man of the theater, had exquisite taste and a keen understanding of how lighting creates ambience and mood. The lighting, both public and private, remains revolutionary even today.

Pentagram's most recent publishing endeavor originated in Pentagram partner Kit Hinrichs's lucky find at an antiquarian book fair. *Hinagata*, a kimono pattern book from 1899, was so beautifully constructed and illuminated with wood block printed imagery that it led the designer to investigate its roots. Yoshiko I. Wada, a fellow at the Center for Japanese Studies at the University of California, Berkeley, was brought in to assist in the search. The rich and graphic kimono designs are quite compelling and visually luscious. It is easy to see why Hinrichs found them fascinating enough to share. Shown are just four of the most recent of the thirty-one books in the *Pentagram Papers* series.

FIRM: PENTAGRAM DESIGN

DESIGNERS: DAVID HILLMAN (PENTAGRAM PAPERS 27), JOHN RUSHWORTH
(PENTAGRAM PAPERS 29), MICHAEL BIERUT (PENTAGRAM PAPERS 30),
AND KIT HINRICHS (PENTAGRAM PAPERS 31)

PARTICIPANTS: CAL SWANN (PENTAGRAM PAPERS 27), GRAHAM VICKERS
(PENTAGRAM PAPERS 29), JONATHAN VAN METER (PENTAGRAM PAPERS 30),
YOSHIKO I. WADA, AND DELPHINE HIRASUNA (PENTAGRAM PAPERS 31)

PHOTOGRAPHY: CAL SWANN (PENTAGRAM PAPERS 27), PHIL SAYER (PENTAGRAM
PAPERS 29), DOROTHY KRESZ (PENTAGRAM PAPERS 30), AND TERRY HEFFERNAN
(PENTAGRAM PAPERS 31)

PRINTING AND BINDERY: ALDERSON BROTHERS PRINTERS LIMITED
(PENTAGRAM PAPERS 27), GAVIN MARTIN ASSOCIATES (PENTAGRAM PAPERS 29),
THE CAMPBELL GROUP (PENTAGRAM PAPERS 30), AND ANDERSON
LITHOGRAPH (PENTAGRAM PAPERS 31)

FIRM: RED CANOE

CREATIVE DIRECTOR: DEB KOCH

DESIGNER: CAROLINE KAVANAGH

ILLUSTRATION: KATHERINE DUNN

PRINTING: STUDIO INK (SILK-SCREEN ON WOOD)
   AND EPSON INKJET PRINTER (BOOKLET, BUSINESS CARD, AND WRAPPING PAPER)

MANUFACTURERS: PAPER MART (NATURAL WOOD EXCELSIOR ASPEN WOOD SHAVINGS)
   AND RED CANOE SITE (ACORNS, WOOD SLICES, AND STICKS)

creative collaboration

Creatives are beginning to realize the promotional potential that results when they join forces on a collaborative endeavor. Such was the case when Deb Koch and Caroline Kavanagh, cofounders of Red Canoe, teamed up with illustrator Katherine Dunn. After creating a Web site design for Dunn, the team of creatives realized they had a lot in common. With shared interests and an overlapping client base, they embarked on a dual-functioning promotion that not only enticed prospects to visit and bookmark Dunn's new site but also drew attention to the interactive design and development capabilities of Red Canoe.

To capture the attention of their mostly creative audience, the promotion had to be interesting enough to stand out from the flood of incoming mailers. To develop something that successfully promoted both companies, the design team went back to their shared inspirational source—nature. Dunn's illustrative Web site, which draws a lot of its key components from natural elements, was in perfect tune with the philosophy and mission statement of Red Canoe. To make a familiar connection, the design team went out into their 350 acres of natural woodland and collected many of the elements that appear on the Web site: wood, sticks, and acorns. This made for a very tactile introduction to the Web site's electronic experience. "The concept was to bring dimension and reality to some of the site's elements, enhancing one's sense of the site as a place that one would immediately feel familiar with," offers Koch.

Acorn tops and bottoms were cleaned and glued back together with biodegradable material. The wood and twigs were gathered from fallen tree branches, cut, and sanded to smooth and brighten their surface. To remove moisture, the slices of wood were baked in a conventional oven until perfectly dry. They were later silk-screen-printed with the Web site's URL. The mini-slices of wood served a secondary function as coasters, increasing the longevity of the piece. A little, illustrated storybook with rhythmic sayings and French-folded pages enticed the recipient to visit the newly developed site. To add character and distinction, the minibook was wrapped with a cover stock and uniquely bound with a rubber band and stick. Wood shavings, shaped into a nest, housed the piece. The package was sent in a white box wrapped by a custom-designed sheet accented with the artist's gestural work. The narrative approach, natural materials, and keen attention to detail helped make the piece memorable and the URL (leaves-no-more-than-i-do.com) something worth exploring further.

For the design firm, collaboration is a way to enrich their portfolio and diversify their capabilities. "Besides the new-blood aspect of creative input, each collaborative endeavor reveals new processes that contribute to the flow of the next project, whatever it may be," says Koch. "It allows clients to see skills and talent that go beyond the generally perceived scope of design, creating unique projects and work opportunities." Although you give up a certain amount of personal ownership when collaborating, a project somehow always goes beyond what it otherwise would have because of the contribution of others.

When embarking on a group endeavor, it is important to be organized from the start. It is essential to set ground rules and to produce a detailed creative brief, outlining the project's intent, overall theme, and working specifications. A solid timeline, detailing individual responsibilities and due dates, will also prove helpful in keeping each participant on track.

When you chose to collaborate, you begin to build relationships and connections to resources that can prove valuable down the road.

FIRM: MILTON GLASER, INC.

CREATIVE DIRECTOR AND DESIGNER:
MILTON GLASER

PRINTING: RASCO GRAPHICS, INC. (POSTER)

MANUFACTURER: NC SLATER CORPORATION (BUTTONS)

making a difference

Because of the tragic events of September 11, creatives around the world have become much more introspective, reexamining the purpose and the role they play in society, not only as businesses but also as individuals. In the aftermath, many felt a great deal of loss and uncertainty. The world was forever changed, and nobody knew quite what to do about it. "After 9/11, I got up one morning and I said 'I love New York' isn't complete anymore as a proposition," recalls creative director and designer Milton Glaser. "I realized that my feelings about the city had changed fundamentally. The city was vulnerable making me realize the sense of potential loss similar to when someone is sick and you begin to recognize just how much you love them." Glaser went back to his original "I love New York" design and added the endearing words "more than ever." In addition, a black stain on the lower part of the heart was made in acknowledgment of the destruction in lower Manhattan.

In an attempt to shift social consciousness, the designer asked the School of Visual Arts (SVA), where he lectures, to produce a poster to be distributed around the city by students. The poster was given to merchants for placement in storefront windows. In addition, the poster was positioned within SVA's vast transit advertising in subways in Manhattan and the surrounding boroughs. To expand the concept, Glaser contacted National Public Radio. "I connected with WNYC, and they used the posters to raise money to assist in the restoration of their antenna," says Glaser. "If you sent in a contribution, you got a free poster. They raised $190,000. I was very encouraged by that."

As a way of continuing the momentum, Glaser embarked on a campaign to preempt a war. "I felt we all had to do something about the extraordinary passivity that exists in this country and the lack of demonstrable opposition to the policies of the government," he construes. "One thing I could do was to give people an instrument with which to express their opinions overtly." To encourage social commentary in a visible way, Glaser contacted the *Nation*, proposing a joint venture button initiative that would be advertised in their publication. To lead the initiative, two buttons were designed, respectively reading Dissent Protects Democracy and Preempt the War. It was a tremendous success, leading to another wave of buttons. Leave No CEO Behind, Secrecy Promotes Tyranny, Oil War, and Surveillance Undermines Liberty became the messaging chosen for round two of the Join the Loyal Opposition campaign. Glaser is currently working on yet another initiative, Together for the City We Love. "It seems to me that unless we are conscious of the fact that we are all in this together, we will never recover," he acknowledges. "It is everybody's responsibility to help the city along by withdrawing from the idea of self-interest and personal opportunism that is destroying everything. If we only think about ourselves, the world is completely doomed. I am galvanized by this sense of urgency."

Creatives choosing to work collaboratively are truly establishing new pathways in what is possible when it comes to promotion.

sweet
impression

Each of the seven gum wrappers features a character expressing such emotions as *happiness*, *sadness*, and *anger*. A pack of five is wrapped in translucent paper and taped shut. The attention-getting collection is used to pique the interest of art buyers to the illustration style of Barbara Lipp.

The Graphic Artist Guild was having a trade show, and participating illustrator Barbara Lipp wanted to make a sweet impression with attendees. "Each artist had a table space for showing their portfolio. I'd never participated in this event before, but I assumed there would be plenty of promotional postcards being handed out," offers Lipp. "I was trying to think of something different and novel." Call it divine intervention or creative inspiration, but the idea of using gum just popped into the artist's head as a unique, portable, and delicious way of presenting her work. "The inherent silliness of using tiny gum wrappers to promote oneself appealed to me," Lipp adds. "It really came out of my desire to offer the people coming to the event something fun and different from all the other freebies." At the trade show, Lipp used the gum promotion to bring attention to her work, giving away approximately two hundred individual sticks to interested art directors and editors.

To produce the whimsical promotion, the artist went to the local grocery store and purchased gum in a variety of flavors. She opened the wrappers, measured and noted the dimensions, and started playing with various designs on the computer. She focused her attention on the faces of characters in her portfolio. Their engaging quality and ability to capture attention in a small-scale format made them the perfect subject matter for this promotion. To add a humorous twist and unify the images, the artist made up titles for each, using emotions like *happiness*, *anger*, and *sadness*. "I like the idea of creating gum that has these magical qualities if chewed," shares Lipp. "I thought I might even do a round of secondary emotions—ambivalent gum, envy gum, and manic gum." To create the finished look, Lipp simply repackaged the silver foil–enclosed gum with her newly designed wrappers, using glue stick as an adhesive. "The trickiest part was aligning the wrappers so that they folded around the edges in just the right place," admits Lipp. "I'd do it at night while watching television. It was like knitting!"

Because of the tremendous response at the guild event, Lipp decided to wrap the sticks into packs of five and mail them to editorial and book publishing art buyers along with a postcard and illustrated client list. "Art directors are absolutely bombarded with promotional mail," comments the artist. "But if they get a package and can feel that there is some little object inside, they will always check it out just from sheer curiosity. This doesn't guarantee you will get work, but it will get their attention." As the market for illustration narrows, the competition will intensify, leading, as Lipp feels, to "even more creative and bolder forms of promotion."

TECHNICAL TIPS

When you are reproducing text and images in a small format, it is important to keep them bold and simple for readability purposes. If you want to print the wrappers in-house, you can easily gang up eight wrapper designs to a sheet. To save money, everything can be trimmed and wrapped by hand. Retain the existing silver foil around the gum to avoid an additional process and expense.

The promotional pack is sent to prospective buyers with a client list and postcard. The illustrated client list serves as a way to show a variety of images from the artist's portfolio in an interesting way. The artist's logo and signature image, entitled the Angry Girl, appears on all of her promotional material as a unifying element.

Lipp has expanded her promotion work to include customized magnets. Each image is applied to self-adhesive business card–sized magnets that can be purchased in packages of fifty or one hundred. Each image is printed on glossy photo-quality paper. It is sent as a follow-up mailing, a reminder of the artist and her whimsical work.

FIRM: BARBARA LIPP ILLUSTRATION

CREATIVE DIRECTOR AND DESIGNER:
    BARBARA LIPP

ILLUSTRATION: BARBARA LIPP

MANUFACTURERS: OFFICEMAX (MAGNETS)
    AND VARIOUS BRANDS OF GUM

fresh
start

"Real, raw and renovated" were the words that staff designer Shawn Murenbeeld used to describe the relocation of DWL's corporate headquarters from an old 800-square-foot (74-square-meter) piano factory to a newly renovated 3,700-square-foot (344-square-meter) space. The expansion marked a fresh start for the company, and what better than to document it with a special gift? "There was this whole new look," recalls Murenbeeld, "and I wanted something fun, unexpected, and memorable to raise the spirits of the staff."

With the fresh theme in mind, Murenbeeld came up with an interesting idea: T-shirts wrapped in meat trays like fresh produce in a supermarket. The designer chose to deliver the message on green cotton T-shirts, silk-screen-printed in red on both sides. The front of the shirt has a bold illustration of meat. On the back, various interpretations of the word *fresh* are outlined, symbolizing the renewed spirit that a fresh start in a new space brings. The sleeve of the shirt simply displays the company's identity. The printed T-shirts were folded and placed on white meat packing trays obtained at a local grocery store. To finish the look, each package was shrink-wrapped and labeled. "I wrapped 250 T-shirts with the butcher for two hours," says Murenbeeld. "He also gave me a whole roll of these labels that said 'ring in meat.' I couldn't refuse!"

The designer also created some labels of his own. "Every time I got meat at the store, I kept all the labels because I wanted to get a feel for the best features of each," notes Murenbeeld. "One thing I noticed about the labels was that they were so random. When the store printed them, no one thought carefully about the placement of the type." The designer tried to simulate that feel by overlapping the type in different areas. The custom label features expressions like *keep cool* and *fresh perspective*, a pseudo price listed as "$F.REE," the moving date masquerading as an expiration date, and a barcode to finish off the overall effect. Also noted is the firm's new address, conveniently positioned where a grocery store address might be found. To reveal the size of each shirt, small circular labels were printed and die-cut on fluorescent orange stock and applied to the outer package.

The T-shirt promotion was distributed to all DWL employees on the day the new office was complete. It was a big hit and enjoyed by all. "Actually, most of the people would not even open them," comments Murenbeeld. "Instead, they put the wrapped package on their wall and on their desk. People were asking for two—one to wear and one to keep. It made me happy."

TECHNICAL TIPS

Be as resourceful as you can be. Start with the best solution and never rule out potential sources, like the local supermarket butcher, who can help you realize your vision. To capture a sense of realism, always spend time researching. Sometimes the tiniest touches make the biggest impact.

1

Each cotton T-shirt is shrink-wrapped onto a Styrofoam tray and labeled, giving the effect of fresh produce in a supermarket. The custom label features various details that help make the package not only interesting but also functional. For instance, the moving date looks like an expiration date, while the firm's new address is positioned where a grocery store address might be found. A small circular fluorescent orange label cleverly reveals the size of the shirt.

2

The silk-screen-printed T-shirts are adorned with a bold and graphic illustration of meat. On the back, the definition of the word *fresh* is detailed to help communicate DWL's fresh start in a new space. The sleeve simply displays the company's name and logo.

1

Ring in MEAT

Real, Raw & Renovated

2

FIRM: DWL INCORPORATED

CREATIVE DIRECTOR AND DESIGNER: SHAWN MURENBEELD

ILLUSTRATION: SHAWN MURENBEELD

PRINTING: THE BEANSTOCK GROUP

alternative
stock

The poster features a graphic optical illusion on the back to complement the intriguing photography on the front. The illusionary effects make the piece not only different but also memorable. Each poster is rolled, sealed with a red sticker, and delivered to prospective buyers in a custom injection-molded tube.

To get prospective buyers to visit, bookmark, and license work from their Web site, Untitled knew they had to come up with a promotion that was a bit out of the ordinary so as to attract attention in the oversaturated stock photography market. Designer Zoe Scutts was pulled in to assist in the creation of an innovative, yet simple, promotional campaign. Taking inspiration from both the world of fine art and the medical industry, Untitled developed a unique presentation for their alternative and experimental work. "The poster was inspired by the abstract artist Bridget Reilly," notes photographer and founder Nick Veasey, "while the mailer was inspired by surgical swabs."

To make a lasting impression, the first mailing took the form of a keepsake. The device chosen to carry the message was a large, highly graphic poster displaying the work of several photographic artists in a unique and intriguing way. Further distinguishing the group, the poster was rolled, sealed, and shipped in a custom injection-molded tube made of 500-micron plastic. This not only provided an interesting presentation for the memorable Web site announcement but also protected the piece from the elements during delivery. "We tried to create something that the target audience would cherish," says Veasey.

A second, attention-getting promotion was sent as well. Round two packed its punch in a small, but effective, package. Sent in a medical swab pouch, the intimate accordion-folded brochure features the work of twelve photographers out of 106 currently represented in the contemporary image library at Untitled. Flexography, a process commonly used in the packaging industry, was employed to imprint the self-sealing bags. To stay within the limitations of this process, the graphics and text were kept simple and straightforward, directing the recipient to Untitled's stock site in a clear and unadorned fashion. Because of the number of folds in the fourteen-paneled piece, 80-gram Skyegloss was the thickest paper that fit within the packet's interior parameters.

With the entrance of large corporate stock houses into the photography business, the industry has seen an influx of mediocre and cliché images into the culture. This overabundant work, delivered at a discounted price, has created a wedge in the market, limiting commission work by building client loyalty through discounted stock sales. To control their destiny, photographers have united, creating alternative solutions for buyers. Taking matters into their own hands, they have created some of the best sources for innovative and creative stock photography available. "I had a few friends who were photographers, a collection of images, some money, and off we went," concludes Veasey. "Untitled is growing and getting better. The word is out, and some very good people are approaching us."

TECHNICAL TIPS

Because the space inside a swab packet is limited, use a thin stock for any promotional material you plan to fold up inside. When imprinting the packets, remember that you need to design within flexography's restrictions.

When custom designing with injection-molded plastic, give the manufacturer an accurate schematic drawing and a mock-up to work with. Always have a working model made to fully test your idea before you go into production.

3

A brochure, sent as a follow-up mailing in an adapted surgical swab pouch, features a range of images from the contemporary image library at Untitled. Two versions are available.

Untitled's stock catalog is quite unique in that it profiles each photographer in his or her own specially designed section. Featured is the opening spread for photographer Nick Veasey's work.

1

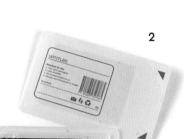

2

FIRMS: UNTITLED

CREATIVE DIRECTOR AND DESIGNER:

ZOE SCUTTS

PHOTOGRAPHY: UNTITLED.CO.UK

PRINTING: SPIN OFFSET (POSTER) AND

PRECISION COLOUR PRINTING (BROCHURE)

BINDERY: SPEMA

MANUFACTURERS: MACPAC (INJECTION-MOLDED TUBE)

AND RIVERSIDE MEDICAL PACKAGING

COMPANY LIMITED (SELF-SEALING POLYETHYLENE BAGS)

3

alternative uses and

add-ons

Designers are reusing existing elements in a variety of ways to complement their promotions. Film canisters, wallet holders, and dog tags are finding secondary functions and miniature spoons, seeds, and customized sound chips are being added as accents—the finishing touch that makes a promotion memorable. Often, the most minute of details can make the biggest impact. "We put a premium on resourcefulness and are always on the lookout for mechanical processes or techniques that can be repurposed and reapplied to create more interest, personality, or a unique character," shares Ron Miriello of Miriello Grafico. "During our travels, we've collected a hand-lettering perforation machine from Milan, a page-numbering stamp from Japan, and a 1930s postage stamp perforator from an antique dealer in Orange County, California. We've also got a small, sewing-machine-size letterpress printer from the 1920s. The tools are a symbol of our interest and respect for personal communications in a time of mass production. When mixed with modern imagery and technique, they can create an interesting tension."

When you choose to supplement your work with add-ons or want to reuse elements in a different way, make sure they enhance your concept in some way. Using something just for the sake of being different is a waste of time and money that only results in a confusing overall message. "The primary impetus for alternative uses and add-ons should always be an effort to improve the effectiveness of a design," offers Marcie Carson of IE Design. "It should unify and complete the design, not clutter it." Never stop asking yourself how you can improve on something you have created. Questioning your efforts will challenge you to strive for excellence each time. When creatives push the envelope and try new things, the industry will evolve and grow as a result.

fictional
correspondence

"I wanted to create a promotion that would identify me as an idea person, someone who can come up with interesting concepts and put things together in a kind of unusual way," says designer and illustrator Charlotte Noruzi. "To get art directors and editors to look at my work, I wanted something that was not only fun but also memorable." Targeted toward the publishing industry, Noruzi developed a series of four direct-mail promotions based on well-known trade book titles. "I did a fictional correspondence between characters from books I thought people would know of and that would be interesting and diverse enough to do a self-promotion with," she adds. *Faust*, *Bridget Jones's Diary*, and *A Handful of Dust* were all illustrated and cleverly presented as postage stamps alongside handwritten envelopes and personalized letters. In each mailing, the reader is a voyeur into the lives of several main characters in the respective books.

The elongated shape of the stamps helped maintain the vertical book cover format, while the hand-lettering and graphics brought interest and intrigue to each mailing. The postage rate, replaced by a telephone number, was the only point of contact. Noruzi enhanced each mailing with prominent storyline elements such as cigarettes, matches, burn marks, dripped wax, and small pieces of cut paper. "Bridget Jones, in her letter to Mark Darcy, gives away her last cigarette in an attempt to stop her vices," shares Noruzi. "There is no return address on the letter to Miss Brenda Last because the writer, Tony Last, was off on a safari in the jungle and had no address." On the back of each envelope, small details were extracted from the selected book covers to maintain visual harmony throughout. Such finishing touches show the illustrator's attention to detail and keen ability to convey key points within each story.

The entire promotional series was printed using a color laser printer. The die-cut details were created by hand with perforated scissors. Each stamp was adhered with glue stick to the appropriate envelope with great precision. If a stamp was not positioned just right, it would not accurately line up with its corresponding cancellation mark, the date each mailing was sent. The complete promotional ensemble was hand-assembled by the artist. "I think it is worth the investment to spend a little bit more time and money on your promotion to create something that will really stand out," remarks Noruzi. The three fictional correspondences were mailed at two-week intervals. A final mailing, showing other examples of the artist's work, served as a follow-up. Only twenty-five pieces were created.

The book, *Bridget Jones's Diary*, deals with the main character's quest to stop her addictions. A cigarette is enclosed to Mark Darcy, another character in the book, as a gesture of Bridget's attempt to quit. The whimsical hand-lettering, graphics, and copy bring out the main character's personality. They also show the artist's ability to conceptualize, design, and, of course, illustrate. This is the first in the series of mailings.

Dear Mark,
Cigarette in this envelope is my last... instead of smoking it though, I've decided to give it you (as token of my 'changed ways'). Tomorrow, chocolate go. My Mondays, alcohol units will be 0 forever. All because of you, darling.
Love,
x Bridget

Bridget Jones
231 Arthur Place #6
London, Eng.
P4X315

Mark Darcy
151 Bond Street
London, Eng.
P4X315

1

FIRM: QUESTION DESIGN

CREATIVE DIRECTOR AND DESIGNER:
CHARLOTTE NORUZI

ILLUSTRATION: CHARLOTTE NORUZI

MANUFACTURERS: KATE'S PAPERIE
(WAX, STATIONERY PAPER, AND ENVELOPES)
AND JAM PAPER (ENVELOPES)

fictional
correspondence

continued

A Handful of Dust is accented by little cut pieces of paper that are adhered to the inside flap of the envelope. The tiny black scraps are symbolic of what the life of Tony Last has become, a handful of dust. The letterhead features Victorian graphics taken from a Dover book. This is the second mailing in the promotional series.

Faust, the third mailing, shows Noruzi's ability to illustrate a very different kind of story, one more dramatic in nature. To create the burn marks, the artist used both a lighter and a match held at varying distances from the envelope. The back of the envelope is accented and sealed with colored wax, which was heated and allowed to drip on.

Designed like a set of stamps, the final promotion ties the previous mailings together and serves as a follow-up device. Each stamp shows a different book cover design, demonstrating the breadth and diversity of the artist's repertoire of work. The follow-up promotion is sent in a white envelope with a perforated label that nicely ties in with the overall stamp concept.

3

4

techno
dog

A mechanical wind-up toy transforms into a techno dog, announcing the *Bark's* newly developed Web site. The industrial-looking canine is distributed in a silver antistatic bag punched with holes to facilitate "breathing." The label, economically printed in-house with an Epson 1520 inkjet printer on high-quality, non adhesive paper, is applied with a spray adhesive to seal the package shut. It also provides operating instructions for the recipient's new pet. The launch and shipping date is stamped in red ink as an accent. The promotion is shipped in a cardboard box custom-wrapped in yellow.

The *Bark*, a San Francisco–based literary arts quarterly for dog lovers, wanted to announce the unleashing of their newly designed Web site to top advertisers, distributors, and investors of the magazine. Red Canoe, developers of the site, wanted to do something a bit different to capture the attention of their client's target audience. "We had just completed two sites. The first one was an investor demo, which was successful enough to lead to a complete site redesign and development," recalls cofounder Deb Koch. "The *Bark's* publisher and editor knew that promoting the Web site would be crucial."

To bridge the gap between the tactile and the online worlds, the design team at Red Canoe started looking through their vast resources in search of the perfect vehicle to carry their message. After discovering this real eclectic wind-up toy with an uncanny resemblance to a dog, the design team had the starting point they were looking for. From there, a bone-shaped dog tag, engraved with the Web site's address (www.thebark.com), just seemed like a natural add-on for the techno pet to wear. "As would any useful dog tag, it provided the doggie's home address information, which in this case was a play on words, given the Internet meaning of *home*," adds Koch. "In the instructions, we suggested that once the little guy was on the move, one might follow him to his new home and, to do that, one had to read the dog tag."

The wind-up dog arrives packaged in a silver antistatic bag complete with air holes for the little metallic creature to breathe through during its journey through the mail. "The nostalgic memories many people have of bringing home a pet in a box and poking breathing holes in it was an experience and a feeling we hoped to be able to bag," explains Koch. A bright yellow custom-designed label provided not only shipping information but also operating instructions for the small mechanical canine. As an additional finishing detail, the shipping date, which announced the launch day of the newly developed site, was imprinted on the labels with a rubber stamp. "All of the wording on the label was reduced to the bare minimum to express a manufacturing and industrial trompe l'oeil," details Koch. "For us, the 'less is more' philosophy is expressed in the details."

The promotion was successful for both the *Bark* and Red Canoe. "In addition to achieving specific advertising goals for the client, the piece also drew attention to our Web site design and development work as well as our identity, branding, and promotional capabilities," Koch concludes.

TECHNICAL TIPS

When utilizing vendors outside the communications market, don't assume they will completely understand your out-of-the-ordinary requests. Be patient, keep in constant communication, and put all of your correspondence in writing so everything is completely clear. To get text imprinted on a dog tag, make sure the wholesale supply house understands that what is to be imprinted has to be exactly the way you have designed it. They have a tendency to change the font size and drop to two lines where they see fit. For punching holes in antistatic bags, a conventional hand-held single-hole puncher works best. Last, always request samples and plan enough time to do things right, thinking ahead at every step.

The doglike toy winds up and encourages the recipient to follow it home. The bone-shaped collar around its neck makes the connection between the canine's home and the Web site home page.

A full-page, four-color print ad was created in addition to the direct mail promotional announcement.

The *Bark*'s Web site, www.thebark.com, and the announcement feature similar design elements to make the transition from print to online a familiar one.

CLIENT: THE BARK

FIRM: RED CANOE

CREATIVE DIRECTOR: DEB KOCH

DESIGNER: CAROLINE KAVANAGH

PRINTING: EPSON 1520 INKJET PRINTER (WRAPPING PAPER AND LABELS)

SPECIAL TECHNIQUES: R. C. STEELE (ENGRAVING)

MANUFACTURERS: KIKKERLAND DESIGN, INC. (WIND-UP DOG),

R. C. STEELE (DOG TAGS) AND ULINE (ANTISTATIC BAGS AND SHIPPING BOXES)

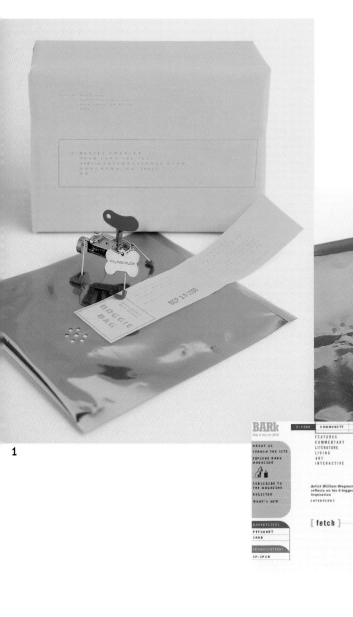

1

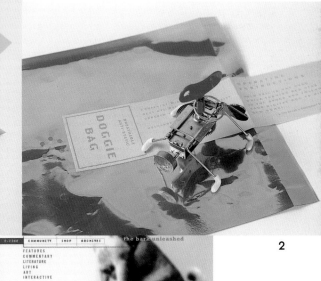

2

4

mini-catalog

Empty film canisters, obtained at a local photo lab, contain minicatalogs featuring the work of photographer Luka Mjeda. Each catalog is offset-printed, hand-cut, and laminated to simulate the look and feel of film. Once inserted and rolled, the catalog is placed in a plastic container.

The impetus for this minicatalog began as an assignment from Igor Zidić, the director of the Modern Gallery in Croatia. Luka Mjeda was hired to photograph several Croatian artists who were to participate in a traveling exhibition. Excited about the resulting work, Mjeda was eager to find a way to package it in a presentation that was as engaging as the photography. The biggest challenge was figuring out how to create an interesting promotional piece that was also lightweight and easily portable. Mjeda and designer Danijel Popović worked together to develop an innovative solution—a minicatalog rolled up inside a used film canister. "I have always had problems explaining to people what I do and why I want to photograph them, and it is difficult to carry my big book around," notes Mjeda. "This catalog is like my business card, and I always have it with me. It's an icebreaker." The fine- and commercial-art photographer always likes to deliver the compact promotion by hand, as he is interested in recipients' reactions to the piece.

Two versions of the promotion were created, one in English and the other in Croatian. Each version was printed on Sappi Magnomat (115 gr/m^2) stock that was later sealed in plastic to simulate a filmlike surface and to protect the piece from tears and scratches. Each printed catalog was hand-inserted into an empty film canister by permanently adhering the piece to the core with clear tape. Once the catalog was attached, it was simply rolled back up, leaving out just enough to give the appearance of the beginning of a film roll. To save money, each catalog was hand-cut and inserted into the canisters by Mjeda. The empty canisters and plastic containers were collected from local photo labs. Mjeda assembled a total of 1,200 promotions.

Referred to by Mjeda as the "canned catalog," the minipromotion features twenty-three Croatian artists, from painters and sculptors to installation and video artists. The slice-of-life portraits reveal the artists' inspirations, their work, and their surroundings. "Looking at them in their studios, you can get an idea about what kind of an artist they are," adds Mjeda. Copies of the catalog reside in the permanent collection of Kodak and the Victoria and Albert Museum in London. A book entitled *Luka Mjeda: Croatian Artists*, published by The Modern Gallery, nicely complements the promotion. The portraits were so captivating that Mjeda himself was included in the traveling exhibition that journeyed through Chile, Brazil, Argentina, and Bolivia.

TECHNICAL TIPS

If you choose to trim the work by hand, you must cut each laminated press sheet one at a time. Because the plastic sheets tended to shift, cutting multiple pieces at once would create a lot of waste. Adhering and inserting a catalog into a film canister takes about two minutes.

The lightweight and thought-provoking promotion captures the world of twenty-three of Croatia's best artists in a variety of disciplines.

A full list of credits regarding the exhibition is on the back of the promotion.

2

FIRM: S.L.M. D.O.O.

CREATIVE DIRECTORS:
DANIJEL POPOVIĆ AND LUKA MJEDA

DESIGNER: DANIJEL POPOVIĆ

PHOTOGRAPHY: LUKA MJEDA

PRINTER: AKD

MANUFACTURERS: KODAK, FUJI, AND AGFA

1

3

meet
the family

Designed to simulate a collection of snap-shots, the series of personalized business cards presents the staff of BBK Studio in a fun and creative way. The piece can remain inside the tin container or hang on a wall. The promotion is distributed in a white corrugated box stuffed with orange crinkle wrap and sealed with the firm's mailing label.

Excited about their new office space, BBK Studio plunged into redesigning their entire business system. To celebrate, the design firm wanted to host a party for clients and vendors alike. But as time went on, the busy studio got sidetracked with other work. Soon, too much time had passed, and a party was no longer appropriate. "We had grown quite a bit, and our clients didn't know about the new people we had hired either," adds creative director and designer Yang Kim. Wanting to salvage their initial idea of an open house, the firm came up with an interesting alternative. "We decided we would do a studio tour, but in an analog fashion," explains Kim.

Because the design firm's new visual identity contained quite a unique collection of business cards, Kim thought that she could use this somehow. "The cards in themselves are almost like miniresumes, listing everyone's different personality and interests," she notes. "I was thinking that the cards, in a way, were a little collection of personal snapshots. It was almost like the proud father who pulls out photos of his family." With that idea in mind, the design firm searched for vendors to create a wallet-style plastic sleeve that could house standard-size business cards. After looking through several options in an array of plastics, the designer chose a custom plastic sleeve that was accordion-folded with a small tab at the top, allowing it to be hung if desired. "I thought it would be useful to be able to put the piece up on a tackboard to reference several people at a glance," remarks Kim. The cards were printed on the front with two PMS colors, metallic silver and bright orange. The backs of the cards were double-hit with the orange for solid coverage. To accent the BBK Studio logo, a clear thermography was applied. The entire piece was coated with an overall aqueous varnish to protect the orange ink from rubbing off the uncoated stock.

A silver tin with rounded corners was chosen to house the pullout promotion. "Because our system was designed using silver and orange, it made sense to use something metallic," acknowledges Kim. "Also, if you decided to take the piece out and hang it, you could reuse the tin for something else." The piece was sent in a white corrugated box stuffed with orange crinkle wrap and sealed with a mailing label. With a little ingenuity, BBK Studio was able to successfully introduce their new look, space, and staff through an upbeat and entertaining promotion.

TECHNICAL TIPS

Certain colors, because of their chemical makeup, dry more slowly than others. If you are looking to double-hit a color, especially on uncoated stock, talk to your printer about potential drying problems. An overall varnish may have to be applied to protect the slow-drying color from later rubbing off.

The business cards provide insight into the various personalities at BBK Studio. They are printed in the firm's corporate colors, bright orange and silver. The backs are double-hit with orange, and clear thermography is applied to call attention to the logo. An overall aqueous varnish is applied to both sides.

The new business system—pocket folder, notecard, various labels, letterhead, envelope, and business card—reflects the energy and enthusiasm of this growing firm. The rounded corners and circular accents throughout play nicely off the dot pattern used in the BBK Studio logo.

FIRM: BBK STUDIO

CREATIVE DIRECTOR AND DESIGNER:
YANG KIM

PRINTING: FOREMOST GRAPHICS

MANUFACTURER: RG CREATIONS

1

2

3

do it
to music!

The mission of Brown & Company Design was to put together a promotion that really communicated how they worked and who they were as a company—fun, energetic, and a bit eclectic. They also wanted to shake things up creatively in the studio, encouraging each other to work outside their comfort zone. In search for a distinctive vehicle to communicate their message, the firm decided to really push the envelope and put their process to music! Because many staff members are musically inclined, the instrumental compositions were a breeze. The real challenge for many was overcoming the fear of performing in a studio, standing alone with headphones on in front of a microphone and singing. "When we handed out the assignments, some people volunteered right up front and others had to be coerced a bit," recalls designer and musician Chris Lamy.

The project was given a set budget, and everyone was assigned a stage of the firm's working process to write lyrics about, a genre of music to be inspired by, and some music to sing to. "We took our process and identified recognizable milestones, from the sales pitch to the delivery," adds Lamy. Every album cover was thoroughly researched so the design accurately represented the colors, typefaces, and imagery indicative of each style of music being portrayed. Each assignment was critiqued by the entire group, giving the overall project a cohesive look and creating a sense of ownership by all.

The first step was to record the music on tape. "The musicians and vocalists performed their tracks, and they were mixed together. Once we were happy with it, the tracks were mixed down from twenty-four tracks to two tracks (stereo) and burned onto a mixed disc," explains Lamy. The next step was to get a premaster made. "DeCato Sound made each individual track the same volume, inserted even spaces between songs, edited the noise, and put the songs in order," continues Lamy. "Upon approval, the premaster was delivered to Crooked Cove for the CD plant, US Optical Disc, to replicate. Crooked Cove coordinated and handled all of the paperwork, legalities, and actual ordering of the CDs." Normally, CDs are put in jewel cases and shrink-wrapped. To save money, the design firm hand-collated and stuffed the CDs in their own sleeves.

By exploring venues of creativity outside their area of expertise, the staff at Brown & Company was able to put together an attention-getting promotion that has not only invigorated the entire group but also gotten them national exposure far surpassing their expectations. "New Hampshire Public Radio had us down at their studios for a show just on the CD. The show was so popular that they reran it during a pledge drive, and it was one of their most successful half hours," exclaims Lamy. "When it all came together, there were sparks flying around here, and everyone was very proud. It really challenged us creatively and paid off in the end." Mission accomplished!

TECHNICAL TIPS

Creating a promotion such as this is no small feat. Many details must be attended to in order for the project to succeed. Time must be scheduled for design, musical composition, writing, rehearsing, and coordinating with all of the various vendors, from the recording studio to the final printing and replication house. In addition, a lot of administrative work must be done to ensure no one else owns the music. Once the music is deemed original, it must be copyrighted to protect it and the label art. (Crooked Cove handled these administrative details in this case). To organize such an endeavor, it is best to treat yourself like a client and follow the protocol that has already made you successful. Set a budget and timeline, and divide the workload among teams.

1 | **2**

Each Kraft CD sleeve, purchased in bulk in a standard design, is hand-printed on the front, inside, and spine with custom-made rubber stamps. The enclosed CD is professionally recorded, mastered, replicated, and printed. Each package is individually shrink-wrapped and delivered to prospective and existing clientele as a self-mailer.

To communicate to clients who they were and how they worked, Brown & Company Design set their process to music. Each insert, representing a different stage of their working process, is designed to look like an album cover. Each depicting a different decade and style of music, the covers cleverly evoke the personality of this innovative and eclectic firm.

FIRM: BROWN & COMPANY DESIGN

CREATIVE DIRECTOR: DAVID MARKOVSKY

DESIGNERS: CHRIS LAMY, MARY JO BROWN, CHRIS HAMER, SCOTT BUCHANAN, JODI HOLT, ANDREA ADAMS, MATT TALBOT, D.J. BURDETTE, CLAUDIA KAERNER, DAVID MARKOVSKY, AND TRICIA MILLER

ILLUSTRATION: ERIC ANDREWS, SCOTT BUCHANAN, AND MATT TALBOT

PHOTOGRAPHY: DAVID GOODMAN, CLAUDIA KAERNER, AND TRICIA MILLER

MUSIC COMPOSERS: CHRIS LAMY AND MATT TALBOT

LYRICISTS AND VOCALS: BROWN & COMPANY STAFF

INSTRUMENTS: CHRIS LAMY (GUITAR), MATT TALBOT (BASS GUITAR, BANJO, AND ACCORDION), DAVID MORRIS (PERCUSSION AND PAN FLUTE), BILL RIENDUEA (ACCORDION), MARY JO BROWN (PIANO), ERIK EVENSEN (SAXOPHONE), AND ALICEN BROWN (BARITONE GUITAR)

EFFECTS: DAVID MORRIS, JODI HOLD, AND CLAUDIA KAERNER

PRINTING: RAM PRINTING (INSERT COVERS)

SPECIAL TECHNIQUES: THE ELECTRIC CAVE (RECORDING STUDIO), DECATO SOUND (CD MASTERING), CROOKED COVE (DISC PRINTING AND REPLICATION COORDINATION), AND US OPTICAL DISC (CD REPLICATION AND GLASS MASTERING)

MANUFACTURERS: CALUMET CONTAINER (CD SLEEVES) AND BOB'S RUBBER STAMPS (RUBBER STAMP)

LISTEN TO THE CD: WWW.BROWNTONE.COM

that
finishing
touch!

"Good Gracious! came into our offices with a folder they had been using—a standard two-pocket piece that was overflowing with clippings, press releases, recipes, and a cover letter," recalls creative director and designer Marcie Carson. "It was not an effective introduction." To get the events company off to a better start, the designer immediately knew she had to create a piece that would not only conceal much of the extraneous paperwork but also make a more memorable first impression overall. "Good Gracious! creates amazing events and focuses on every detail, from the impeccable menu to the imaginative environment surrounding it," says Carson. "We wanted this piece to feel much like the events—captivating, delicious, organized, whimsical, and always, always creative." The target market for the promotion ranged from planners of large corporate functions to intimate birthday parties.

With a clear direction in mind, the designer put pencil to paper and laid out her idea. "I immediately had a vision for this piece. I saw the finished folder in my head before I even sat down at my desk," says Carson. "We did present one other comp to give the client an option, but I knew that this would be the one." The result was a stunning custom die-cut pocket folder that incorporated the company's existing corporate colors and logo mark. "Good Gracious! did not have a brand identity when they approached us. They did have an existing logo that was quite nice, but felt a bit like fast food," the designer admits. "Because they did have some equity in this logo, I felt strongly about utilizing the existing mark as is. In the end, we were able to tie it in nicely, giving it a more elegant place in which to live."

To add richness to the outside of the folder, a double hit of royal purple was applied. A bright red, yellow, and purple sticker sealed the self-mailing package, creating curiosity about what may unfold. Once the seal is broken, the inside reveals a miniature spoon cleverly inserted into yet another enclosure, enticing the viewer to continue to explore. "I am frequently challenging our design team by saying 'That's great, but how can we make it better?'" offers Carson. "On this project, I asked myself that very question, and Good Gracious! ended up with a playful golden spoon—an appropriate addition, as the letterhead design contained a photo of a fork and knife." Underneath, a business card and stationery provide both contact information and a nicely designed environment for support materials. The ethereal and dreamlike montage interior evokes the ambience, elegance, and sophistication that a Good Gracious! event provides. Overall, the promotion is a beautiful blend of both form and function.

TECHNICAL TIPS

When you have a self-mailer that needs to make a memorable impression, always do a test mailing so potential problems can be ironed out in advance. To keep growing as a designer, never stop asking yourself how you can improve on something that you have created. Questioning your efforts will challenge you to strive for excellence each time. Often, the minutest details make the biggest impact.

1

The stunning jewel-toned package is accented by the company's logo, which was applied as a seal. Inside the self-mailer is another enclosure of sorts. A small golden spoon add-on piques curiosity and encourages the viewer to explore further. For durability and protection during delivery, the piece is printed with an overall varnish on 100-lb. Fox River Starwhite Vicksburg cover.

2

The curvilinear die-cut folder is not only attractive but also highly functional. Inside, a business card and custom-designed stationery provide contact and support information, organizing and adding elegance to the overflow of materials that once cluttered the event company's previous collateral. The piece was both mailed and given out by hand.

1

2

CLIENT: GOOD GRACIOUS! EVENTS

FIRM: [I]E DESIGN

CREATIVE DIRECTOR AND DESIGNER: MARCIE CARSON

PHOTOGRAPHY: STOCK

PRINTING: SOUTHERN CALIFORNIA GRAPHICS

BINDERY: CUSTOM DISPLAY

SPECIAL TECHNIQUES: CUSTOM DISPLAY (DIE-CUTTING)

MANUFACTURER: CREATIVE BEGINNINGS (SPOON)

collaborative new year wishes

Motive Design Research LLC, Wordslinger, and Robert Horsley Printing decided to combine their efforts, producing a New Year's promotion as a way to connect and build relationships with clients, valued suppliers, friends, and colleagues. In these uncertain times, the collaborative group thought it was important to shed light on the newfound possibilities that each year brings. "Over the past five years, we have developed a reputation for interesting, giftlike holiday promotions," acknowledges creative director Michael Connors. "But we, like many other people, were in a more somber mood this year and felt we should do something more meaningful."

With Planting a New Year as their concept, the design team began researching books and the Internet, inundating themselves with the practice of gardening. "In a brainstorming meeting, we came up with the idea of using seeds because they represent change, growth, and new beginnings, many of the same things a new year represents," adds Connors. "Adhering them to the cover immediately piqued the interest of recipients, and it was also a good way to incorporate individual greetings from each company." The seeds chosen were a western wildflower mix that requires minimal maintenance—a wise choice for the busy professionals who were to receive the package. "We decided that any one kind of flower—forget-me-nots, for example—would have limited the message to something too specific," Connors acknowledges. "We felt the wildflower mix was not only the easiest to use but was also in keeping with the spirit of the design." The seeds and insert card were packaged inside a small glassine envelope and adhered to the cover by a custom-made label. Throughout the saddle-stitched booklet, subtle relationships are drawn between gardening and the growing of one's future, business and personal. "The parallels between a garden and a life are unavoidable, and there's no time like a new year to make us aware of the connections. You can always do better and you can always do worse," shares collaborator Brittany Stromberg. "Each new year and each garden is what it is, yet they tell us everything about the people who plan, plant, and tend to them."

The greeting of good tidings has yielded new business for the collaborative team. "People we haven't talked to in ages have called and e-mailed to say how happy they were to receive it and that they couldn't wait to scatter the seeds," says Connors. "One former client of ours called and set up a meeting to discuss new possibilities of working together." Only 450 pieces were produced and divided among the collaborators.

TECHNICAL TIPS

When sending seeds, choose plants that are easy to maintain and can grow in the climate of the target audience. If you are shipping internationally, check with Customs for pertinent regulations. When packing seeds make sure the envelope or container is tightly sealed, as seeds are tiny and find their way through the smallest of holes.

1

The saddle-stitched promotion commences with the presentation of seeds, a beautiful mix of low-maintenance wildflowers. Along with the seeds, a customized card is included, individualizing the package for each company. Both are housed in a glassine envelope and adhered to the cover with a custom-made label. Each booklet is placed in a drawstring bag and distributed to clients, prospects, suppliers, friends, and colleagues.

2

The little book takes the reader through the entire process of gardening, starting with good compost, sowing seeds, watering, maintenance, and, of course, watching the wildflowers grow and change. The layout is a nice mix of utilitarianism and elegance.

2

ideas are

seeds.

1

TO

ORDER NO.

RETURN POSTAGE GUARANTEED
POSTAGE HERE

Planting a new year

Motive
wishes you
a wild,
thriving
and
optimistic
new year.

FIRMS: MOTIVE DESIGN RESEARCH LLC, WORDSLINGER,
AND ROBERT HORSLEY PRINTING

CREATIVE DIRECTORS: MICHAEL CONNORS AND KARI STRAND

DESIGNER: PETER AUGUST ANDERSON

ILLUSTRATION: PETER AUGUST ANDERSON

PHOTOGRAPHY: TOM CONNORS

COPYWRITING: BRITTANY STROMBERG

PRINTING: ROBERT HORSLEY PRINTING

BINDERY: SEATTLE BINDERY

MANUFACTURERS: ULINE (DRAWSTRING BAG), WILDSEED FARMS (SEEDS),
AND PAPER MART (GLASSINE ENVELOPE)

fresh start

To connect with clients, prospects, and friends, the creative team at Miriello Grafico wanted to make a year-end promotion that would touch people. "We were looking for something to symbolize the close of a difficult and challenging year for most everyone," remarks creative director Ron Miriello. "The idea of soap as a new, clean start fit with our search for a handmade and personal item that people would value."

To make the piece special, the creative team worked with a skin- and body-products specialist to design and develop an original blend of soap. After testing several recipes, a combination of such natural ingredients as oatmeal, lavender, coconut, and essential oils made for a soothing and sensual bath bar. "When asked what we wanted to be channeled into the soap, we said extra peace and prosperity," recalls Miriello. To further personalize the soap, the design team explored various shapes and signature engravings. However, when manufacturing limitations confined the soap to a traditional rectangular shape, they began to examine packaging alternatives to make their mark.

Because of the soap's unrefined texture, the team went in search of natural materials that conveyed a handmade and unfinished quality. A Kraft box with metal closures, available standard, was the perfect vehicle. To accent the surface, a customized mailing label and adhesive seal were added. Inside the box, a muslin drawstring bag imprinted with rubber stamps provided yet another layer of packaging, further piquing the recipient's curiosity. To give the promotion an artistic flair, each bag was individually numbered with a signature impression made using an automatic counter, traditionally used by manuscript editors to number document pages. "We liked the unique numbering system so much that we decided to apply it to the outside label on the box as well," adds designer Dennis Garcia. To deliver the message of a fresh and clean new year, a customized hang tag was attached to the drawstring of each muslin bag. The tag also served as a place to list the ingredients used in the making of this premium-blend bath bar. To lock in its sweet aroma, each bar was shrink-wrapped with a custom die-cut label adhered on top, adding just the right amount of decoration to the natural surface.

For the design firm, the intimate and personal gift was a huge success, reinforcing their reputation for being innovators. "We're still getting requests and handing out select samples to new prospects over a year later," concludes Miriello.

1

2

The giftlike promotion is concealed in a muslin drawstring bag whose raw texture and natural coloring add to the handmade and tactile quality of the overall piece. Custom-made rubber stamps are used to imprint the surface. In addition, each piece is individually numbered with an automatic counter, giving it the feel of a signature limited edition. To deliver the message of a fresh start for the new year, a custom-printed label is adhered to a hang tag and fastened to the drawstring bag. To complete the package, the promotion is placed inside a Kraft box and filled with packing tinsel. A decorative mailing label wraps the box, and an adhesive strip provides additional sealing support.

The handmade soap, a premium blend of essential oils and natural ingredients, is shrink-wrapped and decorated with a custom die-cut label. Its organic properties are said to bring peace and prosperity to those who use it.

1

2

FIRM: MIRIELLO GRAFICO

CREATIVE DIRECTORS:

　RON MIRIELLO AND MARK MURPHY

DESIGNER: DENNIS GARCIA

ILLUSTRATION: DENNIS GARCIA

PRINTING: NEYENESCH PRINTERS INC.

SPECIAL TECHNIQUES:

　NEYENESCH PRINTERS INC. (SHRINK-WRAPPING)

MANUFACTURERS: PEGGY RICHARDS (HANDMADE SOAP),

　MASON BOX COMPANY (BOX AND PACKING TINSEL),

　SAN FRANCISCO HERB COMPANY (DRAW STRING MUSLIN BAG),

　CALIFORNIA STAMP COMPANY (CUSTOM STAMP),

　AND GYPSY OFFICE SUPPLY COMPANY (HANG TAGS)

brand
survival

The brand-survival package contains an instructional manual, emergency rations, inspirational imagery, a pocketknife, and a flashlight. It is distributed in a silver pouch that is heat sealed and labeled. The color scheme, text, and icons are all inspired by safety graphics. Only 150 were produced. They were either hand-delivered or mailed to both existing and prospective clientele.

"To survive in the business world today, with the brand-conscious consumer, it is essential to have in place a well-designed identity implemented effectively and consistently," says creative director and designer Alexander Lloyd. "To that end, we wanted to show how our company could help businesses achieve this." To create an awareness of the importance and value of branding, Lloyd's Graphic Design and Communication put together a survival kit of sorts. The idea plays up on the need for companies to survive in a marketplace that is stagnant and starving for distinction. To make the package fun and memorable, a humorous twist was introduced. "As in many of my promos, I use a lot of tongue-in-cheek humor, playing the theme to its extreme," admits Lloyd. "In this case, I refer to how many business corporate identities are in such a bad state that they are really in need of emergency repair and should immediately consult a design professional qualified in brand aid, brand resuscitation, and corporate identity crisis management." Lloyd's Graphic Design and Communication to the rescue!

The brand survival kit contains the all-important spiral-bound manual, which begins by sharing insightful information on the need for companies to build brand recognition. It closes by showcasing the design firm's strong brand development capabilities through a diverse array of identity work. To push the playful concept a bit further, a pocketknife, flashlight, and emergency rations are included as the appropriate essentials for surviving the jungle of today's volatile marketplace. Each of the add-ons was sourced from a local retailer. The outer sleeves of the brain- and brand-stimulating candy bars were removed, and custom self-adhesive labels were applied. As stated on the back of the bar, "It will put you in the right frame of mind to tackle any brand design or redesign traumas you may face." Lloyd observes, "The strong yellow- and black-text-oriented graphics have a practical, no-nonsense, utilitarian feel that reflect the nature of safety information and official survival literature." To shed a light of hope for the truly brand-impaired, a CD-ROM of inspirational imagery was also included.

The promotion was delivered in a heat-sealed, reflective silver pouch reminiscent of a survival blanket. A custom-designed label and a small note enclosed the silver package, reminding recipients of the blessings a new year brings. The promotion was distributed to both existing and prospective clientele in need of immediate brand assistance or resuscitation. Let's hope they survive!

TECHNICAL TIPS

Think of the promotions you put out as an extension of your personality. It is just as important to reveal something about yourself and what it might be like to work with you, as it is to show what you are capable of. When you seek clients, you are also developing relationships.

Each French-folded page of *The Ultimate Brand Survival Manual* juxtaposes insightful text with visually compelling imagery to deliver the brand-building message. In the back, the spiral-bound manual showcases Lloyd's Graphic Design and Communication's portfolio of brand development work. It comes wrapped by a bellyband with an inspirational CD-ROM.

A chocolate bar, a flashlight, and a utility pocketknife all serve as concept-enhancing add-ons to the brand survival package.

1

2

3

FIRM: LLOYD'S GRAPHIC DESIGN & COMMUNICATION

CREATIVE DIRECTOR AND DESIGNER:
  ALEXANDER LLOYD

ILLUSTRATION: ALEXANDER LLOYD

PHOTOGRAPHY: ALEXANDER LLOYD

PRINTING: BLENHEIM PRINTING CO.
  AND BOS PRINT (ADHESIVE LABELS)

BINDERY: BLENHEIM PRINTING CO. (COPPER SPIRAL BINDING)

MANUFACTURERS: CAS-PAK PRODUCTS LTD. (FOIL POUCHES)
  AND LOCAL RETAILER (FLASHLIGHT, POCKETKNIFE, AND JEWEL CASES)

has been dominated by programmers and engineers who know very little about branding, type, image, and hierarchy of message," claims Riordon. "Corporations are at a point where they want the same level of sophistication online that they see in print. We see it as a tremendous opportunity. Like most design firms, we are looking at other ways to promote our services to that medium."

Technology has also created a new venue for the licensing of stock online. Because of the negative effect that corporate stock houses have had on illustrators and photographers, they have taken matters into their own hands and developed some of the best sources of innovative stock available. Unlike the cumbersome corporate stock catalogs that feature generic prefab imagery, interactive, artist-controlled group sites allow access to a vast selection of high-quality work with customized keyword searching and an instant retrieval system, where buyers can purchase from anywhere in the world at any time. If creatives maintain control of their intellectual property by refusing to sign all rights contracts, they can further reap financial benefits from their work down the road through licensing. When interactive TV, video-on-demand, and shopping-on-demand become mainstream and publishers find a way to make money through online subscriptions, an even greater scope of work will open up.

Every successful business has one eye on the wheel and the other on the future. It is important to the longevity of your business to make time, on a regular basis, to focus on ways in which to keep your company on track and moving forward. Do not get so caught up in the day-to-day routine that you allow opportunities to pass you by. The future will bring many challenges to hurdle, but for those who are willing to learn new skills, opportunities abound. Whether through merchandising, client partnerships, or the multitude of options available in the new media arena, creatives will continue to flourish, and they will do so on their own terms.

With the advancements in technology, electronic media has spurred an alternative market for visual communicators to move and grow.

merchandising endeavor

For years, the team at Form had been designing merchandise for musical bands in the United Kingdom and struggling to persuade them to do anything creative. "We decided to create our own designs and be our own client, setting up a separate company called Uniform," remarks creative director Paula Benson. "It supports itself and allows us to express ourselves without client restraints. It is also great to work with another medium apart from paper or screen."

About fifteen designs were created and sampled onto T-shirts, with the best going into full production. Safe-T UniForm, a custom-designed line of T-shirts, is all about safety. "We love utilitarian signage such as airport graphics, hazard symbols, and safety signs," offers Benson. The unusual print placements, interesting use of materials, and strong graphic appeal make the line of streetwear a must-have.

To promote and launch the Safe-T line, UniForm sent promotional T-shirts to bands, disc jockeys, celebrities, and the press. "This gave us something to write about on our Web site," adds Benson. "It also gave a celebrity endorsement to the range." To be eye-catching, the highly graphic T-shirts were delivered in clear air packs along with a poster, presenting the eccentric line in a far from traditional way. As a play on the overall safety theme, the back of the poster demonstrated how the shirts could be used in case of emergency—as a sling,

bandage, breathing aid, smoke excluder, or fire blanket. With the tagline "Be seen, be safe," the unique line of streetwear gives new meaning to wearing a shirt. The humorous disclaimer "UniForm accepts no responsibility for any misguided or delusional people who may injure or cause harm to themselves by attempting to use their garment in such a way as shown above" just adds to the overall appeal of Safe-T. The innovative promotion attracted a lot of attention, building massive Web site traffic and landing numerous feature stories for the newly formed company.

UniForm, which started as a sideline, has now become a booming business with global distribution, selling through their fully secure Web site (www.uniform.uk.com) and a number of retailers in the United Kingdom. "A lot of Form's clients have seen what we are doing with UniForm and have asked us to design clothing lines for them," acknowledges Benson. "Since we now have a lot of experience in what works and what doesn't, our clients can buy into our experience when they commission us." Because of the success of UniForm, Form is now exploring other merchandising avenues.

FIRM: UNIFORM/FORM

CREATIVE DIRECTORS:

PAULA BENSON AND PAUL WEST

DESIGNER: CLAIRE WARNER

PRINTING: HERONSWOOD

MANUFACTURER:

GREEN ISLAND (AIR PACK)

entrepreneurial mindset

With a passion for fashion, partners Pam Williams and Lisa House decided to diversify their business and open a high-end retail boutique selling signature apparel and accessories. Before they took on the venture, they thought hard about what they really wanted to create—and, most important, did their homework. "We started by doing qualitative research on the name of the store," says creative director Pam Williams. "We were interested in understanding how Moo would play among potential shoppers." The next step was to determine the customer profile—a confident woman with a keen sense of humor. "She is someone who knows what she likes and seeks out pieces that are unique and fresh," adds Williams. "Our customer needed to respond to the name in a positive way. If she laughed, she got what the store was about. Fashion is fun, and our name needed to reflect that."

To launch their new retail endeavor, Williams and House needed a flexible core identity system that not only conveyed the true spirit of Moo but also could be built on over time. "The biggest challenge was visually and aesthetically balancing a sense of humor with important elements of sophistication and style in one identity," Williams admits. To begin the design effort, the creative team researched an array of specialty processes and materials that could add character and distinction to the Moo brand. "The research helped us determine what would be possible and what effects we could achieve," notes Williams. "To us, using just the right materials represents the difference between a bound-button hole and a machine-stitched version."

When it came to color, the team looked toward classic simplicity. "A great wardrobe starts with basic black and white pieces, and so too would this identity," Williams interjects. "Accent colors were later incorporated, much like the way accessories add a finishing touch to an ensemble." To bring in the look of fabric, highly textured materials and knits were purchased, scanned into the computer, and added as accents to the various collateral. The resulting identity includes custom die-cut stationery, hang tags, and grommet-bound gift certificates; each element utilizes embossing, foil stamping, and perforation of Via Pure Smooth white paper. The business system is not only fun but sophisticated, a true reflection of the Moo brand.

To ride the wave of instability in the marketplace, many are diversifying into other areas and, essentially, becoming their own client.

FIRM: **WILLIAMS AND HOUSE**

CREATIVE DIRECTOR: **PAM WILLIAMS**

DESIGNER: **RICH HOLLANT, CO:LAB**

PRINTING: **THE POND-EKBERG COMPANY**

SPECIAL TECHNIQUES: **THE POND-EKBERG COMPANY**

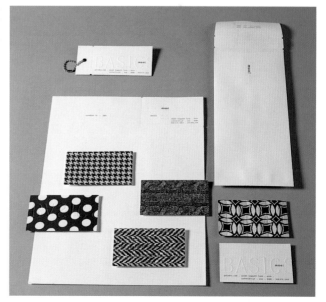

in our leisure

Starshot, a company that specializes in the sports and leisure market, was formed when a retired biking professional, Kai Stuht, joined forces with MAGMA, a cutting-edge German design firm. "In the beginning, the idea of Starshot was that Kai Stuht would go out and take photographs of biking—specifically mountain and racing—stars," explains creative director Lars Harmsen. "The pictures, along with one editorial interview, were put together in a small magazinelike booklet and sent to various trade publications in the biking industry in Europe and the United States." Each booklet came complete with a CD-ROM containing both the text and images so interested publications could easily integrate the content into their magazine. "We saw that selling to magazines was a hard business, and we had to be on the phone a lot," adds Harmsen. "So we decided to create our own magazine, and that is how we came up with *Byke Style Mag.*"

With complete creative freedom, the design team at Starshot push themselves each issue to produce something innovative, boasting the latest techniques. *Byke Style Mag* 4, for instance, opens with an orange fluorescent ink accent by a holographic foil-stamped logo that is also embossed off the surface in select areas. To make the cover photo pop, the same holographic material is applied to the surface as a gold foil stamp. Inside, the excitement continues as foil stamps are creatively mixed with fluorescent, metallic, and process offset colors. To achieve different tones of silver, various inks are printed with the metallic color later applied on top.

Byke Style Mag 5, also an experiment in production, uses glitter to accent key graphics and action imagery. To achieve the effect, glitter is added to a gloss varnish in varying degrees. The varnish and glitter mixture is then applied through a silk-screen printing process to various areas throughout the magazine. According to Harmsen, the glitter works best on a darker solid or an area of continuous tone. Because the magazine uses an array of techniques and equipment, the layout must be carefully planned to make everything come together smoothly in the end. In many cases, each thirty-two page signature must go through numerous processes: offset printing, silk-screen printing, and foil stamping. "I need to know exactly which colors and techniques will be printed on each page. It is a lot of work because of the different printing machines being used," comments Harmsen.

The magazines are distributed free to the public through large bike retailers, mail order companies, and railway stations all over Germany. "We made a joint venture with a bicycle builder who has a big distribution net," notes Harmsen. A total of twenty-five thousand magazines are distributed four times a year. "They are a great way for us to explore and show our work," Harmsen concludes. "We have gotten projects from well-known companies in the industry who have seen our magazine." They were recently asked to design a signature line of aluminum water bottles for SIGG Switzerland's 2003 collection. By creating a vehicle for their work to penetrate the marketplace, Starshot built name and market recognition in the industry, attracting top clients to their doorstep.

It is important to the longevity of your business to make time, on a regular basis, to focus on ways in which to keep your company on track and moving forward.

FIRM: STARSHOT

CREATIVE DIRECTOR: LARS HARMSEN

DESIGNER: TINA WEISSER

TYPE DESIGNERS: LARS HARMSEN, BORIS KAHL, AND FLORIAN GÄRTNER (WWW.VOLCANO-TYPE.DE)

PHOTOGRAPHY: KAI STUHT

EDITORIAL: KAI STUHT (EDITOR IN CHIEF), TOM LINTHALER, FRIEDER MEIER, CHRIS STEURER, AND TINA WEISSER

PRINTING AND BINDERY: ENGELHARDT & BAUER (STARSHOT *BYKE STYLE MAG* 4) AND GREISER DRUCK GMBH & CO. KG (STARSHOT *BYKE STYLE MAG* 5)

SPECIAL TECHNIQUES: ARBEITSKREIS PRÄGEFOLIENDRUCK (HOLOGRAPHIC HOT FOIL STAMP AND EMBOSSING), RIEKER DRUCKVEREDELUNG GMBH & CO. KG (SILK-SCREENING OF GLITTER INK), AND FRANZ SCHMITT KG (HOT FOIL STAMP)

MANUFACTURER: SIGG SWITZERLAND AG (WATER BOTTLES)

PART II

Innovative

All new! Sometimes a promotion is striking for its originality. It gets us to exclaim our appreciation: "Why, I've never seen anything quite like that before!" The sheer newness and freshness of the promotion is what ensures that it will be noticed, appreciated, and remembered.

Design Firm **Strawberry Frog**
Client **Onitsuka Tiger**
Project **Tokyo 64 Hero Breath**

Question: Meditation Session . . .

Close your eyes. Imagine you're at the top of the world. Breathe in, deeply, slowly. Count to three. Now, exhale. Good. You might find yourself using this exercise to relax your mind during a hectic day at the office. Or, if you're a 1964 Olympic gold medalist from Japan, you're probably rehearsing these meditations while breathing into a bag. What for? For canning your breath, of course.

Onitsuka Tiger, an affiliate of ASICS, was releasing a line of athletic footwear called Tokyo 64—shoes commemorating the Japanese gold-medal athletes from the 1964 Olympic Games in Tokyo. So, they asked Strawberry Frog, a design firm in Amsterdam, to spearhead a promotional campaign for their retro soles. The goal was to capture the spirit of the 1964 Games and to create product appeal.

The target audience consisted primarily of European males age 25 to 30 who were opinion-forming individuals. Mark Chalmers, the creative director of the project, provides some psychographic insight into the target audience: "[These people] help define trends and strongly influence early adopters on the street, through their press and social networks." With that in mind, the folks at Strawberry Frog knew they had to come up with a fresh, novel approach that would attract the interest of these young and highly selective trendsetters.

Onitsuka Tiger was releasing a line of athletic footwear called Tokyo 64, shoes commemorating the Japanese gold-medal athletes from the 1964 Olympic Games in Tokyo. The goal was to capture the spirit of the 1964 Games and to create product appeal.

. . . Or Clever Promotion?

So, late at night with a deadline approaching, the creative team came up with their "Hero Breath" idea, a campaign that would capture the spirit of the 1964 Tokyo Games in the most literal sense. During a limited-time promotion, customers who purchased a pair of Tokyo 64 shoes would take home an aluminum can that would resemble an energy drink container—packaged with the actual breath of 1964 Tokyo athletes.

The process of capturing this "hero breath" involved athletes first reconstructing the 1964 Olympic Games in their minds, then exhaling into a tube that was connected to a bag. This was no hoax—skeptics could visit the official Tokyo 64 website and download a video of these breath-capture ceremonies to see for themselves.

With the canning of the breath such a production, you would think that printing on the cans themselves would be relatively easy. Not so, according to Chalmers, who recalls, "It's easy to print on filled cans. It's less easy to print on a limited run of filled cans. It's almost impossible to print on a limited run of cans containing nothing but breath. We had to be very charming . . ." So, charming they were—charming and clever. And Hero Breath cans they printed.

Answer: A Clever Promotion

The end product was a tangible, handheld advertisement that resonated in people's minds. Both playful and ironic, Hero Breath cans invited consumers to learn more about the Tokyo 64 heritage. And, as a unique and highly collectible item, they quickly made their way into online auctions on eBay.

Now, at the count of three, you will open your eyes, feeling energized and refreshed. If you're a Tokyo 64 athlete just lending a hand—er, a pair of lungs—to the Hero Breath promo, you can stop breathing into that bag now.

During a limited-time promotion, customers who purchased a pair of Tokyo 64 shoes would take home an aluminum can that would resemble an energy drink container—packaged with the actual breath of 1964 Tokyo athletes.

Close your eyes . . . breathe in, deeply, slowly. Count to three. Now, exhale. Good. You've just re-created a ceremony to can your breath.

According to Mark Chalmers, creative director at Strawberry Frog, "It's almost impossible to print on a limited run of cans containing nothing but breath. We had to be very charming."

Design Firm Chimera Design
Client Tennis Victoria
Project Tennis Victoria Annual Report

How many cups of coffee does it take to come up with a creative breakthrough? Have enough coffee and perhaps it will lead to an idea beautiful in its simplicity—to deliver the annual report for Tennis Victoria, a Canadian nonprofit sporting organization, in empty tennis ball containers.

Follow the Bouncing Ball

The inspiration, besides the coffee, was the client itself. Tennis Victoria wanted to do something that, in its words, was "Strategic Radical," pushing the bounds of creativity while working with very limited resources. The strategy was simple—to position Tennis Victoria as youthful, progressive, and community based. But as if telling the creative team to push the boundaries of creative wasn't enough, the client also delivered a box of tennis accessories, asking if any of the elements could be worked into the final artwork. Imagine the creative team's surprise when they opened the box and discovered an assortment of tennis components including strings, balls, racket fittings, canisters, vibration dampeners, and grips, along with a note that said, "This is everything I could find . . . have fun."

Next came the aforementioned cups of coffee over multiple brainstorming sessions. The tennis ball canisters seemed the easiest way to provide the annual report with a strong visual point of difference and an effective packaging vehicle.

The client delivered their 2002 annual report in empty tennis ball containers—an "ace" concept served up by Chimera Design.

Nothing Is Ever Easy

Of course, as any creative design team knows, nothing is ever really easy. The first challenge was "How many canisters can we get for free?" The answer came several days later when the client rang with an exciting breakthrough: four tennis academies had agreed to donate their empty canisters. In the end, more than 500 canisters were sourced, either metal or transparent plastic, in varying sizes.

Because beggars can't be choosers, the creative team had to deal with the reality of the variations in the containers. The transparent canisters showcased the report and simply required a good cleaning. But the metal tubes were more challenging because they were covered with branding. It was determined that the key to continuity was to produce a single sticker for the metal canisters, which was cut to fit over the existing branding. Matching circular stickers for the lids were also developed.

The printed report itself presented its own hurdles. The cost needed to be kept to a minimum, so the decision was made very early to keep the printing to two color. Having previously developed Tennis Victoria's corporate branding, the creative team knew that the deep blue and yellow green of the logo was a good combination. Experimentation with bold bitmap imaging in the two vibrant colors led to a unique look that felt very "sporting" and the decision was quickly made to use that look throughout the piece.

Recycling Is Good

To further stretch the report's unique look, the decision was made to use a combination of raw brown and crisp white stock. This look also enhanced the underlying recycled theme that came from the use of the recycled canisters. The finishing touch involved binding the report with side singer stitching to imitate a tennis court net and racket strings.

The response from all who received the final piece was invariably, "Wow!" and set the scene for Tennis Victoria to sell itself as the province's premier tennis body.

The annual reports were printed in deep blue and yellow-green printing. This simple, two-color execution resulted in a look that felt very "sporting."

Design Firm   R2 Design
Client   Teatro Bruto Theatrical Group
Project   *Krampack* Brochure

A highly successful play by the name of *Krampack* was making its debut in Spain. The storyline goes like this: Four young friends, three boys and one girl, decide to live together. They install themselves in an apartment and decorate it together. While they are doing this, the quartet continually plays games with each other's feelings. So as the apartment gets progressively better, the relationships between the four of them get progressively worse. By the time all the redecoration is done, they realize they cannot bear to live together under the same roof. At a certain point they actually play Krampack—an invented and very aggressive game they used to play in their childhood.

A promotional brochure was produced by Portuguese design firm R2 for the opening of the critically acclaimed play Krampack.

The brochure features perforated boy and girl paper dolls, which the viewer can punch out and play with.

The Design Team Enters the Stage

Enter, stage left, a Portuguese design firm, R2. Task: to produce an innovative brochure in a very short time and on a very limited budget. This brochure was designed to be given out during the first showing of play the to the press and then sold to the public during the other performances.

The brochure had to be produced in an inordinately short amount of time—one week for concepts and a second week for production. This, however, did not stop the designers at R2 from having a flash of inspiration: the entire brochure for the play would be presented like a game. Because a game is the idea around which the play revolves, R2 wanted to design something that the public could also play at the end. Four paper dolls are perforated into the cover, each one cut into a picture of the actors and actresses. The idea is that people can play with them over the large fold-out apartment drawing that can be found in the middle of the brochure. This drawing is an imaginary apartment based on the actual set.

The program ended up being 16 pages, plus a big vegetal sheet (16¼" x 17" [41.3 cm x 43.5 cm]) and a cover in A5 (5⅞" x 5¼") format. It was offset printed with a Cromo cardboard. The inside was Munken linx paper in two colors, with architecture project paper in one color.

A Standing Ovation

Krampack, the play, premiered at the Sitges International Theatre Festival. It was so successful that Jordi Sanchez was awarded the special prize of the Barcelona critics association. Subsequently, the play toured all over Spain.

The brochure received an equal number of accolades.

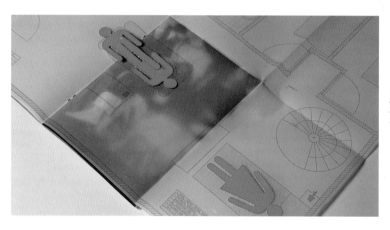

The paper dolls are designed to be used over the illustration of the apartment, which folds out from the middle of the brochure.

The striking visual effect of the doll cutouts is continued throughout the rest of the 16-page brochure.

Design Firm | **Amoeba Corp.**
Client | **Amoeba Corp.**
Project | **Amoeba Corp. Identity**

Amoeba. 1) A single-celled organism. 2) A design firm not afraid of doing things differently and working hard to achieve near-impossible results.

More on the Second Definition

The Amoeba Corp., a design firm in Toronto, Ontario (Canada), was looking to promote itself with an original, innovative, and artistic flair. They wanted to redesign their identity in a way that would highlight the company's multidisciplinary approach to graphic design problem solving. When working for corporate clients, Amoeba must often design around rigid guidelines, yet they are always able to infuse a sense of art into the solutions. Their identity needed to communicate that ability—simply and graphically.

At the cornerstone of the identity are two dot matrix grids that overlap and interact. The rigid grid represents the ordered, systematic methods of problem solving for communications whereas the fragmented grid represents the more artful, creative, though less-structured methods of graphic architecture.

Making It Stand Out

Experimentation ruled the process of design. Unorthodox paper stocks were explored. A variety of different production processes were included to create a more tactile and approachable presentation. Odd color combinations reflect the essence of the company's portfolio, the culture of their youthful client base, and the company's interest in concept over aesthetics.

The business card is the only piece with die-cut holes. Creative director Mike Kelar notes, "We liked the idea of stretching the notion of the matrix on the cards for impact. Even though the grid is formalized in a different manner, the overall impact is impressive and the relationship to the other forms is apparent and makes sense."

The Amoeba Corp. stationery and signage was a labor of love, experimentation, and trial and error. A variety of printing processes, papers, and production techniques were used.

One piece of the identity considered exceptionally important is the business card. Amoeba believes the business card is the most important piece of stationery. According to creative director Mike Kelar, "It is your spokesperson and billboard when you are not present. It is important that it stand out when placed within the confines of the Rolodex or business card books of potential clients. For this reason, we felt that by indulging in both the design and production of the cards and by taking liberties—which most companies would see as cosmetic and wasteful—we would maximize the potential to stand out and minimize the possibility of not being noticed." The card therefore became the flagship piece of the stationery kit— the smallest piece printed, yet the one with the most dimension and voice.

A Few Challenges

Such an ambitious project is bound to have its share of production problems. Amoeba discovered, for example, that the many production processes caused the paper stocks to become brittle with repeated passes through the printing press. But the biggest hurdle arose from the desire to have a vibrant green printed over the chocolate brown cover stock. Multiple passes of white were required before numerous hits of green could be applied to obtain a color match with the rest of the stationery items. Throughout the process, a number of alternatives were attempted to achieve a bright green on dark brown stock. A green foil would have been an ideal finishing process, but the color did not match to Amoeba's satisfaction. Artistic integrity has a stubbornness all its own.

A Learning Process

Producing something new and different requires a huge amount of patience, cooperation from suppliers, and a willingness to be flexible. As Kelar notes, "We learned a lot along the way, including the way physical properties of paper can have erratic effects on production, and just how much a dark uncoated stock can really absorb ink when trying to match colors." Words spoken by someone who truly believes that hard work can achieve perfect results.

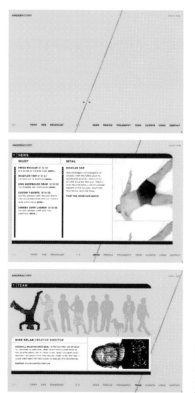

The Amoeba Corp. identity promotion was in production for about a month and in press for two weeks. The overall design required three months of work.

The dot matrix grid was designed to reflect the duality of the company's abilities, and from it all graphic elements are hung. The grid moves, changes colors, and is varied yet retains its integrity across all media.

Design Firm   Dinnick + Howells
Client   Dinnick + Howells
Project   Juxtapose Self-Promotion Cards

Let the Pictures Do the Talking

Holy cow! How do you tell someone they are a sex machine, or tell them to have a great trip, or invite them over for cocktails in a way that's not clichéd?

Don't use words—use pictures. Juxtapose two visual images to create a puzzle that can be funny enough to make people laugh out loud. That was the idea behind the self-promotional cards designed by Dinnick + Howells.

The Juxtapose Cards are a set of cards that the Toronto agency sends to their clients, contacts, colleagues, and friends. Each set contains a dozen or more cards, and they have become a yearly tradition for the design firm. The cards offer a visually rich blend of entertainment, provocation, and usefulness. The idea is for the recipient to be able to pass them along whenever they find that "words themselves are not enough."

The Juxtapose Cards were designed by Dinnick + Howells to "help you express yourself when the right words are difficult to find. We hope you enjoy figuring out and using these images to tell others how you really feel." Cocktails, anyone?

The cards are intended for a visually literate audience that's savvy, urban, and age 25 to 45. Definitely not over the hill.

Assuming a Certain Level of Intelligence

The audience for the cards tends to be those who are familiar with and interested in contemporary design and art, and are, therefore, more visually literate than the regular person on the street. Which is good, because the cards require interactivity to solve, unlike normal, store-bought, pretty cards that come, go, and are quickly forgotten. As creative director Jonathon Howells notes, "Some people get frustrated with them, while others seem to breeze through. It is all the way people are wired." The design firm did realize that the collection from the first year might have been a little too tough to solve. Some were difficult to solve in part because the visuals were either too obscure or of too low quality—the source material is anything and everything, but with a definite preference for "lo-fi" printed ephemera. The cards of year two, although still containing a few doozies, were easier to solve than the first series. Of course, for the indecipherable ones, answers could always be found at dinnickandhowells.com.

Hard Work . . .

The greatest design challenge was finding the exact images needed to support the messages. With access to two of Toronto's best visual reference libraries, designers searched for hours to find the proverbial needle in the haystack. In this case it was more like finding that "perfect old parking lot image that is just bleak and empty enough and is not in color but sepia!" The criteria the designers set for themselves were very tough and unforgiving. The obscurity, yet specificity, of images sought became rather hilarious, especially to bleary-eyed designers who'd had multiple cups of coffee.

. . . Earns Rewards

The response has been very good. The cards have wound up in a number of designer journals and award annuals, and the firm intends to distribute them in design and gallery shops around the world. But the real reward is that people laugh out loud when they finally solve them. Some days, isn't that all you need?

People who are not afraid of being seen as a bit risqué might want to tell someone that they are a sex machine.

"Holy Cow!"

Some were designed to offer simple and sweet sentiments to others, such as "Best wishes . . ."

. . . whereas others were intended to be slightly more provocative.

On the back of the cards are these simple instructions: "Just read the pictures and their meanings will appear before your very eyes." The answers are not given on the cards themselves, but people are directed to the Dinnick + Howells website if they get stuck.

You're a child. You like to play, have fun, and interact with things. You like games that move and include sound. You like characters that are consistent in your life. Although you probably don't have an awareness that you're being marketed to, many people believe that you started to develop a mental image of corporate logos and mascots as early as six months of age. Certainly, by age four you know how to request brand-name products. And once you do, you're as brand-loyal as can be.

Marketing to children is tricky business. There is a special responsibility expected of all marketers to children, but especially those who market to children under age 12. Yet, it's a huge and growing market. By some estimates, if you can create a lifetime customer at an early age, that customer might be worth more than $100,000 to a company over the course of a lifetime.

And nobody knows this better than McDonald's.

Design Firm   **Zoesis, Inc.**
Client   **McDonald's**
Project   **McDonald's Advergame**

An advergame that Zoesis created for client McDonald's is uniquely designed for
the 4 to 12 age bracket. The singing burger will sing faster or
slower depending on how fast the child moves the mouse.

When Zoesis, an interactive design firm in Boston, Massachusetts, wanted to design an "advergame" for McDonald's, their strategy was to bring actual products to life in the form of compelling characters. So, for example, a cheeseburger becomes a friendly face with whom children can sing or play tag. By bringing a product to life, kids have the opportunity to make a connection and bond with the product. This bond allows kids to develop positive feelings about the product and the associated brand.

The thinking was simple enough, which is probably why it's such a big hit with the under-12 set. As Laura Elia at Zoesis explains, "We wanted to develop characters that were intrinsic to the McDonald's offering; when you think of McDonald's, you think of burgers and fries."

The other thing they did with this advergame to make it appeal directly to this age group is to make the characters unique and seemingly alive, unlike video games in which characters are wooden and play back scripted animations. The characters react with unscripted emotional and physical responses depending on how kids interact with them. A character will act differently each time a child interacts with it. Because of the awareness of the children's actions, the characters seem more alive.

It is challenging to find ways to get your product into the places where children play. But once you do, just help them have fun!

The actual products, such as cheeseburgers and fries, come to life and interact with the child. The burger and fries take turns being "it" in this game of tag.

Each product is programmed to respond differently depending on how the child reacts. For example, when the child is doing well with the game, the characters will react with big smiles . . .

. . . and when tagged, they will react sadly because the child was able to "catch" them.

No "Air Quotes" Here

Combine a Swiss reinsurance company, a new initiative called The Centre for Global Dialogue, and an internationally recognized English design firm, and what do you get? A stunning identity system in which the cornerstone idea is oversized quotation marks that come together in the shape of the Swiss flag.

Not that it was easy.

"The hardest part of any job is coming up with the right idea, and this was no exception," states designer Matt Willey. "However, once we had developed the graphic using quotation marks in the shape of the Swiss flag, everything else just clicked into place. It was one of those beautifully simple ideas that just worked."

The Centre for Global Dialogue was founded by leading international reinsurance body Swiss Re as a forum for events, programs, and conferences dealing with global risk issues. The facilities and services offered by the Centre attract business leaders, politicians, risk analysts, and other industry experts from around the world.

The design challenge set forth to Frost Design was to develop a corporate identity that would convey the role of the Centre, the diversity of its facilities, and its relationship with Swiss Re clearly and consistently across all promotional material. The solution needed to "appeal to a broad, industry-based audience, while retaining a 'human' element to reflect the nature of the Centre's activities."

Since its inception in 1994, Frost Design has grown into a multiaward-winning, internationally recognized graphic design studio, renowned for its bold approach and distinctive use of typography.

Communication and quality are the inspiration behind Frost Design's stunning new corporate identity for the Centre for Global Dialogue in Switzerland.

A Solid Identity

Niels Viggo Haueter at Swiss Re explains further: "At the Centre for Global Dialogue we deal with a range of complex risk and financial services related issues. So when defining the specifications for our new visual identity we were looking for an expression that helps to structure our topics and activities rather than complicating or confusing the content. At the same time it needed to express an invitation for dialogue at the Centre."

Central to the new identity is a distinctive logotype derived from the Swiss flag, using speech marks as the framework. The speech marks are inspired by dialogue and interaction, key characteristics of the Centre. This graphic forms a grid that can be used on a range of material and literature, from stationery to conference reports to menus and price lists. In fact, it's exactly the type of solution Frost Design is known for—a bold approach with a distinctive use of typography.

Design Approach

The Centre has been designed to the highest standards with strong emphasis on quality and attention to detail. Frost's solution reflects this by using the best quality materials; innovative design for print; and a simple yet bold color palette of red, black, white, and gray. The materials are also recyclable or biodegradable wherever possible, to demonstrate the Centre's commitment to the environment, a subject of major concern in risk assessment.

Vince Frost, who led the project, said, "I have always been inspired by 1950s and 1960s Swiss design, which is based primarily on clean, simple lines and strong grids. With this project I wanted to acknowledge this heritage and create a logo that was worthy of the building and its surroundings."

"This project is proof that identities can be design led rather than strategically numbed," notes Vince Frost, creative head at Frost Design.

A variety of papers and materials are used, all recyclable or biodegradable where possible, to keep with the Centre's ideals.

The design grid is based on the simplest of elements—the grid of the Swiss flag.

"The Centre is a fantastic building in stunning surroundings and to see what we have created at work is a real pleasure. This was a wonderful project to work on from start to finish," says designer Matt Willey.

Design Firm Bubblan Design

Client Stiftelsen FöreningsSparbanken Sjuhärad Bank

Project Stiftelsen Promotion

A Generous Client

A bank in Sweden wanted to create a continuous promotional campaign that would visualize and provide identity to the bank in an innovative and engaging way. But this is more than the story of innovative design. It is the story of how a bank can give back to the community in ways that are also innovative and engaging.

Stiftelsen is head owner of the bank FöreningsSparbanken Sjuhärad. As a bank owner, he gets a certain amount of money; he gives this money back to local projects that help develop Sjuhäradsbygden, a part of western Sweden. The projects awarded are both small and large, in the areas of science and research, culture, trade and industry, and sports. Over the past six years, Stiftelsen has given in total an astounding 67 million crowns (nearly 9 million US dollars) to projects in the area.

The bank soon realized that this was a competitive advantage and should be marketed as such. No other bank has a Stiftelsen. But the irony was, apart from those who actually received money at the annual celebrations, nobody knew anything about Stiftelsen—not even that he existed.

This intriguing series of images is designed to symbolize the many projects that Stiftelsen, head owner of the Swedish bank FöreningsSparbanken Sjuhärad, helps to support. The pole represents Stiftelsen's support for the projects he assists, which are represented by the growing tree.

Everything Symbolic

So Bubblan Design was called in to promote the fact that the bank had a Stiftelsen as a symbolic force. They did so with a series of intriguing images. At the center of the illustrations was a stanchion, or pole, which symbolizes Stiftelsen. The posters had four parts, which showed a progression of the growth of a plant up the stanchion. Each part symbolized the growth of the projects, the people, and the community that Stiftelsen helped.

Additionally, every spring Stiftelsen has a grand evening when the selected projects are awarded and the money given. Stiftelsen wanted to give a gift to every project, as a memento for years into the future. The gift: a 12 cm by 12 cm (about 5" by 5") black cube, handmade from stoneware with a 6 cm (about 2½") seeding made of soft plastics. An illustration of this was also used as a symbol in printed matter, badges, bags, and T-shirts at the celebration.

Stiftelsen also wanted to give awards of honorary distinction to projects that were extremely well developed. Bubblan's idea was an apple with a stairway, symbolizing the fact that learning is a journey with steps you must take to reach your goal.

The apple is larger than normal and was made of ceramic clay and wood. With so many to create and each one handmade, it was impossible for the artist to make the apples look the same. But the design firm came to a resolution; because the receivers and their projects are all unique, so is the apple—a material that is living and individual.

Everyone engaged in the project with Stiftelsen realizes that it takes time to enter the minds of people. The bank wants to be known as a company that takes part in society, inspiring the possibility to develop positively, for a long time to come. Still, there are some immediate results to report. For example, the day after the latest awards were given, Stiftelsen got their biggest media attention ever.

Generosity becomes a seed for so many things.

Bubblan created a black stone cube with a plastic seedling growing out. This was used both as poster illustrations . . .

. . . and as actual gifts to the recipients of Stiftelsen's generosity.

Another object created to promote Stiftelsen and the bank is this ceramic and wood apple, signifying the steps taken while learning.

Design Firm   Carter Wong Tomlin
Client   Howies
Project   Howies Wardrobes

"What is rubbish to some is useful to others."

Abandoned wardrobes covered with political statements don't often make a promotional vehicle. But thanks to design firm Carter Wong Tomlin and client Howies, a clothing company, they made quite an exceptional one.

A Joint Effort: Part 1

Howies is a small, ethical clothing company based in Wales. A married couple, David and Clare Hieatt, started the company determined to link their beliefs with their products. Environmental consciousness, organic farming, less dependency on nonrenewable energy sources, and recycling were some of the many things they wanted not only to practice but to spread the word about.

Carter Wong Tomlin used abandoned wardrobes as an innovative point-of-sale promotion for clothing company Howies.

All the wardrobes were deliberately kept quite raw and unfinished, apart from the illustration. Each was fitted with a basic neon light tube, mirror, and label explaining the particular theme.

When commissioned to create point-of-sale, fourteen illustrators responded to the brief, which was to interpret a different "Howies Belief" onto an actual wardrobe.

A Joint Effort: Part 2

An innovative way to do that came in the form of a project to design a point-of-sale piece that could house T-shirts in stores. Howies turned to Carter Wong Tomlin, which had just designed the packaging for those shirts. The packaging's theme revolved around discarded furniture that kids use as ramps and other trick-inducing obstacles for skateboarding and BMXing. Carter Wong Tomlin thought it would be a good idea to carry this theme through to point of sale but wanted to push it further.

Phil Carter, creative director and principal of Carter Wong Tomlin, and a believer himself in the dictum that one more bike is one less car on the road, was making his daily cycling commute to his studio. He started to first notice and then photograph various pieces of abandoned furniture that he passed. Carter liked the idea of these pieces appearing out of context and started to mull *Inside Out* as the potential title for a book.

But suddenly it occurred to him that the abandoned wardrobes would make a perfect promotional vehicle for Howies. The wardrobes were found in a variety of places—highways underpasses, dumps, and in junk shops for £20 or less.

A Joint Effort: Part 3

Carter then involved good illustrator friends (friends being the operative word—being a small company, Howies isn't cash rich) by bribing them with Howie's T-shirts and the promise of good PR. Then, the word spread to other interested parties. The artists were given a list of themes and beliefs dear to Howies, and they chose the one they wanted to do. All in all, fourteen wardrobes were created.

The project took about four months from concept to fruition. Carter Wong Tomlin had the artists come into the studio, which was a bit like having an artist in residence and great fun for all their designers. All the wardrobes were filmed in 360 degrees on slow time video and can be viewed on the Howies website.

Carter Wong Tomlin insists it doesn't have a philosophy; it's a design firm that just wants to do work that pushes the client as well as create work that's innovative. But most importantly, they want to have fun and enjoy designing. Carter says, "I usually take this as a good sign of good work if you've really enjoyed the process of doing the project, the wardrobes being a case in point." But it doesn't hurt to try and make the world a better place while you're at it.

On this wardrobe, Jeff Fisher illustrates Belief #3: "Reclaim the streets. A bike is one less car on the road. The air we breathe is choking us as cars have been proven to cause asthma."

The target audience was Howies customers, who are environmentally aware teenagers mainly into skateboarding, biking, and other adventurous pursuits. The wardrobes were used to house organic T-shirts, whose packaging Carter Wong had also designed.

Creative director Phil Carter ended up getting into the act, designing a wardrobe himself with the assistance of two of his colleagues. His "belief" illustrates the probable extinction of the sparrow if things don't change.

Design Firm R2 Design

Client Alexandra Martins

Project Identity

The Importance of Proper Punctuation

Everyone agrees that punctuation is important. But how many would think to turn it into an entire promotional identity? That is a question worthy of both a question mark and an exclamation point, is it not?!

Alexandra Martins is a journalist responsible for the public relations and public management of important Portuguese businesses. Her company is a relatively small PR firm that works for big companies, and she promotes and organizes events, provides most of the clients' communication needs, and does everything related to successful promotions.

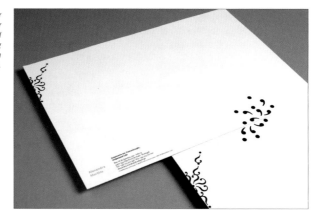

The simple yet effective color scheme of black, cyan, and silver is in keeping with the sophisticated tone. It also reinforces that feeling that much of communication hinges on the writing.

This set of stationery using punctuation marks as graphic elements promotes Portuguese PR maven Alexandra Martins in a surprising way. Because much of what she does is write texts, this was a clever and appropriate concept for her identity.

The Gestalt of It All

So an identity program where commas, periods, question marks, and exclamation points dance across the page and come together in a gestaltlike fashion—an identity where the sum is greater than the parts—seems particularly fitting.

R2, a design firm in Matosinhos, Portugal, started with the idea that although what Alexandra Martin does on the big picture level is communicate and promote business concepts, what she does most often on a day-to-day basis is simply write texts. From there it was a quick conceptual step to thinking of punctuation marks as a bold yet lovely graphic element. According to Liza Ramalho, who directed the art of the project along with designers Artur Rebelo and Nadine Ouellet, the use of punctuation marks "generated truly organic forms that had symbolic meaning alone but even more meaning when viewed together." The punctuation marks "work like a germ," linking several different promotional components together. When placed side by side, for example, the back of a business card fits together with a sheet of stationery-like puzzle pieces. One is reminded of a sophisticated design exercise done in an advanced typography course.

An Elegant Look

The stationery was printed using offset printing on a rich paper stock called Munken Linx. It was printed in three colors: black, cyan, and silver, which was designed to keep with the elegant and sophisticated tone suggested by the design. Plus, the black-over-white paper conceptually reinforces the writing perspective.

Amazingly enough, the entire project took only three weeks from start to completion. It was one of those seemingly magical projects that fell together perfectly. Just two weeks for the creative and design process and one week for the printing. And then it was done, period. Exclamation points, anyone?

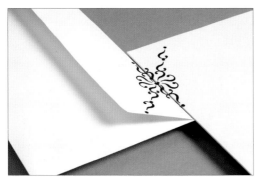

The pieces work together in unexpected ways to create a whole that is greater than the sum of its parts.

Elegant, stunning, visual—but conceptually it's all about communication.

The entire project took a mere three weeks from brief to printed pieces.

Design Firm   Metal
Client   Betterbay
Project   Interactive Movie

People are visual creatures. So while you can tell them things like "Hey, if we continue to pollute our waterfront, bad things will happen," it's never quite as effective as actually showing them.

Which is precisely why this promotion is so effective.

Devastating Visuals

In just 60 seconds, one gets a vision of devastation far greater than words could explain. Through a clever use of collage animation, a beautiful bay area is transformed into a seething, dirty, industrial mess. The mess is then cleaned up, and a much better solution is put in place before the viewer's very eyes.

An innovative promotion often comes out of an innovative message. Betterbay is an ambitious, ongoing project put on in part by the Army Corps of Engineers, whose goal is to enhance Galveston Bay in Houston, Texas, both environmentally and economically through the responsible and creative use of materials dredged during the expansion of the Houston-Galveston Navigation Channel.

An idyllic landscape appears on screen in this Flash piece created for the ongoing project Betterbay. The Army Corps of Engineers heads this project in an effort to enhance Galveston Bay in Houston, Texas.

Gradually, the scene becomes cluttered with machines, pollution, and industrial waste, until the scene is a virtual wasteland.

Email for More Information

The original strategy of this project was to develop a brief, intriguing teaser that would drum up interest in the viewer about the project and drive him or her to a website for more information. The project was intended to be an embedded Flash piece (400 x 300 pixels) that would be emailed to anyone interested in receiving information about the project as well as anyone of relevance as decided by the client.

The target audience included anyone who would be interested in finding out more about better air and better water, and the effect they have on people. People residing in the surrounding areas of the project, who would be directly affected by the process, were also part of the target audience.

Using Recycled Materials

Metal fabricated the entire scene out of elements from a variety of still photos.. The scrapped and collaged technique gives the whole piece a slightly surreal look. It's a creative, metaphorical representation of progress handled responsibly, which in a nutshell sums up the project. The time-lapse treatment is something that has yet to be tackled in this medium, which makes it unique.

As Peat Jariya, principal and creative director at Metal, notes: "The birth of the idea was actually a result of several brainstorming sessions concerning how to convey the project goals in a captivating, atypical way. We had explored several different directions and decided that this one was the most interesting and effective."

Producing the piece ended up being quite a challenge, and most of the challenges involved file size. Metal knew they had to keep it within a reasonable range or else the viewer would have difficulty downloading the spot. They overcame the problem by limiting the number of layers of activity in the scene as well as editing the piece to only the crucial frames necessary for the spot to work.

The other challenge was figuring out how to do the technique itself. One of the most interesting things about this project is that the treatment resembles a time-lapse movie in which a camera is set up at a designated spot and rolls for an extended period of time to show what was captured in an extremely accelerated way. They were able to capture this feel by using only collage technique and stop-motion animation.

Jariya concludes, "We were pleased with the results. We feel we were able to address the original objectives in a very brief spot. It not only is aesthetically pleasing, but effectively shows the goal of the Betterbay project."

The scene starts to reverse itself.

The scene ends with a reversion back to the original landscape with the addition of very civilized buildings in the background. In this case, the picture truly is worth a thousand words.

Design Firm   **Strawberry Frog**

Client   **HoeGaarden**

Project   **Promotional Beer Campaign**

Want to Try a New Beer? Take a Seat.

Who could imagine that the best way to promote a beer might be by building furniture? The folks at Strawberry Frog, a design firm in Amsterdam, that's who.

The beer is HoeGaarden, and the design firm had gotten the brief to introduce the brand to the opinion-forming audience. HoeGaarden's audience is young and spirited—guys and girls in their twenties and thirties, predominantly working in creative and media industries. This was an audience whose members had a refined genuine taste, who were into art and music, who made it their mission to stay one step ahead, and who have a finger on the pulse of underground culture.

Getting a Share of Headspace

The HoeGaarden brand itself had a lot going for it—it had been around since the 1400s so it had a lot of heritage, and it has an unusual but refreshing taste. It was equally popular among men and women. And it had as one of its brand values the single word "curiosity."

The design firm took an interesting approach. They didn't consider the rest of the beer market as competition. Instead, they looked at other things that provoked curiosity, other things that "took up the headspace" of their audience, as Mark Chalmers, creative director on the project explains. So instead of looking at other beers, they looked at what other items provoke curiosity—art, fashion, books, magazines. And, yes, even furniture.

Looking at it this way, the design firm realized that people would be able to come across the beer through the things that they loved.

Who could imagine that the best way to promote a beer might be by building furniture? The folks at Strawberry Frog, a design firm in Amsterdam, that's who.

Custom-designed furniture was built by Droog Design, an internationally recognized collaboration of Dutch designers. The installation then traveled around Europe, creating little venues in which the beer could be sampled by the target audience.

Welcome to the HoeGaarden

And so an idea was born. Take the brand value of curiosity and combine it with the hottest summer on record for 100 years, and the Strawberry Frog team just couldn't resist the opportunity to make the beer garden and café terrace fashionable again. And thus began the "Welcome to the HoeGaarden" campaign. Custom-designed furniture was built by Droog Design, an internationally recognized collaboration of Dutch designers. The installation then traveled around Europe, creating little venues in which the beer could be sampled by the target audience. As Chalmers notes, "Communicating the need for six foot 'high chairs' for adults wasn't always easy." The end result is festive and captivating, and even includes such touches as a bird feeder that dispenses nuts that can be enjoyed with the beer.

How well did the furniture promote the beer? Incredible buzz and PR were generated. The initial investment was tripled in terms of PR coverage received. And within the first months, the promotion achieved its objective of site visits and signups. But the true value was in the brand loyalty achieved—the audience was surprised and delighted, and appreciated a brand that could talk to them in the right way, playing to their interests in an authentic way, without overselling. According to Mark, this is an agency philosophy: "If we can make you smile, have a bit of fun, we've done a pretty good job—consumers respond best to brands that have fun."

Have a seat, and welcome to the HoeGaarden. And don't forget to smile.

The end result is festive, captivating, and even includes such touches as a bird feeder that dispenses nuts that can be enjoyed with the beer.

Have a seat, and welcome to the HoeGaarden. And don't forget to smile.

Design Firm Wink
Client Blu Dot
Project Blu Dot Catalog

Fun. Sophisticated. Lively. Clever. Good-looking.

Sound like your perfect soulmate? Yes? Well, how about your perfect furniture catalog? Wink design knows that just as people have personalities, so do objects. And just like a personality trait can cause us to like or dislike a person, it can cause us to like or dislike mere objects, furniture included. Wink thus tries to create brands that "inspire people to relate to them."

The Brand Personality

Blu Dot is a furniture design and manufacturing company that offers high-end products at accessible prices. Besides being a company that offers "design you can actually afford," they also believe that they have a brand personality that is "clever, sophisticated, and modern." When Blu Dot approached Minneapolis-based Wink to create a catalog for them, they wanted it to not only express their unique brand personality but to have a modular and easily updated grid, and a modern and contemporary tone and feel.

"It all starts with a great product, but the personality of the company and the product needs to come across in every aspect of brand," states Wink founder Richard Boynton.

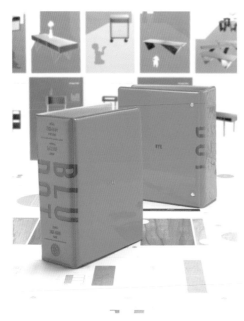

The accordion fold inserts make the whole program modular and easily updated.

Blu Dot's bright orange binders are designed to be impossible to miss when looking at the shelves of furniture distributors.

Wink's solution was an orange binder with each product line on its own three-hole punched, accordion-folded section. The orange is not only a fun and lively color, but it also "can easily be spotted on nearly all their distributors' shelves." The accordion-folded section allows future additions to be printed and added with ease to the end of each section. Each individual section conveys a specific tone and feel that plays off the sensibility of the various furniture lines themselves. The wit and sophistication of the company's personality comes through in the catalog's humorous copy and unusual propping choices. This entertaining writing, along with the vivid orange binder and the inspirational aspect of the furniture, has made the promotion nearly impossible for distributors to throw out.

Creating Personality Through Humor

This idea of the personality of a company being shown through its catalog is perhaps the most interesting part of this project. The fact that the personality of the Blu Dot designers is contained within the product descriptions of the furniture show that this company's personality, spirit, and creative expression are consistent. According to Wink, most of the time, a client will say that they want it to sound like them but then back off and revert to something a little more safe. However, with Blu Dot, "all of the humorous bits" that Wink threw in, they kept, "which is shocking as some of the lines are pretty ballsy," the designer confesses. For example, how many catalogs would have products with names like "felt up chair" or "flip me table?" Or describe a bookshelf as perfect for "books that you're looking for but cannot see, despite the fact that they're right in front of your face?"

Wink claims that it has been recently pointed out that much of their work tends to be "clever, compelling, and witty. This might be attributed to the fact that we don't try to remove our personalities from the process." These words seem to sum up the success they had with Blu Dot's catalog. Wink knows how much we associate ourselves with brands. Fun? Smart? Sleek? What brands do you associate yourself with?

Reality check—actual color chips and wood grain samples are conveniently packaged and displayed right next to the product illustrations.

Humor

Go ahead, laugh. That's exactly what the designers of these promotions would like you to do. And the louder and heartier, the better. It's hard work being funny, but the hard work pays off in these cases. And laughter, as you know, is good for the soul.

Design Firm **Nesnadny + Schwartz**
Client **Cleveland Institute of Art**
Project **Cleveland Institute of Art Direct Mailer**

Turning a Cookie Cutter Industry on Its Head

When you're an institution trying not to look like an institution, what do you do? Look like an institution, of course.

The ultimate challenge for every marketer is breaking through the clutter to reach a particular target. For a college or university not named Harvard, trying to reach students thinking about their next matriculation is particularly difficult. Most institutions seemed to have resigned themselves to slapping together materials with photographs of students perched atop library bell towers and mascot-laden rugby shirts laid out on campus lawns. Leave it to a small art school in the Midwest and their design shop to change the way recruitment campaigns are handled.

For a new system of direct mail material, the Cleveland Institute of Art (CIA) wanted a concept that would "challenge the audience, be courageous, and set a new standard for college recruiting materials." They wanted the piece to create such a buzz that it would almost become a keepsake for the students. To achieve these lofty goals, the designers at Nesnadny + Schwartz determined that they would need to appeal to their audience with a sense of familiarity, while packing an element of surprise. Their solution? A whimsical parody of a standardized test.

Anxious high school seniors can't relate to an average college brochure like they can to a Mad Lib.

An Innovative Way to Break the Ice

The potential problem with this concept was that while every prospective student could identify with it, the likelihood that they would discard it was high as well. At first glance the two-color mailer looks like an SAT booklet, with a pocket holding different weights of papers inside. However, upon further inspection, one quickly sees that it is an interactive platform, with fill-in-the-blank answers to seemingly straightforward questions. In Mad Lib fashion, the inside reveals a quick, first-person narrative about a high school senior's angst about getting into school, with the answers from the straightforward questions on the front, filling in the blanks. This was the hook to get people in, and in focus groups students loved the fact that, unlike most college brochures, the CIA actually took the time to "break the ice."

Inside the piece, the standardized test parody continued and expanded, with large type, over-the-top word problems, and common symbols to guide the reader to "continue" and eventually "stop" for the answers. All of this reflected the unapologetic message of the CIA, which of course, came in the form of a multiple-choice question:

The Cleveland Institute of Art is:

>   a) Five years of hard work

>   b) Fun but intense

>   c) What you make of it

Of course, it's "d) all of the above." Much like their recruitment brochure.

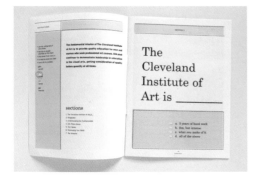

The brochure spelled out the Institute's unapologetic message in no frills, multiple-choice fashion.

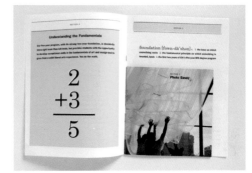

Turns out, this is not your parent's SAT booklet. A vibrant, 14-page color insert waits inside the brochure, just in case anyone takes things a little too literally on the outside.

"True or False? You belong at the Cleveland Institute." Some early applicant screening in section 6.

Design Firm Renegade Marketing Group
Client Panasonic
Project People Against Fun Campaign

Do as You're Told . . .

Don't have fun! Fun is no good and must be avoided at all costs! And whatever you do, don't buy Panasonic products because they will cause you to have way too much fun!

Propaganda? Promotion? Fun?

People Against Fun is a fictitious (thank goodness), sarcastic, witty, online promotion created by Renegade Marketing Group for Panasonic. It was created in response to a strategy stating that the Panasonic brand needed to be "coolified." The strategy needed to get males 18 to 24 years old to love the Panasonic brand. This demographic is the MTV generation that has made extreme sports popular, and has grown up watching edgy shows like *Jackass* and *Punk'd*. This generation has also grown up with computers and Internet access and has a sarcastic, even caustic, sense of humor, and responds best to irreverent and self-deprecating humor.

. . . Or Not

So here's a target audience that questions authority and does not like living with restrictions or being told what to do. They are increasingly independent and marketing savvy, but remain cynical of mass messaging and corporate commercialism. Their disdain for their parents, their teachers, and our leaders fuels their skepticism. People Against Fun, with its spokesperson, Bob Paffersen, are parodies of the killjoys they resent and rebel against. And so the target appreciates and is more likely to identify with a brand that pokes fun at itself.

The People Against Fun was part of a bigger promotion being run by Panasonic called "Save Your Summer," which directly talked about the fun that Panasonic products could deliver. But therein lies the dilemma faced by the creative team. It quickly became apparent that it's very difficult to talk about fun to the teen and young adult audience—the very act of saying you are fun makes you "unfun" in the eyes of such a cynical target. So Renegade Marketing Group brilliantly turned this liability into an asset and "unfun" became the cornerstone of the online efforts.

People Against Fun is a fictitious, witty online promotion created by Renegade Marketing Group for Panasonic.

This simple, two-color logo created for People Against Fun made a bold, sarcastic statement. Clockwise, it reads "creating a better world without fun."

Taking Risks

Then came the meeting where the idea had to be sold to the client. And believe it or not, there were actually people at Panasonic who thought that telling people not to buy your products was a bad sales strategy. So what finally convinced them? Well, as Drew Neisser, the president and CEO of Renegade explains, "Timing is everything. Our client had just attended a seminar on what makes teens tick. He was in the room and saw in People Against Fun what he had seen in the teen presentation: a counterculture to which he didn't much relate. He became an advocate for People Against Fun as a counterpoint to the more traditional fun site. Our client took the risk with us and helped to sell it into the rest of the company."

Once the site went live, the fictitious persona that was Bob Paffersen, chairman of People Against Fun, elicited a tremendous response—positive as well as negative. Generally speaking, the positive responses came from the site visitors that fell within the target demographic. In on the joke, they lauded People Against Fun for its "diligent dedication to the eradication of amusement and other recreational fun agents." Others expressed antipathy towards Paffersen and the "cause."

"Buzz" is difficult to measure, but it did not take long for the site to be the subject of news stories and several pages of Google results. Various elements of the site were designed to be viral, from Paffersen for office videos to the downloadable "Paffirmation," a guide to a life without fun. These and the URL for the site spread like wildfire. In the end, the site received millions of page views and far exceeded everyone's expectations. And we refuse to believe that it wiped out fun altogether.

The online promotion was created in response to a strategy stating that the Panasonic brand needed to be "coolified"—it needed to get males 18 to 24 years old to love the Panasonic brand.

Believe it or not, there were actually people at Panasonic who thought that telling people not to buy your products was a bad sales strategy.

Research showed that the target appreciates and is more likely to identify with a brand that pokes fun at itself.

At this age, it's all about being cool. Really, what else is there? When you're a teenager, it doesn't seem to matter where in the world you live, what your income level is, or where you go to school. You share the same feelings of teens all over the world. You want to be seen as smart, hip, fun, and aware of the trends. You want to be liked, accepted. You want to belong to a club or a group, even if it's a group that's rebelling against all other groups. You want to fit in somewhere. Again, you want to be cool.

One way to be cool when you're a teen is to join a group of people who speak your language. Not just your native language, but your "teen" language—the language of your peers.

So Weiden + Kennedy teamed up with Plazm Media and created a poster campaign that ran for Nike—one that embraced adolescents' unique dialect.

"All cotton" is a basketball term. Those in the know know that it's a term for making a shot without hitting the backboard. So in teen talk, the All Cotton Club is where beat meets the street.

Design Firm **Plazm Media**

Client **Nike**

Project **All Cotton Club Poster Series**

Teens, more than almost any other target audience, want to feel like they belong. Joining the All Cotton Club is a double entendre—"all cotton" is a basketball term; the "Cotton Club," a famous nightclub.

The concept played on the history of the original Cotton Club posters.

But at the same time, the Cotton Club conjures up images of the famous Harlem nightclub of the 1920s—the club whose clientele consisted of the wealthiest, most influential, and most notorious people around. Many of the early black entertainers got their start at the Cotton Club—Duke Ellington and Lena Horne, among others. So if you're *really* in the know, the All Cotton Club has many levels of meaning, embracing all things of interest to teenagers: sports, music, culture, clubs that exclude, clubs that include. (And just in case you're *not quite* in the know, the posters include plenty of other teen trigger words such as McNasty, Booger, Bad Times, and Boogie Nights.)

To make the promotion even more topical, the posters ran only in New York City, in the bus shelters and subways around the area where the original Cotton Club first opened its doors. It was what Nike and Weiden + Kennedy called a "City Attack" campaign—blanket a small area that has your core target audience and make it impossible to ignore. And the look of the posters was hand drawn, the way it was on the original Cotton Club posters.

Specifically, the posters were designed to promote the benefits of two new performance basketball shoes by Nike. The Air Powermatic is a basketball shoe specifically designed for power and an inside game, whereas the Air Flightposite shoe is designed for fitness and the outside game. But, much, much more important than that is the fact that the posters made teens feel like a part of something. They were a way to make teens feel cool.

The posters employ a mix of
street ballers and professional
New York basketball players.

Authenticity is very important to
the design firm Plazm. It's a good
thing, because savvy teens can
spot inauthenticity a mile away.

Design Firm   Wasserman & Partners Advertising Inc.
Client   Vancouver Fringe
Project   Fringe Festival Posters

The Big Presentation Day

How do you think the following client meeting would go? The design team stands up to present the concepts. In one, there's a series of visuals where two men in karate uniforms break into a Rockettelike dance. In the second, a couple engages in Tantric sex only to have an elephant hand the woman a large knife. In the third, a young man demonstrates how to make balloon animals out of condoms.

Yes, condoms.

Well, the only thing you can say about client meetings is that you never know what to expect.

And "You never know what to expect" happens to be the tag line for the Vancouver Fringe Festival, which is what the aforementioned posters and ads were designed to promote. Since it is the Fringe Festival, after all, a bit of provocation is in order.

The Vancouver Fringe Festival has more than 100 performances in and around the Granville Island area. And as the tagline states so eloquently, "You never know what to expect."

The Main Event

The Vancouver Fringe Festival is a yearly event that features over a hundred different artistic performances. Browse through a program listing and one can see why it's a bit fringe. Performance titles like "Sketch Comedy for Dummies," "Sex, Violence, and the Meaning of Life" and "Sh*t Happens When You Party Naked" are the norm.

The festival had a lot of recognition in the local market, but little consistency in their messaging. People look forward to the festival every year, but in the past the events were stretched across the city, and thus a hassle to get to. In a bid to answer that issue, the festival relocated to Granville Island. But in doing that, they were in danger of alienating its core crowd, an artistic community, which had supported the event from its inception. Granville Island was more for tourists and West-siders.

The Contender Steps into the Ring

So Wasserman & Partners, a Canadian design firm, understood the challenge set forth to them: The work they produced had to have stopping power; it had to appeal to tourists and slightly more conservative folks, and yet it also had to remain true to its fringe element.

The concepts, once they got approved, were run as ads in Vancouver's urban weekly, placed in washroom stalls, and developed into T-shirts that were then sold at the Fringe Festival itself.

The birth of the idea came by accident. After a few weeks and reams of recycled paper, someone said one thing but the others thought he meant something else. Voila—an idea was born. That idea was to have someone show you how to do something a bit outrageous and then do a little bow at the end. The illustrations reinforce the concept because they're reminiscent of the safety instruction manuals you might find on airplanes.

This promotion took almost four months to complete. This process ended up being a bit complicated due to client inexperience, number of pieces, and number of people involved. Luckily, the design firm was able to overcome those problems "through diligence, sheer willpower, and pain."

Take a Bow

Back to that first infamous client meeting. Wasserman presented three creative platforms, but this project was the strong recommendation. As far as the sexual references are concerned, the client reacted perfectly. At first they were a little shocked, but inherently knew it was cool and it would appeal to their younger, core crowd. You know—the ones on the fringe.

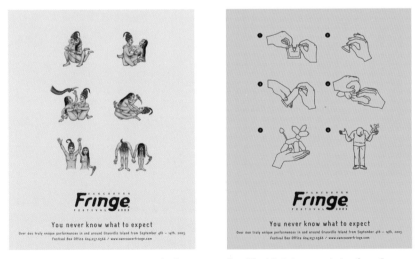

The concept for the campaign was to have someone show the viewer how to do something outrageous and then end with a little bow.

Three different illustrators were used—Lorne Carnes, Jimmy Woo, and Alanna Cavanagh. The concepts fit together, however, because they are all "instructions with a twist."

Design Firm   Squires & Company
Client   James Bland
Project   Promotional Mailer

The Essentials

Voodoo dolls. Test-tube beauty queens. A flesh-eating alligator about to meet its match by a scantily clad vixen. What would a promotional piece be without those things?

To say that photographer James Bland wanted to do something different when he called upon design firm Squires & Company to create a promotional mailer would be an understatement. There is nothing understated about the old pulp magazine covers re-created by the design firm and photographer. They are fun, funny, engaging, and sure to be noticed.

A Pretty Package

The mailer is an accordion-fold mailer of individually perforated cards, each measuring 4¼" x 6¼" (10.8 cm x 15.9 cm), and contained within a glassine envelope that also holds business cards and an info card. The elements were then enclosed between two pieces of cardboard, and packaging tape sealed the whole thing together. The piece was sent out to designers and art directors of agencies and magazines, with the hope that people would be intrigued enough to open it up and see what was inside. In fact, the entire piece was designed with the goal of preventing the "toss effect" at any step of the way.

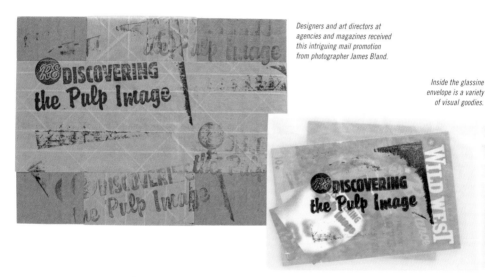

Designers and art directors at agencies and magazines received this intriguing mail promotion from photographer James Bland.

Inside the glassine envelope is a variety of visual goodies.

Business and info cards complete the set.

The promotional piece came about when photographer James Bland—based in Dallas, Texas—wanted to show that he could create thematic photographs. The design firm presented several ideas, but none was as exciting as the idea to re-create old pulp magazine covers with actual models, sets, and customized typography.

Originally, the promotional piece was supposed to be mailed in just the glassine envelope, but the post office nixed that idea, stating that it would rip in mailing. But by that time, Squires & Company had already sealed the envelopes with the contents—all 2,500 of them. Brandon Murphy, creative director on the project, really wanted to keep the see-through envelope, so the design team sandwiched the envelopes between two pieces of cardboard and taped them together. They then rubber-stamped the outside with the return address and added type to convey more character. This process protected the contents and alluded to the roughened nature of the envelope's contents. It also added to the intrigue factor.

Achieving the Look

Amazingly enough, the only Photoshop manipulation used was on the *Mystery Science* image with the test-tube beauty. All the other models and backdrops were shot with a camera. The typography and the stressed look were added later via Adobe Illustrator and Photoshop. Even the logo has that retro sci-fi look.

Oh, yes, and the alligator *is* stuffed.

The promotion piece, designed by Squires & Company, has at its heart an accordion-folded set of perforated postcards, each painstakingly set up and shot by the photographer to re-create old pulp magazines.

Design Firm **Duffy Design** (London)
Client **British Telecom**
Project **British Telecom Book** *A Complete Guide to Making Yourself 50% More Popular*

"I'm Popular or You're Fired"

British Telecom wanted to run a relatively straightforward promotion telling CEO's of major corporations that they could give their employees an opportunity to buy a PC for home use at a fraction of the normal price. Yet the end result is a laugh-out-loud book titled *A Complete Guide to Making Yourself 50% More Popular*. Within the foil stamped covers of fake leatherette are CEO bumper stickers, a banner to let employees know that you offer them free water daily, and pithy sayings you can adopt such as "I'm popular or you're fired." The kicker, of course, is that while all of those ways might help to make a CEO more popular, nothing really does it like offering employees reasonably priced computers for their home.

Believe it or not, the idea to create such a book was arrived at very quickly. When sitting around, discussing the promotion, there was an adamant belief that the British Telecom promotion *would*, in fact, make CEO's more popular with their employees. As soon as the initial idea jelled, it took about four days to create the prototype, which looked almost exactly like the final version. As Tim Watson of Duffy Design notes, "Once we had the overall idea, each page was a joy to create." It then took approximately four months to produce the whole book and get it printed.

Tim Watson of Duffy Design notes, it appears to be a "free Christmas desk diary—the sort of gift you get sent by some obscure supplier who has produced these things for 20 years and is under the misunderstanding that everyone loves them."

These bumper stickers are guaranteed to increase any CEO's popularity by 50 percent.

The Gift That Nobody Wants

The details are all well thought to make the piece look very tongue in cheek and over the top. The idea for the look of the piece was to make it appear to be a "free Christmas desk diary—the sort of gift you get sent by some obscure supplier who has produced these things for 20 years and is under the misunderstanding that everyone loves them," notes Tim, drolly.

The entire piece ended up being more than 100 pages long. The idea was to have it feel "slightly lavish, but in a naff sort of way." This was done through the use of bold colors and foldouts with interactive pieces such as stickers. The piece ended up being nine colors throughout. The paper stock took a bit of experimentation in the proofing stage. The design team finally chose a G.F. Smith paper stock called Zen because the definition of the shots appeared to be the best against it, and they thought a more traditional feel to the stock would be most appropriate. The most difficult part of production, perhaps surprisingly, was to find a sticker backing stock that could be printed on the reverse side. Most sticker stocks, it turns out, have a repeated print of the brand name on the back. But dilemmas such as that aside, the overall production process went quite smoothly, and the books were hand delivered to the CEO's of the top 100 companies in the United Kingdom.

Although it's too early to tell actual results, we're quite sure there are many newly popular CEO's in the British Empire.

The details are all well thought out, making the book very tongue in cheek and over the top.

While CEO's can learn how to become more popular with this handbook, nothing really does it like offering employees reasonably priced computers for their home.

Design Firm Nolin Branding and Design
Client Domtar
Project Boring Paper Promotion

Two Different Audiences, Two Different Approaches

Every communication piece a company creates says something about their business. And ideally, every piece should complement the others. The best way to ensure that this consistently happens? Being honest and straightforward with all of your audiences all of the time. The design firm Nolin, and their client, Domtar, a paper producer, executed a textbook example of this with two very different pieces to two very different audiences.

How Many Clients Would Be Willing to Admit Their Product Was Boring?

For a new Domtar trade show brochure, it was determined that the main goal should be to communicate the company's distinctive personality and capture the essence of their new tagline: Domtar. A different feel. The company is proud that their employees are fun to do business with and don't take themselves too seriously. After all, they deal with paper—a plain, flat substance that just doesn't do too much. A substance that is, in a word, boring.

Nolin creative director Barbara Jacques explains, "We wanted to show that paper needs people. Paper needs inspiration, creativity, and feelings." From this directive, the "boring" brochure was born. It's a good-humored, visual piece that comes right out and admits that paper is indeed boring, but in the process succeeds in screaming that Domtar people most certainly are not.

The Boring brochure maintained a clear and simple look, featuring colorful typography and large images. This clean design allows the audience to recognize that the paper is a vital part of the layout.

Nolin creative director Barbara Jacques explains, "We wanted to show that paper needs people. Paper needs inspiration, creativity, and feelings."

Although their products might be boring, the people at Domtar certainly are not—just take a look at their brochure.

Met with almost instant approval, this concept was the only one ever developed. The final brochure was received extremely well by both Domtar clients and employees. For the record, our sources tell us that not one person claimed that Domtar was boring.

The Canvas May Be Boring. The Results Are Not.

When it was time to create the Domtar annual report, Nolin and the client understood that this piece would be talking to an entirely different audience. One that may not appreciate the "boring" message as much as the trade show set. The annual report would go out to investors, shareholders, and company employees. In an effort to keep what could have been a stodgy piece out of the recycling bin, the agency and client decided to take a step away from the ingrained perception of the pulp and paper industry as being old-fashioned, straightforward, and well, boring.

The idea was to position Domtar as a dynamic and contemporary company, a leader in the industry. Jacques explains, "In spite of a very tight timetable, we knew immediately that we were on the same wavelength. We had hit on the perfect concept: Pulling together . . . we planned on the symbolism of the forest, identifying it with team spirt and creativity." Not to mention trees and paper. Like the Boring campaign before it, the annual report presented an honest view of Domtar.

Designers employed bold and modern colors to bring the piece to life, and the team made an effort to highlight the company's vision for the upcoming three years.

From briefing to delivery, the entire project took less than three months. Jacques confirms, "Everything went well at every step." And along with honesty, quality, and a sense of humor, what more could you want from your paper company?

The company's annual report went out to investors, shareholders, and company employees, and it positioned Domtar as a dynamic and contemporary company, a leader in the industry.

Using an insert—something not often seen in run-of-the-mill annual reports—the piece clearly states company objectives and their overall commitment to quality. The client would eventually print more inserts to distribute among the employees.

Design Firm **Kolegram Design**
Client **Buntin Reid**
Project **Rocks Invitation/Poster**

Rock, Scissors, Paper, Shoot!

Rock

The Hard Rock Café—the perfect place for a party when you really want things to rock!

From this location a promotion evolved to invite people to this event and get them excited by it. How excited? The promotion shows seven different "rock moves" they can learn to do that will essentially "guarantee rock stardom." Created by Kolegram in Ottowa, Canada, the promotion had as its mantra: "We believe a rocking attitude is what makes things happen."

Paper

The client is Buntin Reid, a paper distributor. They often organize events to show off their new and existing products. The event they organized was a paper show, but a hard-rockin', fun-lovin' paper show. The promotion, printed on paper, naturally, was a cyan-magenta-yellow-black (CMYK) flyer that opens up to be a 19½" x 27½" (49.5 cm x 70 cm) poster. It was printed on Luna Matte 100-pound text, and it was shrink wrapped to be sent out in the mail. The piece was sent to graphic designers, agencies, and people working in the communications industry.

But what makes this promotion remarkable is the fact that you actually want to read it! The content and pictures are fun and amusing—a sure-fire recipe to encourage readers to keep reading and maybe even save it or at least look at it more than once. This is especially important since the target audience is a very design-savvy group of graphic designers, project managers, printers, and other paper customers from the Ottawa region.

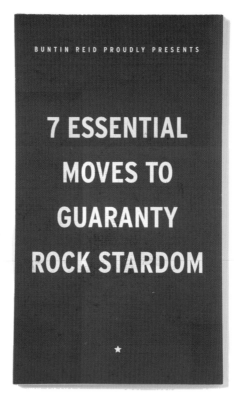

Who wouldn't want to attend a hard-rocking party for a paper show after seeing this humorous and engaging promotion?

Scissors

As for problems encountered in the production process, there were only three—budget, budget, and budget. The budget meant things just had to be cut, and the designers had to live with it. The original strategy was to have a saddle-stitched booklet with the content inside, and the full-sized poster folded and glued in the inside back cover. Unfortunately that feature had to be cut because of budget. The piece also had to be resized many times due to the changing budgets, and at one point the design firm had to switch printers.

Shoot!

Creative director Mike Teixeira directed the promotion. He put on the rock star outfit and posed for photographs (the fact that he played in a rock band himself definitely helped). He knew he could do the rock star moves and wanted everything to be exaggerated and grand. Teixeira describes the shoot: "I had a blast at the photo shoot. The photographer and I laughed so much. We did the photos in a few hours, right after some department store's shoot, using the same white background. It worked!"

And the Winner Is . . .

In the end, everything worked out great. The paper show was a hit. The promotion really got people in the rock and roll mood. There were life-sized banners of all the moves hanging inside the Hard Rock Café. Kolegram knew the promotion had to be energetic and humorous if they expected people to show up, and that's exactly what happened. Rock on!

Due to budget constraints, Mike Teixeira, the creative director of the piece, donned the rock-star outfit. His over-the-top moves make this piece hysterical and memorable.

"Graze on some excellent grub, see the latest cool papers, win prizes, and check out the cool guitars on the wall." Whether you're into rock and roll or papers, this party had it all.

Design Firm	**Duffy Design (Minneapolis)**
Client	**Archipelago (ARCA)**
Project	**Direct Mail Campaign**

We could introduce this next promotion by using some clever, unexpected hook to draw you in. Then, we could ramble on for a bit about joke and gimmick shops—maybe even propose a new theory or two on the educational value of toys. This segment certainly has the potential to develop into a very interesting preamble. But there will be none of that. Because, as you'll see, this next promotion does just that: It captures the audience's attention right from the start and makes them want to read on and learn more. And it does it so well that there's really no point for us to try.

Turning a Potentially Boring Assignment . . .

So, imagine your ad agency or design firm has just been called on to develop a promotional direct-mailer campaign for a stock exchange. Your initial thought might be, "A financial account! This is just going to be *loads* of fun." And quite understandably so. Well, Duffy Design, a company of Fallon Worldwide, was the lucky design firm assigned to the job. And this project was loads of fun.

Their client was Archipelago (ARCA), an electronic stock exchange that competes with NASDAQ, NYSE, and ASE, as well as alternative trading systems. Before the new campaign, ARCA was primarily trading NASDAQ volume. So, in short, the goal was to expand into the NYSE, an unrealized territory.

Prime campaign targets included both current and prospective Archipelago traders. Jennifer Jagielski of Duffy describes what these people are all about: "[They] are work-hard, play-hard guys with short attention spans and little time to pay attention to advertising messages." And, with that in mind, the creative team developed a whole line of toys—er, marketing tools.

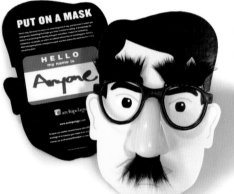

Want to remain anonymous? Then put on this mask—and learn about trader anonymity.

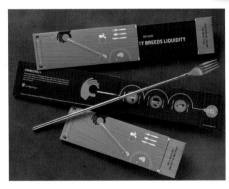

The connectivity fork is a piece all about how Archipelago reaches out and finds the best prices for its customers.

The Electronic Naturals sing about the benefits of electronic trading.

. . . Into a Fun One

Each direct-mail piece was essentially a different gag—and each carried a unique selling point. Jagielski explains, "Each piece played off a different 'weakness' of the NYSE, and leveraged ARCA's strengths." One mailer, for instance, was a mysterious blue envelope. Pull a tab, and out came a telescoping fork. This piece, as the copy on the packaging explained, was all about connectivity; it represented Archipelago's ability to reach out and find the best prices for its customers.

In another example, one piece in the campaign was a cardboard cutout of a face wearing a Groucho Marx–esque disguise—complete with a fake nose and moustache. The header on the back read, "Put on a mask," and below that was a nametag that said, "Hello, my name is Anyone." This particular piece highlighted yet another one of Archipelago's strengths: their ability to preserve trader anonymity.

In the end, the client was very pleased with Duffy's work; the campaign, they reported, generated a lot of positive talk and email messages among their target audience. And the folks at Duffy must have been thrilled, too—their campaign was an easy sell to the client, as outlandish as it was. Jagielski says, "[Archipelago] are willing to take risks and communicate in an unexpected way . . . and they were very helpful in explaining many of the 'industry inside' hot buttons and language to make our pieces really strong."

No More Joking Around

Okay, we gypped you out of a decent intro. So, in a few words, we'll sum up the moral of the story for you: If you're looking for an easy career in advertising or design, make sure all your clients are as receptive to bold and wacky ideas as Archipelago. Alternatively, consider this: Unexpectedness is a definite attention grabber.

Remember the buzzing handshake? This is to remind traders that there is always open access when trading with Archipelago.

Unlike Miss Princess Fun Brick here, Archipelago believes in promoting and maintaining a competitive environment.

Archipelago's lightning-fast electronic trading system means you'll never find yourself trading at the speed of this guy.

Unexpected

Surprise! The promotions in this section make one's eyes widen. No matter what the category, target audience, or format is, an unexpected promotion is one that is sure to make someone say "Wow, I wish I had thought of that!"

Design Firm **Templin Brink Design**
Client **Target**
Project **Michael Graves Design Collection Promotion**

Imagine coming up with an idea for a promotion. You're sitting around, brainstorming with another designer, and one of you says, "How 'bout we do a pop-up ad insert?"

Blood, Sweat, and Tears

Fast forward a month. Twenty-one 13-person teams are working eight-hour shifts for four weeks to make your promotional idea happen. And that doesn't even include the Web and sheet-fed print portion of the job—that's just the folding part, the part of the process that needs the actual "popping up." A bit mind-boggling—just think about it—13 people had to touch each and every part of your promotional piece to make it happen.

But then again, the promotion was for Target, a company that "merely" sells good quality merchandise at low prices, but has a brand that transcends that, a brand that is mod, trendy, bold, hip. Declared by a recent USA Today poll as "in," Target is *the* place to find the latest trends at the best prices.

Templin Brink, a San Francisco design agency, was assigned a specific promotional project for Target. The strategy behind this promotion was to reinvigorate the Michael Graves Design Collection, a collection of products sold exclusively at Target. The Michael Graves brand had been around for a few years and the impetus was to get people jazzed again about this incredible line of products.

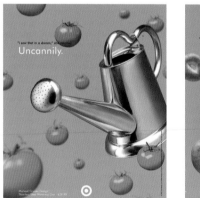 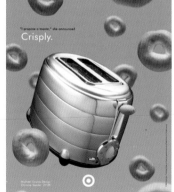 

The target audience is primarily women in the 25- to 44-year-old age group. Joel Templin, creative director, notes: "I think the campaign, like any Target campaign, is appealing because it's fun and has bold energy."

Everything Works Together

The promotional campaign was fairly extensive, involving the creation of a print ad campaign, direct mail (that was sent out to a list of Target's Graves shoppers), a press kit, and other innovative PR and marketing ideas. And what Templin Brink did so well was to conceptualize and execute all the various components into a seamless campaign, one that gave the Michael Graves Design Collection a fresh, updated feeling while still staying true to the core Target brand.

Templin Brink Design has an agency philosophy of linking together a brand's history and destiny together. A perfect philosophy in a case like this. Target has a bold and colorful history and seems destined for continued success—it was started in 1962 in Roseville, Minnesota, and has since grown to 1,107 stores across the United States.

Sometimes the Best Ideas Just Pop Up

The campaign has been extremely successful in capturing people's imagination and creating brand awareness. Templin Brink is currently on their third year of the campaign. Part of the assignment is always coming up with extra credit ideas, events, or unusual ways to promote the collection. This year the Michael Graves Design Collection included freestanding pavilions that would be offered only at Target.com. So, in a typical creative brainstorming session, the design team attempted to create an innovative promotional idea that would showcase those pavilions. And one designer says to the other, "Hey, how 'bout we do a pop-up insert?"

And the rest, as we know, is history.

The press kit went along with the other materials to create a seamless, visually vibrant campaign.

The infamous ad insert was "incredibly complex to produce from a paper-engineering standpoint taking twenty-one teams of thirteen people each working eight-hour shifts for four weeks to put it together."

Design Firm **Plazm Media**
Client **Portland Institute for Contemporary Art**
Project **Pink Posters**

Artistic Expression

Severed body parts. It's hard not to be provocative when designing posters using actual body parts. Add to that the word "severed," and it's nigh impossible. Of course, being provocative is just what Plazm Media set out to be when they designed a series of posters for the Portland Institute of Contemporary Art (PICA).

First, just for the record, the body parts were already severed when they were photographed. No magic of Photoshop was used here. The photographer, Christian Witkin, had a difficult time finding available body parts to photograph, as one might expect. But then, art has always been about dogged determination.

Art in the Public Sphere

The purpose of the posters was twofold. On one hand, they were designed to promote Portland's Contemporary Art Museum and raise awareness of it. But they were also designed to attract people to an exhibition called "Counter Canvas," which is all about art in the public sphere. And what better way to promote art in the public sphere than to create art in the public sphere that gets noticed and talked about?

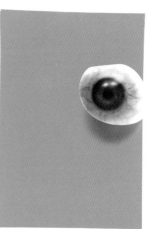

The posters were a visual metaphor. Each one represented one of the five senses, this one being touch, with the Portland Institute of Contemporary Art becoming the sixth sense.

The actual printing was a combination of litho and silk screen. The body parts were printed litho as a tritone using silver and two blacks. The pink is a silkscreen trapped to the image. The image shadow overprints.

One can only wonder what was served for lunch at the photo shoot where severed body parts were photographed.

Around 1,000 posters were printed and wild posted around the streets of Portland, Oregon.

Joshua Berger of Plazm Media likes to give credit where credit is due. According to him, the real inspiration for the idea came from PICA itself, who has a willingness to raise questions yet respect the audience's intelligence to reach their own conclusions. The art museum strives to embrace the unknown, to push people in the direction of a more open mind. Even when a more open mind means approval of a layout that shows severed body parts on hot pink backgrounds.

Berger, who collaborated on the posters with creative director John Jay, becomes animated when he speaks of the project. "The very color itself elicits political, sexual, and gender overtones. Combined with a severed finger, ear, tongue, eyeball, or nose, the hope was to create a new provocation in the street. The purpose of these icons of the human senses was to ignite the first step of the creative process, the spontaneous act of thinking. Rarely does one consider the act of provocation through elegance. To beautifully lull one into danger . . . into the gallery of PICA."

The Work on Display

The posters went up one at a time over a six-week period and were posted on construction walls and any surface legally available. There was no copy, only a logo on the last poster to go up. People were left to figure out the puzzle by piecing together the five senses—an eye, an ear, a nose, a tongue, a finger—with PICA metaphorically becoming the sixth sense. Along with the posters, small 2" x 3" (5.1 cm x 7.6 cm) cards were also produced using the images. PICA and Plazm staff got cards each week and were asked to surreptitiously hand them out and leave them in public places. They were also mailed—one a week for six weeks—in unmarked envelopes from the central post office to various media sources.

As for the reaction—like the best art, the posters evoked extreme reactions in people. Love 'em or hate 'em, they did get a response. Many posters were defaced and others were appropriated by other artists. In the gallery, PICA had an entire wall painted pink with each poster mounted across the length of the wall. And, true to form, someone actually tagged the gallery wall itself.

All That Matters in the End

The client, on the other hand, was very pleased. They have since been seen using pink for other promotions.

Once viewers were "seductively lulled into the gallery through provocation," there was an area of the exhibit that had a bright pink wall where all the posters were displayed.

The only copy appeared on this final poster with the logo, which went up during the last week of the six-week blitz.

It's not easy being on the brink of adulthood. You might have just completed college, or have been working for a couple of years. You are suddenly responsible for more things than you ever thought possible. Perhaps you are just buying your first car, or even buying your first house. Maybe you're thinking of getting married. But one thing is for sure–you don't want to give up on the fun stuff. Some days, you still have the urge to be a kid. Some days, you just don't want to be old.

Designers and marketers targeting this age group need to be aware of this duality. This age group knows it needs to make certain decisions responsibly. So it's a group that seeks out more information about certain products and services than it used to.

But at the same time, members of this age group lead incredibly busy lifestyles. So brand names mean something because they are the ultimate time-saver. Yet unlike the younger demographic, they no longer use brand names to be a part of the club.

Design Firm   Sandstrom Design
Client   The State of Oregon (USA)
Project   X-Pack Smoking Cessation Program

The X-Pack is a self-help smoking cessation kit, packaged in a way that is attractive to the target audience— young adults aged 20–26.

And one other thing to remember—you can't talk to them like they're not still hip. After all, young adults still want to have fun.

Sandstrom Design needed to talk to this age group with an incredibly challenging project—to get young adults in the state of Oregon to stop smoking. Research confirmed the conflicting stresses of this target: they had started smoking in their more carefree days and now were beginning to regret their decision. They needed help, but help came with a caveat. It needed to be fun, also.

Enter the X-Pack. A self-help smoking cessation kit, packaged in a way that is attractive to the target audience, with a mix of quick, simple information along with fun things to do instead of smoking.

Among the components: a youth-oriented smoking cessation guide complete with a quit plan and quit day checklist; motivational messages; testimonials of successful quit attempts by peers; information on nicotine replacement therapy. And, of course, the fun stuff: various products to keep the hand and mouth busy during the quitting process (gum, cinnamon toothpicks, stress putty); and an incentive for registering the product (a Borders Books and Music gift certificate). All materials were based on the best medical practice, combining insights from both adult and adolescent smoking cessation research.

And everything was packaged in a way that said "we know you are still hip."

Among the components: a youth-oriented smoking cessation guide complete with a quit plan and quit day checklist; motivational messages and, of course, the fun stuff—gum, cinnamon toothpicks, and stress putty.

The goal of this project was to get young adults in the state of Oregon to stop smoking through an informative, yet fun, approach.

Design Firm   Amoeba Corp.
Client   Jill and Steven Miller
Project   Wedding Invitation

A wedding. A time of great tradition. Stuffy, scripty invitations on plain cream stock are not usually seen in a book on promotions. But this was a wedding that was promoted in a most unusual way.

An Untraditional Announcement

Jill Furnival and Stephen Miller, a happy couple about to be married, wanted an invitation that was different from anything they had seen before and that would leave a lasting impression on their guests. The couple contacted Michael Kelar of Amoeba Corp. because they were aware of his design work as well as his personal artwork. The creative brief was pretty brief (excuse the pun); Michael was given a blank canvas—a designer's dream. He sold the couple on an idea to create an invitation package that would be "an eclectic mix of vintage/modern elements that would take the viewer through a dynamic visual story rather than just displaying the simple facts." It was a form of anti-design—invitees would have to work for the information rather than have it presented to them in a straightforward fashion. The concept for the invitation was a reflection of the couple's personalities and eclectic tastes, much like the actual wedding event itself. The concept was to create a package that had many formal aspects but was not traditional in its content. The project took a little more than two months from concept to completion.

From the moment the guests received the envelope in the mail, they could guess this was not a traditional wedding invitation. And they were not disappointed.

The concept for the invitation was "an eclectic mix of vintage/modern elements that would take the viewer through a dynamic visual stay."

Adding a Personal Touch

The production process was as unconventional as the invitation itself. Due to a limited budget, the 150 wedding invitations and associated collateral were hand assembled. From hand litho mounting 1960s vintage wallpaper to each invitation card to trimming and assembly, the entire production process took more than two weeks to complete. Four sets of skilled hands, many long nights, and a lot of take-out was needed to accomplish such a feat—a true example of limited edition in the world of art and design.

Kelar notes that the most interesting part of the project was the attention to detail—each piece that was created for the wedding was highly customized and unique. Graphic elements, textures, typography, and the vintage etchings were never duplicated throughout the entire package—every element was customized and hand manipulated to emphasize the unique qualities of the couple's personalities and their wedding party.

Another interesting note was that few guests actually returned the RSVP card and instead kept the entire invitation package. But luckily they did show up!

A Happy Couple

There are lots of things to be nervous about when planning a wedding, including the presentation of concepts to the bride- and groom-to-be. When they first saw the design, the couple reacted exactly like clients who see something truly unusual. They gasped, took a few minutes to recover, and then joked about whether anyone would show up. They had asked for something different, and different is what they got. And when all of the pieces were designed and the full package was presented as one cohesive idea, the couple saw the method in the madness. The wedding was a huge success and the invitations were the subject of many conversations. And the couple is still very happily married.

The design theme was carried through to the celebration, with menus, gift CDs, and thank-you notes included in the cohesive theme.

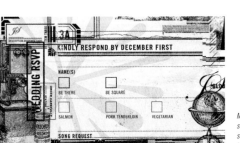

Many of the guests liked the package so much that they were reluctant to send back the RSVP card and destroy the integrity of the package.

Design Firm   Emery Vincent Design
Client   Emery Vincent Design
Project   September 11th Anniversary Posters

Designers Unite

It was a year after the September 11th tragedy. The people of New York City and Washington were remembering what happened. It was an event that shocked the world. So is it surprising that halfway across the globe, in Sydney, Australia, people were remembering, too? As Sharon Nixon of Emery Vincent Design states, "Everyone was touched by the tragedy in some way whether through clients, the extensive media coverage, or the loss of friends—the effects were global."

Strategy and Execution

So Emery Vincent Design decided to take action by creating a series of posters that would mark the anniversary. The office as a whole became involved in the project. The design firm felt that a visible public response, in a medium that has been typically used for expression—the street poster—was an appropriate vehicle. The thinking was that the posters would be partly about giving the studio an opportunity to express its reaction to this significant world event, but also would share this anonymously with the wider community as a catalyst for debate. The posters were designed to be an urban statement that came from the street. They were placed on telegraph poles along a busy inner-city street in a guerilla-style campaign. The street posters in their own right are subversive. There was a guerilla tactic in putting them up in Sydney where there is a policy of no street pole posters—and yet there are many. The posters were placed anonymously; there was no reference to Emery Vincent Design. The idea was to make a social comment and spark community debate.

Posters commemorating the anniversary of September 11th were placed on telegraph poles along busy inner-city streets in Sydney, Australia, in a guerilla-style campaign.

Their tactics were somewhat subversive because in Sydney there is a policy of no street pole posters—and yet there are many.

So all along the roads in inner urban Sydney—areas with different demographics and psychographics—the posters were placed. Emery Vincent consciously chose a variety of communities to try to spark a variety of personal responses.

The Message and Content

The posters were part of a studio project, which generated 15 designs. The studio collectively selected three designs to be produced. Everyone was uniquely affected by the tragedy and responded in a different manner ranging from graphically aggressive, political, and antiterrorist to compassionate and peaceful expressions. Each of the three posters that were chosen promoted and represented one of three common themes—commemoration for those who died; compassion, and the need to pursue peace; and a political commentary on America's stand on terrorism.

The posters were restricted to a two-color palette and a limited screen-printed edition. The stark use of red, black, and white adds to the impact of the design. And as for the response, Sharon Nixon simply states, "Public reaction is difficult to gauge as the lifespan of these posters is generally short and often undocumented. Hopefully, for the instant they are up, there is engagement, review, and a personal response."

Public reaction was difficult to gauge due to the lifespan of these posters, which is generally short and often undocumented. One can hope that these designs caused engagement, review, and a personal response.

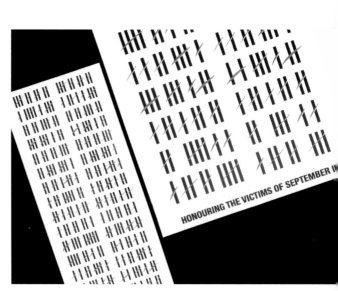

Everyone was uniquely affected by the tragedy and responded in a different manner ranging from graphically aggressive, political, and antiterrorist to compassionate and peaceful expressions.

Lush

There's a certain indescribable richness about a promotion that's designed to be lush. Regardless of what the actual budget is, the person receiving the promotion feels as if no expense has been spared. It is evident in every little detail: maybe it's the weight of the paper, a precious piece of typography, a stunning photograph, or deep, opulent colors. The end result is something that can be treasured long after the promotion is over.

Design Firm **Riordon Design**
Client **Riordon Design**
Project **Personal Calendar**

"365 new mornings. 8,760 hours to spend. 525,600 passing moments. One full circle of time."

The Day That Never Ends

And so begins one of the more poetic promotions to be found, a lowly personal calendar, elevated to new heights through design, poetic writing, and a most unusual production technique.

Every year Riordon designs a custom gift to give to their existing client base and prospects. For 2004, it was a personal calendar, measuring 6½" x 8½" (16.5 cm x 21.6 cm), featuring simulated velvet pastel blue book covers with silver foil stamping. Sandwiched in between the covers is a two-color accordion calendar insert and, holding it together, a wide rubber band with the pi symbol imprinted on it.

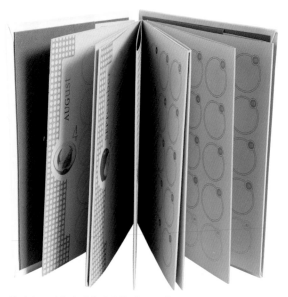

When Riordon sets out to design each year's custom gift piece, part of the criteria is to design something that showcases the design firm's capability in presentation design—something memorable, something that people will keep around and not be quick to discard.

The designers at Riordon find projects like this personal calendar fun to do. It's the kind of project that not only showcases the imaginations and skills of the design team, but it's essential for internal morale building.

Half-Time

One thing that makes this piece unique is that the year is split in the middle. The first six months of this calendar book start at the front cover and go to the middle. For the second half of the year, the user flips the book over, and starts all over from the back cover. This not only complements the circular theme, but was a clever solution to a production quandary. As Ric Riordon, design firm founder, explains: "We wanted to create a continuous linear layout of the calendar year and the only way to achieve this on one sheet of stock was to set it up in this fashion."

The theme of the personal calendar is a playful yet philosophical look at the concept of infinity and the circle. According to Riordon, using the mathematical formula pi and its "interwoven presence in all the designed universe, the implied association is made that infinity, or eternity, exists in tandem with all matter and our measurement of time." Lest one think that is too esoteric, keep in mind that the piece was designed to appeal to a target audience consisting mostly of smart corporate professionals and entrepreneurs.

Timing Is Everything

Ironically enough, the biggest problem in producing a piece like this was the timing. The assembly of the piece was more intense than first anticipated. The various elements were produced by three different vendors, and then the 400 books were assembled and wrapped at the studio. The book covers were late. The die line for the insert calendar was off, which required hand trimming with an X-acto blade in order to slip them into the covers. The bands weren't perfect when they arrived. Some had messy printing; others were a little tight on the finished book. So everyone had to sort through the bands and do a quality purge. Fortunately, there were plenty of extras.

We hope that the first entry into Riordan's new personal calendar is an early starting date for next year's promotion.

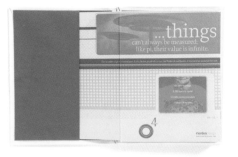

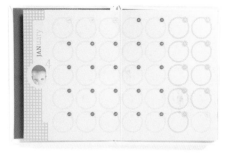

Beyond being creative, the goals of the piece were that it "needed to showcase intelligence, serve a function, and fulfill a purpose," notes Ric Riordon, founder of the design firm. The following quotation from Jonathan Swift highlights this perfectly: "I'm up and down and round about yet the world can't find me out; though hundreds have employed their leisure, they never yet could find my measure."

Design Firm Anvil Graphic Design, Inc.
Client Anvil Graphic Design, Inc.
Project Gift Wrap

Have you ever thought about the creative process that goes into creating gift wrap?

Do you imagine it to be an easy process, one that simply involves designing a single pattern that can be repeated over and over on a large roll of paper?

Did you ever think that each design might have to be critiqued in numerous formal presentation scenarios and go through many rounds of revisions, until a team of designers feels it works?

Well, this is the real story . . .

A Gift for You

Granted, this is not just any gift wrap—it is gift wrap that is designed to be used as a promotional tool for Anvil Graphic Design, a design firm in San Francisco. Each year, they give the wrap to their clients as a gift in a promotion that involves the entire agency. For one thing, all the patterns come with names, and the names are varied and fun. Here's a sampling of the gift wrap names: Champagne, Tile, Geisha, Elephants, Monkeys, Octopi, Nightgown, Mints, Heat, Blossom, Flourish, Matrimony, Chill, Sputnik, Light, Cubist. Because naming the wraps is such a fun project, everyone in the studio participates in the naming process. As for the design itself, the inspiration comes from traditional Asian art combined with Modernism and a bit of contemporary Japanese graphics mixed in.

Anvil's promotional giftwrap started with 1,500 gift sets. Each year they increase the amount produced. They also partner with vendors so they can produce the gift wrap economically.

The project takes approximately four weeks from concept to completion. Ratliff explains, "The goal is always to produce the gift wrap in time to use as a holiday promotional gift for our clients. The short timeline also keeps our studio (labor) costs in check."

Alan Ratliff at Anvil describes the process: "We give the paper depth through use of varying color, line weight, scale, and opacity. The paper is designed to keep your eye moving so no matter how you wrap the gift the pattern will look beautiful from every angle. It's much like designing a scarf." To create the design is not simple and involves countless sketches, research, and lots of the aforementioned presentation meetings within the design firm. Ratliff notes, "Our biggest challenge was trying to select just six designs to include in our promotion. With everyone's enthusiasm and interest in the project, the staff produced more than fifty designs."

The gift wrap was a promotional idea that Alan had wanted to do for several years. "It not only promotes our creative capabilities but it provides a useful gift to the recipient. Because most of our work is in the high-tech industry, this was also a great opportunity for us to work on something completely different from our day-to-day projects."

Plans for the Future

So that's how it started. But it turns out that projects like this have a momentum all their own. Anvil received many compliments and won several awards. In fact, they got such great feedback from clients that they chose to test the waters of the wholesale market. In 2003 they sold the Neo Tokyo gift wrap line as flat sheets. For 2004 they decided to turn this into a business venture using national sales reps to sell the gift wrap in rolls and flat sheets. In an unabashed plug for the wrap, Ratliff adds, "Look for Anvil gift wrap at a design-conscious store near you or go to www.shopanvil.com for a list of stores and representatives."

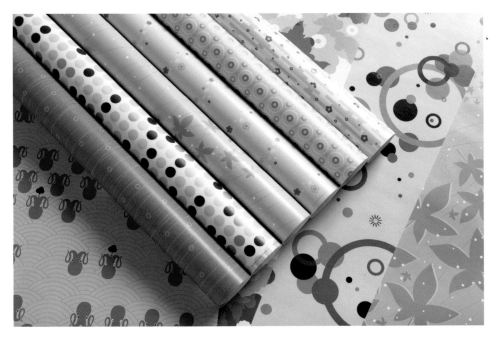

The gift wrap is a great reason to build relationships. Clients reveal personal information about who they wrapped a gift for and for which occasion. This window into their lives builds bonds, which strengthens client loyalty.

Design Firm **Noon**

Client **Noon**

Project **Lunch-at-Noon Promotion**

Anyone Want to Go to Lunch?

"There once was a time when Monday's lunch was Sunday's leftovers or a cheap sandwich." —from Noon's website

This is no longer the case, thanks to a promotion by Noon, a San Francisco design firm with six designers and a philosophy based on "distinction, intelligence, and charisma." The group is close knit, and "agrees that we will always inform each other the day we begin to dread coming into work and we will always strive to do our best," notes Cinthia Wen, founder of the firm. This attitude extends even to the lunchtime hour, an hour particularly meaningful to an agency named Noon.

Cinthia explains. "We, as a group, do enjoy our time with each other and make the effort to spend lunch hour together daily. Thus, we created a 'game' where we each contributed to a collection of ingredients in a bowl. Then we each drew an ingredient from it weekly and brought a dish that we made with the ingredient the following Monday for a great big pot-luck lunch."

A promotional mailing announcing a new website filled with recipes and food facts was created by Noon, a San Francisco design firm. The outside of the very personal-looking envelope is die-cut with a tiny place setting.

The aroma of dried rosemary greets the viewer when opening the package. The card merely states the Web address elegantly.

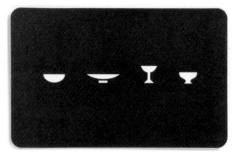

The announcements were sent mostly to friends and family as well as to a select group of clients and contacts. The mailing was simply to keep in touch with contacts, introduce a new project, and reinforce the studio's reputation of creative thinking.

The lunches at noon became so popular that it wasn't long before the team decided to create a website that would document all the recipes and photographs of the dishes. At first there was no intention in making the site public, but "the end product was surprisingly dear to us so we were compelled to share."

The Promotion That Almost Wasn't

And so, a promotion was born. The birth of the idea came from endless discussions among the designers about whether they should or should not announce the website upon completion. Eventually they agreed that if they could find a cost-effective and unique method for introducing the site, then they would. The criteria were that the promotional vehicle had to reflect the lunch-at-noon process itself as well as to have the look and feel of a special invitation.

Ahh, the Smell of Rosemary

The announcement itself is an intimate little card (5" x 3¼" [12.5 cm x 8 cm]) enclosed in a cream-colored envelope with die-cut icons of a knife, fork, and spoon on the front. When the recipient removes the card, they immediately are hit with the unmistakable smell of rosemary, as some dried sprigs are included with each card. The copy is nothing more than the website itself.

Two hundred and fifty of the promotions were created with a total teamwork effort. Hand-punching the die-cut envelopes got a bit painful, so everyone took turns. Drying the rosemary so that its oils didn't rub off onto the card was something that was taken into consideration and tested extensively.

For a promotion that almost wasn't, it ended up being amazingly successful. Soon after the mailing, the site was noted on the Yahoo! Hot List and Creative News. To Noon's surprise, the record hit on the site was 130,000 per month. Testament, perhaps, that when an idea is born out of true passion it always touches people in some way.

The website itself has dozens of recipes that were created by the designers at Noon. All recipes were tried and tested. In fact, each shot was taken moments before the designers dug in to eat.

Alignment

After writing *The Art of Promotion,* (Rockport Publishers, 2003) artist, author, and national lecturer Lisa L. Cyr was inspired to pursue a distinctive promotion of her own. "I was looking to attract the attention of the graphic arts industry from the major organizations, conferences, and universities to the trade media," recalls Cyr. With her eye for talent, she turned to Red Canoe as the firm of choice. "I love their sense of integrity, keen attention to detail, and most of all, their ability to communicate even to the most sophisticated audience," she adds. Cyr approached Deb Koch and Caroline Kavanagh, cofounders of Red Canoe, ("The Canoeists" as they like to be called), with a synergistic collaborative proposition.

After establishing a shared baseline measure for excellence under mutual philosophical and practical benchmarks, the two collaborators went to work and a promotional idea enthusiastically began to take shape. "Red Canoe believes that any promotion or brand extension must reveal an honest representation of the client's character," explains Koch. "In our research, we discovered that Cyr's writings and lectures consistently evolved around certain key words." For the *Axioms* promotion, the design team focused their attention on three in particular: Challenge, Pursuit, and Commitment. "These expressions are underlying constructs for any successful endeavor," comments Koch. "That is why we chose to use them as chapter headings, prominent themes in the promotion."

The French-folded front and back covers encase the hand-crafted, custom piece; all components were printed on an Epson 2200 printer. As a finishing touch, it is bound with screws and posts, securing actual rulers that accent the theme of measurement carried graphically throughout. The piece came mailed in a custom-fitted and labeled box along with a cover letter, business card with custom sleeve, and reply card. Order forms were also created to be sent as a follow-up on replies.

The book breaks down into three distinct chapters: Challenge, Pursuit, and Commitment. Challenge relates to not only the challenges that the industry faces but the challenges one makes venturing out with a unique voice and vision in a very competitive marketplace. Pursuit unfolds insight into how to stake a lasting claim in the often volatile business of visual communications. Lastly, commitment sheds light on how to put into action one's thoughts, goals, and dreams.

Structure

Because of the visual sophistication of the audience, the promotion had to far exceed the confines of a typical brochure. "When considering the approach, we were in pursuit of a visual vernacular that communicated on multiple levels with layered and interactive messages—interpretations that allowed a certain degree of audience definition," notes Koch. "Design, illustration, photography, and copy—these creative crafts always consider and reapproach perspective and context." The architecture for this promotion is structured with a keen attention to information design, from the title to the thought-provoking and almost definitional brain teasers that support each chapter heading. In addition, timeless, inspirational quotes are eloquently intermixed with real-world insight from seasoned professionals in a two-tiered typographical manner, an appropriate framework for Cyr's words of wisdom. The piece juxtaposes timeless, story-telling photography against vibrant, dynamic, and emotive illustrations. It was also important for the piece to display innovative production qualities, as the subtitle of *The Art of Promotion* is *Creating Distinction through Innovative Production Techniques*. The French-folded pages, tipped-in signature images, bindery, and custom identity elements each gave the recipient a sense of the kind of promotional vehicles that they were to experience in the book or at a lecture. All the details, both conceptual and production related, worked together to create an engaging and memorable experience.

Measure

Tackling the creation of a promotion entitled *Axioms* that is by definition "a proposition whose truth is so evident that no process of reasoning, of measuring, of demonstration can make it plainer—as the whole is greater than the parts" was surely not an easy course to take. But, in the end, it became a true measure of character. It not only talks the talk—it also walks the walk!

The theme of axioms—self-evident, abstract truths—sets the tone and pacing of the book.

Each chapter opens with a salient quote from a significant industry professional juxtaposed against archival photographs enhanced with relevant schematic elements and accented by defining copy. The monochromatic, classic look of the photography is contrasted by the vividly colorful, more impressionistic art by leading contemporary illustrator Brian Cronin.

Design Firm **Angelini Design**
Client **Angelini Design**
Project **Corporate Brochure**

The Importance of First Impressions

First impressions are a make it or break it proposition in today's overmarketed, oversaturated world. And it's especially important when it's a design firm making the first impression, since image is all they have. The first impression needs to be something that will make a potential client comfortable enough to want to spend tens of thousands of dollars on a design project.

Angelini Design knew they wanted something that could be delivered to potential clients to get them to accept the first telephone call. Something that would not only make a great first impression, but would clearly say that the design firm had a strong bias for high quality creative work and was passionate about the details.

Details, Details, Details

And the details of this particular piece are particularly noteworthy. Measuring just 5¾" x 7¼" (14.5 cm x 18.5 cm), the small, case-bound book has a black "shagreen" canvas cover and an engraved metallic badge carrying the Angelini logo on the front. The inside pages carry four-color printed images on 170 gr ivory Old Mill paper. The effect is elegant, rich, and tactile.

The brochure then gets packed in a black box and hand-delivered by courier directly to a database of marketing directors, top managers, PR managers of targeted companies, and advertising agencies. Each delivery is followed by the necessary telephone call. But by the time the phone rings, the potential client has a reason to remember Angelini Design.

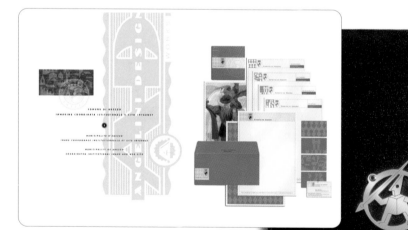

First impressions are a make it or break it proposition. For a design firm, image is everything!

This small, case-bound brochure measures only 5¾" x 7¼" (14.5 cm x 18.5 cm) and has a black "shagreen" canvas cover. The engraved metallic logo on the cover and 170 gr ivory Old Mill paper on the inside make this an elegant, rich, and tactile piece.

As Angelini designer Mariagrazia De Angelis notes, "Clients appreciate the strong personality of the brochure and the sense of prestige it communicates."

Mariagrazia goes on to note that the idea behind the brochure came from the *schetck book* (sketch book) that every Italian designer always keeps in his pocket and uses to spark creative inspiration throughout day. That's the reason why every page carries an unpublished *schetck* next to the published project. So not only does the client gain an appreciation for the finished design, but they also get to see the thinking that goes into an Angelini Design project firsthand.

Presentation Is Everything

And the showcased projects are many and varied—logos, brand identity, catalogs, company literature, brochures, packaging, trade shows, Internet graphic design, and point-of-purchase displays. There is packaging for Air Alitatia's snack box that actually makes airline food look good. Equally difficult, but equally well done, is packaging for a bra company logos and for Sony PlayStation and Peugeot. Samples of unusual design projects such as free-form-shaped mouse pads and cactus shaped salt and pepper shakers are also included.

What a beautiful way to package up such an eclectic mixture of projects!

Angelini's projects are many and varied—logos, catalogs, brochures, packaging, and point-of-purchase displays are just a few types of design work showcased in their brochure.

Like Client, Like Promotion

A historic commercial property rich in texture and heritage deserves promotional material equally rich and textured, yes? That's certainly what Emery Vincent Design thought, even though most promotional materials in the commercial real estate category usually rely on high-color, glossy marketing materials.

Located at Wharf 8/9 on Sydney Harbour, Australia, the property is at once prestigious and unique, qualities that are echoed throughout the rich black-and-white photography and the sophisticated production. For example, the pages of the booklet were French-folded and bound together with silver interscrews, whereas the text on the cover was foil-stamped and debossed. The handmade slipcase also features foil stamping and debossed text.

The design strategy was to create a high-quality publication that was more like an art catalog than a sales brochure. A sense of elegance and sophistication is achieved through the use of black-and-white photography and is supported by abstract color imagery. This is reinforced by the restrained typography, which also references the buildings' historic past.

Most promotional materials for commercial real estate are glossy four-color pieces. Emery Vincent Design took a unique and tactile approach to highlight a property that is itself unique and tactile.

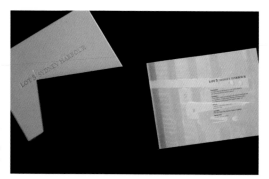

A sense of elegance and sophistication is achieved through the use of black-and-white photography and the restrained typography, which also references the buildings' historic past.

Sending It Out

The brochure was mainly distributed by direct mail to top 500 Australian companies, with a particular emphasis on entrepreneurs with a potential interest in securing a one-off location on Sydney Harbour. It was thought that these people would most likely appreciate the uniqueness of the property itself: it is the last intact complex of its type in the world and the best example of early 1900s Sydney port infrastructure.

The brochure needed to promote the opportunity to buy a unique slice of historic real estate right on Sydney Harbour—a never-to-be repeated offer. But there were certainly barriers to be overcome. For example, communicating the exact location and its future potential was a challenge, given that the rejuvenation of the area was not yet complete and the location did not have a strong identity. Also, the brochure was effectively asking someone to buy in an up-and-coming location (for which they would normally expect a discount) but at a premium price.

In this instance, ego was an important button to press. The idea was that there would be very few individuals who could afford such an exquisite yet underdeveloped location. And the design, with all its rich details, spoke to that ego.

What's in a Name?

The name Lot 3 was chosen because the development is located on Lot 3 and the property is unique enough not to require a clever metaphorical. It also leverages the Sotheby's connection (offered through Sotheby's International Realty), a company that deals in historic rarities for wealthy individuals. The end result is a brochure that feels rich and rare and one of a kind.

The design strategy was to create a high-quality publication that was more like an art catalog than a sales brochure.

Design Firm Sandstrom Design
Client Portland Center Stage
Project Identity System and Promotional Materials

Designers to the Rescue

Portland Center Stage is the largest live theater production company in Portland, Oregon, yet it was plagued by static attendance and growing financial problems as it entered its fifteenth season. So when the theater company hired a new artistic director, Chris Coleman, it was clear he had to do *something*. And with the help of Sandstrom Design, they did something remarkable.

The To-Do List

The goals were challenging: first, to improve the quality and diversity of the performances, and second, to build a national reputation. Although Portland Center Stage took responsibility for the first goal, Sandstrom Design quickly attacked the second. They began to redesign the identity system, as well as all promotional materials for Portland Center Stage. The identity system included a new logo and stationery, and general guidelines for their usage on mailers, print ads, banners, and apparel. The promotional materials included posters, flyers, mailers, print ads, playbills, and many other pieces. The lead piece was a small 56-page flyer that outlines the play schedule for the 2003–2004 year. It was mailed to all previous subscribers and potential customers on a targeted mailing list, handed out at every performance, and distributed as a rack brochure in a variety of venues around town.

A poster series with a unified graphic look helped the Portland Center Stage achieve its goal of national recognition. Powerful graphics, bright colors, and evocative images were used to showcase each performance.

Flyers to promote future events were bundled up like newspapers and given out at performances.

Performing arts communities are fairly small, often less than 4 percent of a city's total population. The upside to that statistic is that it's fairly easy to identify that target, which makes it efficient to market to them. They are educated, urban dwellers who periodically attend the ballet, opera, and symphony. They range in age from 25 to 65 and tend to sample the arts first and then subscribe later. Because the performing arts are dependent upon donors to stay afloat, many of them are charitable givers and convert to donors after becoming subscribers.

Breaking Away from the Competition

The concept used for the flyer stressed the fact that this is live theater. This distanced Portland Center Stage from television and movies as an entertainment option. Live theater is more compelling, tends to involve the audience more intimately, and often allows them to interact with the performers and positively affect the quality of the play.

The copy states: "The experience, at its core, is a provocative relationship. The actors take the stage and offer themselves up to the audience. They tell a story, evoke an image, and conjure an emotion. The audience reacts, and from this energy emerges a performance that can never again be replicated. You are cordially invited to shape the following performances . . ."

This concept came directly from an interview with the artistic director. Coleman talked passionately about live theater as a total sensory feedback experience. His love of his work and his level of dedication inspired the designers to bring his insight to the attention of the subscriber base.

Money is always an issue with performing arts groups, and that's when reality hit the production process. Sandstrom's recommendation was significantly above Portland Center Stage's budget, and there needed to be a reduction in colors, size, and pages to come closer to it. The end result was close approximation of the original design, and other elements of the marketing program were eliminated to cover the costs.

Building Awareness

To achieve the goal of national recognition, Sandstrom recommended that the poster series be consistent through the year. A concept was created that was based upon rock band poster art. Powerful graphics, bright colors, and evocative images were used to showcase each performance. Larry Jost was hired to illustrate each poster, and each poster is more powerful than the one before. You might say that the posters come to life, just like the theatrical presentations.

Larry Jost illustrated each poster in the style of rock band poster art, and each poster is more powerful than the one before.

The lead piece was a small 56-page flyer that outlines the play schedule for the 2003–2004 year. The concept revolves around the fact that this is live theater, and the copy "cordially invites the audience to shape the following performances."

Design Firm Viva Dolan Communications & Design Inc.
Client ArjoWiggins Fine Papers
Project Curious Direct Mailer

How do you make someone curious?

a) Give them something to open that's wrapped up like a giant stick of gum.

b) Prominently feature a bald guy and a penguin.

c) Show four unique kinds of paper.

d) All of the above.

Yes, all of the above. Well, it certainly made *us* curious.

So, what is this project that invokes such curiosity? It is a direct mail piece. It's sized to fit in a standard DL envelope. It's printed on a representative cross-section of the Curious Collection of papers. And it was produced in 12 languages for 20 markets worldwide with the target audience being the European design and advertising community.

It's hard to resist opening something wrapped up like a giant stick of gum—silver foil with pinking-sheared edges.

Inside are four inserts with engaging visuals. The only copy is the word new *printed in seven different languages.*

The Beginnings

The project started when ArjoWiggins Fine Papers, design firm Viva Dolan's Anglo-French client, consolidated several legacy brands under one umbrella to create the Curious Paper Collection. This consolidation strategy was subsequently adopted worldwide, with Viva Dolan acting as the lead branding/design firm. The Canada-based design firm provided creative direction, graphic design, writing/editorial, and intensive production management for a program of swatchbooks, brochures, and packaging. The program was aimed at twenty markets in twelve different languages, using seven printers in four countries. The aim was to make the Curious Paper Collection the most effective, smart, visually striking, strategically branded, beautifully produced project imaginable.

When ArjoWiggins Fine Papers asked Viva Dolan to help them with the launch, they had been a client since 1991, so the design firm had a good understanding of what was needed. They produced a boxed set of introductory swatchbooks, which visually spoke to the unique characteristics of each paper, as well as a print advertising campaign and a website using the same design strategy.

Stop Teasing

So where does this small promotional piece fit in—a piece meant to be a teaser, designed merely to arouse curiosity in the Curious brand? It's a piece that uses snippets of the imagery (without giving too much away) from the Curious Collection swatchbooks due for release later in the year.

The piece is a series of five simple samples of the paper with minimal copy and the curious illustrations on them. Each piece was designed, printed, and photographed according to a tight pencil sketch. The photographer and illustrators had access to the sketch and produced precise images that fit into the layout. The end result is a whimsical promotion cool enough to have been featured in British *D&AD* and *AIGA*.

Now for Something Trivial

And as for that bald guy: He's a French-Canadian named Jean-Luis; he was the model for a Metallics hair dye box that Viva Dolan designed. They dyed his hair gray for the shot, and when he attempted to dye it back to his natural color, it turned blue. He then shaved his head in frustration.

Just in case you were curious.

The inserts are printed on a variety of papers: "Translucents patterned with diamonds and snake scales. Particles that shimmer and vanish with body heat. And a textured sheet that ripples and droops like damp floppy fabric."

At some point, you become an adult and things start coming together. You make choices and realize they are your choices and no one else's. Perhaps you do the proverbial "settling down" or perhaps you travel the world. You've found a career calling that suits you or you hop around trying new ones. Responsibility is not the heavy word with a capital R that it once was. Sure, you have responsibilities, but in the end, that's just day-to-day life. You make choices about yourself, your family, your future, and you live with them. And so most of the people in this age group have at least a semblance of having life figured out. And it's great.

Market to the adult age group, and you're casting a wide net. This group is not tied together by age as much as teens are. Still, there are some commonalities. People in this age group are making wise choices, and they are making them more and more intuitively. They have a variety of interests but are not so set in their ways that they won't try new things.

So when a tiny arts center in the United Kingdom wants to get its name in front of as many people in this age group as possible, what do they do? They come up with an innovative promotional idea, and then run with it.

They blanket the Great North Run—Britain's biggest running event—with signs that tap into the psyche of this demographic. Playing off the B in the name, the Baltic Contemporary Arts Centre sponsors an entire campaign that revolves around the way people of this age feel. *B.Great. B.Determined. B.Lucky. B.Excited. B.Limber. B.Ready.*

Design Firm **Blue River Design**
Client **Baltic**
Project **Baltic Centre B.Great**

When the Baltic Contemporary Arts Centre wanted to appeal to the 27- to 45-year-old target, they blanketed one of Britain's largest race events with banners that spoke directly to the psyche of the audience.

The signs evoked the curiosity of many spectators, who asked about the Baltic Center or even volunteered to hold some of the signs.

This well-known half marathon was identified as a suitable vehicle to use to take the Baltic brand outside of its usual environment and engage and interact with an audience directly at street level. The half marathon's audience and emotion levels matched those of the Baltic Contemporary Arts Centre. The race also offered huge audience figures with its 47,000 runners plus the potential to capitalize on the guaranteed national and regional media coverage. The starting point of the race was in close proximity to the Arts Centre, which added an extra element of fusion on the day of the race.

Baltic was able to tap directly into the carnival-style feel at street level, bonding with both runners and spectators. The team of banner holders was frequently questioned about the banners as well as the activities, exhibitions, and projects at Baltic. Some of the public spectators even offered to hold the banners. The banners provided an approachable, friendly face for Baltic. Baltic was, without a doubt, able to engage directly with its target audience and help them develop a strong emotional bond with the Baltic brand.

A great way to B.Great.

The promotion not only got the attention of more than 47,000 runners and spectators, but there was extensive media coverage, which often included shots of the simple, yet powerful signs.

Design Firm   Hornall Anderson Design Works

Client   Widmer Brothers

Project   Blonde Ale Promotional Collateral

What makes a promotion successful? Roll the dice and find out . . .

Everything a Client Could Ask For

From a "drinking game cube" to a draft beer tap handle that includes the svelte curves of a woman on the handle, Hornall Anderson Design Works, a design firm in Seattle, created the promotional materials that would successfully brand Widmer Brothers' Blonde Ale. The agency designed everything from the beer's six-pack carrier, bottles, poster, metal sign, beer tap handle, T-shirt, and fact sheet to the drinking game cube.

Not only do the promotional collateral pieces incorporate the look and feel of the brand, but they do so in a creative way. For example, the drinking game cube is a memorable and whimsical way to promote the brand because it actually serves a purpose. Customers can keep the item, instead of receiving just another flyer or card advertising the brand that begs to be thrown away. The blonde character on the tap handle becomes very recognizable when lined up with numerous other tap handles in a bar or pub. It speaks for the brand not only through its name, but also through its visual impact.

The drinking game cube is a fun and interactive way to keep the Blonde Ale name in front of drinkers. Roll the dice . . . then propose a toast, add a new rule, or ask a buddy to drink.

Speaking Out to a Small Crowd

The target audience for this beer is relatively narrow—males, ages 21 to 28, and consumers of microbrew beers. So, you have a beer named Blonde Ale, and you have males who are just past the drinking age and . . . well, suffice it to say that using images of svelte blonde women and encouraging the target to play a drinking game was inordinately successful.

Brand Image Is Key

But the successful Blonde Ale brand had an interesting history. It proves the point that success or failure of a beer is never based on taste alone; it is the resulting brand image that surrounds any given flavor that makes it successful in the marketplace. This particular flavor of beer was originally launched by Widmer under the name Sweet Betty, and a brand character was created around a 1940s-era woman. When launched, however, sales of the beer were notably lackluster. It was determined that not only did the character not appeal as much to the target audience, but the name Sweet Betty left consumers assuming it was a sweet-tasting beer as well. Sweet Betty, had to go. Christina Arbini, media relations manager at Hornall Anderson, explains, "To find a stronger appeal in the marketplace, we renamed the beer 'Blonde Ale,' and reintroduced the character as a svelte, hip, sophisticated woman. This new brand appealed to both male and female consumers."

A Satisfied Customer

The project started out as a packaging and collateral request only. As the design project developed, the client felt that the concept and execution were so strong that the project extended itself to a tacker sign, table tent, drinking cube, and a tap handle. The client thought that Hornall Anderson Design Works created the perfect package solution that represented not only the personality of the Widmer Brothers brand of products but also dramatically improved the current sales records for the Blonde Ale line. After all, beer sales speak for themselves.

The promotional materials were designed for Widmer Brothers Blonde Ale after it was determined that the original flavor name—Sweet Betty—simply did not resonate with the target audience.

The new character was the perfect match for their target market, 21- to 28-year-old males.

Design Firm Ph.D
Client Primary Color
Project Eight-color Press Announcement Posters

The Machine Age. An era when machines enhanced living and mass production, and glorified streamlining. According to Michael Hodgson of Ph.D in Los Angeles, California, the Machine Age "was the most important iconoclastic revolutionary movement of the last century."

Eight Is Enough

And so a trio of posters, all titled "eight," celebrate the look of graphic design in the Machine Age. The reason for their being is apt enough—to announce the acquisition of a new eight-color Heidelberg Press at printer Primary Color. As copy from the posters proudly proclaims, "Primary Color brings an eight-color machine of opus proportions to the forefront of its own operation. Surrounded by specialists with keen eyes and unsurpassed attention to details. Light speed ahead."

The Machine Age period of design occurred from the middle 1920s through World War II, an era that swung between euphoria and sobriety. Machine Age graphics were usually black-and-white, with the odd spot of color. Ph.D wanted the posters to have the look of their original counterparts, but be produced in lavish, luxurious ways. According to Hodgson, "Most printers overplay their hand . . . we wanted people to see these posters, touch them, and ask 'How the hell did they do that?'"

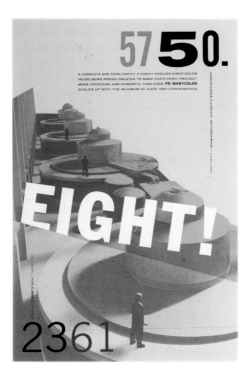

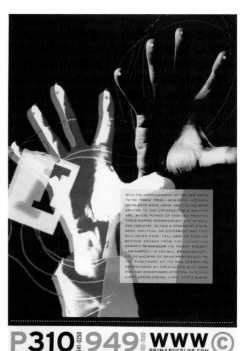

The idea behind this set of three bold posters from Ph.D was to highlight the eight-color press capabilities of printer Primary Color.

The look for all of the posters was based on Machine Age graphic design.

A Gala Event

The series of three 24" x 36" (61 cm x 91.4 cm) posters was distributed at a gala event. At the same time the press was being put in place at Primary Color, Ph.D was busily designing a new identity for the printer. An open house was held to announce the new identity, and at the event posters were rolled and presented to clients and vendors along with goodie bags. Also, large-format versions of the posters were made to grace the walls at the open house.

Ron Slenzack photographed two of the posters. For the one titled "eight" (whoops, they're all titled "eight") the design firm obtained the rights to use a Tennessee Valley Authority photograph, which "playfully suggests the importance" of the new press. The figures along the disappearing sight line were retouched over the original photo. Also of note is that each poster was printed on a different paper type, ranging from an 80# gloss cover to a 50# smooth text to a 92# metallic anodized cover. A range of spot colors, Pantone Matching System colors, varnishes, and foils were also used, albeit sparingly to demonstrate the printer's range.

History Repeats Itself

"History is being made once again cycling back around to the unforgettable Machine Age. Where points of view and printing tools worked synonymously with science and industry." So states another blurb of copy from the posters, with the posters themselves being testament to that statement.

From start to finish, the project took three months to complete. Printing on that new eight-color press, however, was a breeze. After all, light speed ahead.

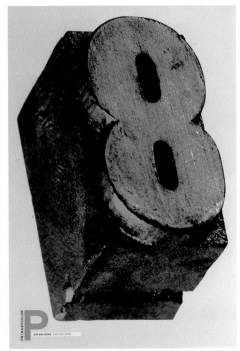

Ph.D likes to produce work that has "a cleverness to it and perhaps a sense of wit," remarks Michael Hodgson, who helped art direct the piece along with Clive Piercy and Heather Caughey.

Design Firm   Ph.D
Client   Roxy
Project   Roxy Vibe Promotion

A photo shoot that lasts four days and is held on the Big Island of Hawaii. Ahhh, life is good!

Calling All Girls

The shoot was for a promotional piece for Roxy, the junior girls' line of Quicksilver's apparel and a leading brand for active girls. It's designed for the "junior customer with progressive style who embraces all elements of life," explains Michael Hodgson, of Ph.D, Quicksilver's design firm. The Roxy girl is "involved in beach sports and snow sports and demands a girly fit and functional wear." The line is designed by Dana Dartez, who designs clothes ranging from basic surfwear for sport and style to vintage-inspired, forward-looking sportswear. The brand was launched in 1991 with a line of swimwear, but quickly expanded to include surf clothing, snow wear, denim, footwear, accessories, fragrances, and skin care. Tying all the product lines together is a soulful, spiritual vibe that defines the more ethereal nature of the brand Roxy.

Roxy sells a complete line of products for young, active girls in the United States, Europe, and Australia.

A Soulful, Spiritual, Surfing Feeling

And so that youthful, soulful, spiritual, surfing feeling—part girly, part vintage, progressive, embracing-life feeling is what California-based Ph.D wanted to capture in a promotional piece to be given out at trade shows. The idea they created is a 30-page, 5½" x 8½ " (14 cm x 21.6 cm) booklet that has gorgeous four-color photography interspersed with vellum sheets. On the vellum sheets are lovely brush illustrations by Ann Field. The photographs show through the vellum, and they interact with the illustrations to add an element of whimsy and surprise. For example, an illustration of a surfer is deep blue with ominous shadows behind it. When you turn the page, you realize the photography below the vellum is an underwater shot of two surfer girls kicking on top of the water.

The idea for the illustrated vellum sheets grew out of the fact that Roxy's new branding image involves a sense of transparency—there's a sense of always seeing through to the next level. This comes across in the vellum, the images of water and sky, and the illustrations, which are done in watercolor to further enhance the idea of transparency.

Hard-working Models

The catalog is also notable for the fact that the Roxy models are all excellent amateur or professional surfers. Megan Abubo, for example, is part of the World Championship Tour of surfers. And Lisa Anderson is a four-time world champion and the first woman to be inducted in the Hall of Fame of Surfing. In fact, Lisa is often credited with changing the image and perception of the sport of women's surfing, according to Roxy's website. She "became a role model for young women and girls everywhere, proving that a girl can rip and still possess femininity."

The entire piece took just three weeks to create from start to finish. The short time frame created a frenzied pace, a fact the designers lamented.

But then, don't feel sorry for them. After all, there was that photo shoot in Hawaii.

The promotional piece was designed with vellum inserts, which add a layer of transparency and interact with the photographs in surprising ways. This piece was created to be given away at trade shows.

All Roxy models are amateur and professional surfers. Lisa, for example, is a four-time world champion.

Salon. A word that reached its height of popularity around the turn of the century—the long-ago turn of the century in 1900, that is. A salon was a place where prominent people from the worlds of literature, art, music, and politics met on a regular basis.

A Thoroughly Modern Salon

More than a hundred years later, we now have, appropriately enough, a "Digital Salon." The intent is still the same as the salon days of yore, but with a thoroughly modern twist. In this case, Salon Digital opens its doors once a month at the Cross Media Lab of the Academy of Art and Design in Offenbach, Germany. Two prominent academics, Rotraut Pape and Bernd Kracke, invite between 100 and 150 well-known artists, producers, and designers for a *jour fixe* with professors as well as students. The invited guests show actual film, video, or other media projects and then discuss their insights with the audience. Different topics are presented, such as streaming projects of the Berlin music scene and independent media projects in international political context.

Such an event needs to be promoted on a regular basis to inform and attract the people most likely to attend—the students, the people from other academies and universities, and, of course, all persons generally interested in culture. Posters are the perfect promotional vehicle to grace the halls of academia where the target audience hangs out.

A series of posters designed to promote Salon Digital, a monthly gathering of prominent people from the arts and academia who gather together to discuss, in this case, streaming media.

Two hundred posters are produced for each run. Although they are created using only simple lines, the posters have a rich quality due to the fanciful type and illustration and the black and gold color scheme.

Squiggly and Baroque

The design firm Hesse, a 16-year-old institution in the German design scene, was called in. They wanted to pick up on some design conventions that echoed the feeling of the turn of the twentieth century. Klaus Hesse, a principal of the firm and a designer, teacher, illustrator, and typographer, has a love of type that extends back to his student days at the Bergische Universität Wuppertal. Klaus says that what he loves most about design is "the idea and the second view." Thus, it was immediately apparent to him that the style of the type and illustration should be "a little squiggled and baroque" to echo the original time period of the salon. And because the lecture series is known as Salon Digital, the type and illustration are done with one tool that is both artistic and digital: Freehand.

The posters are monochromatic (the first three were in gold and the fourth in black). Although they are done in lines only, they have a richness all their own. The design is flexible enough to accommodate different needs yet retain its design integrity. At the beginning of a new series with new guest speakers the colors might shift, along with a variation in the style of illustration. Still done with Freehand, still squiggly, but a variety of looks can be created within those parameters.

The response has been overwhelming. Visitors of the Salon Digital not only had a great salon experience, but they took the posters home afterward. Out of 200 that had been produced, not one was left at the venue.

The "squiggly and baroque" style of illustration was done using the designer's favorite tool, Freehand.

Klaus Hesse, principal of the design firm and also typographer and illustrator of the series, has a love of type that is very apparent in his work.

Design Firm Giorgio Davanzo Design
Client Giorgio Davanzo Design
Project The Hidden Agenda of Dreams Book

Look through the exquisite bound book with the intriguing title *The Hidden Agenda of Dreams*. You will see that dreams containing trains often represent opportunities in life, dreams containing clowns often represent "a deep and heavily camouflaged sadness or dissatisfaction," and dreams containing boats suggest a subconscious thinking of problems in romantic relationships. In analyzing these dreams and their meanings, we might also wonder: what does a dream, dreamt by Giorgio Danvanzo, about a handbook of dreams suggest? As it turns out, it suggests a startlingly effective self-promotional piece, in the form of a very real 4¾" by 6⅜" (12 cm x 16.2 cm) booklet. A booklet whose sole purpose seems to be to analyze dreams.

Enticing the Reader

The Hidden Agenda of Dreams, at first glance, looks like a book of the sort you might find in an antique bookstore run by an enchantress. It is simple and elegant, a mere 26 pages long, mostly black and white, with a gold title and no author. However, upon further inspection, one can see that not only is it a book, but it is a tool with a dual purpose. For the receiver, it is a tool for analyzing dreams. For its creator, Giorgio Davanzo Design, it is for promoting his design company in the simplest, most effective way—promoting yourself by not promoting. Instead of promoting with the usual tools of loud graphics and attention-grabbing colors, he used a "compelling subject matter, refined art direction, and high production values." The compelling subject matter took twelve images that routinely appear in dreams and analyzed their deeper meaning in a few sentences.

The Hidden Agenda of Dreams *is a self-promotion piece for Giorgio Davanzo Design that is cleverly disguised as a beautiful little book that analyzes dreams and their meanings.*

A Promotion That's Like a Dream

This simplicity and beauty was able to "seduce even the most promotion-resistant" audience, which in this case consisted of 500 existing and prospective clients who received the handbook in a cream-colored, cloth shipping bag. Giorgio Davanzo Design wanted to show clients what the design firm could do in an "unusual and memorable way." At the same time, there was also awareness that these clients were bombarded every day with thousands of advertisements and designs in the form of everything from pop-ups to logos on sweatshirts. Knowing that by using the same tactics, it would be too easy to get lost in the chaos of promotions, Giorgio decided that there was no need to shout when he could convey his message more powerfully in a whisper. As he states, the beauty of the book is that "it's so gutsy in its subtlety."

However, the greatest irony is the similarity in the triangle of dreams, the handbook, and promotions. The prologue of the handbook ends with "In your lifetime, you will have over 150,000 dreams. What are they trying to tell you?" A promotion is just like a dream. You will see thousands. What are they trying to tell you? Which ones will you remember? Which of them will come back time and time again to haunt you, in ways that make you unlikely to forget?

The refined art direction and high production value came in the form of elegant typeface, and beautiful photography—duotones and black-and-white photos that were attained by painstakingly searching through the Library of Congress website.

What will you dream of tonight?

"Dream No. 11. Boat. Traveling on water is common when we are dreaming about romantic relationships or interpersonal conflicts. Water is associated with deep emotional feelings. Sailing is a metaphor for how you feel currently about your life, your degree of control, and your level of satisfaction. Are you at the helm?"

The idea literally came to Giorgio in a dream. But after designing the piece, he "realized in horror that all the dreams were in Italian. He needed the help of a writer. But not just any writer. He wanted Gretchen Lauber, the über-talented copywriter, jetsetter, renowned art collector, and Pinot Noir expert."

V Pliant is a company that sells clothing and bags that have an interesting, edgy combination of vintage textures and materials. So it only makes sense that the promotional materials for such a company would also have an interesting, edgy combination of vintage textures and materials. From vellum to old postcards to grommets to metallic thread to rubber stamping on variable cloth, the promotional materials are a recycling dream come true. If it works, use it.

Clothing That's Recycled and Reconstructed . . .

A small, independent company producing what they call "reconstructed clothing," V Pliant sells one-of-a-kind items made from vintage, unusual, reclaimed materials. The identity system likewise incorporates industrial, old, and modern elements and handcrafting techniques. The company information, for example, is rubber stamped onto the back of the business card and hangtag, which is layered with paper ephemera using grommets. The logo is also stamped onto various cloth squares to create sew-in labels, and the letterhead is printed onto vellum and backed with varying pieces of paper ephemera.

. . . And an Identity That's the Same

Not only does the creative approach mesh with that of V Pliant, but also it's a philosophy that Dynamo Art & Design embraces with all clients. Nina Wishnok, principal of the Boston-based agency, has four guiding principals for great design: 1) Don't self-edit too much early on in the process because you never know where something's going to lead; 2) Look anywhere and everywhere for inspiration; 3) Leave plenty of room for (and welcome!) happy accidents; and 4) Stay flexible.

It took five months from the initial meeting to completion of the project, which included hangtags, sew-in labels, business cards, and letterhead. The pieces are used for products, shows, resellers, direct-sale customers, and correspondence.

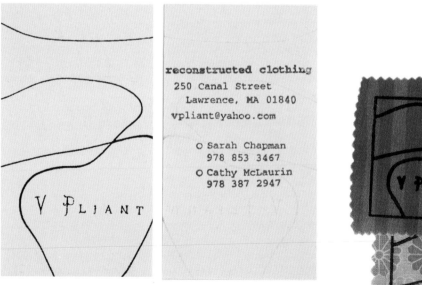

reconstructed clothing
250 Canal Street
Lawrence, MA 01840
vpliant@yahoo.com

O Sarah Chapman
978 853 3467
O Cathy McLaurin
978 387 2947

V PLIANT

The look of the promotional materials for V Pliant takes off on the definition of the word "pliant," which calls to mind lines and movement, which led to the abstract line work of the logo, a mark that suggests metal wire or thread.

The sew-in labels for the clothing were made from various scraps of leftover cloth that were then rubber stamped.

An Idea Is Born

The birth of the idea came through intellectual discussions at the first meeting. The client and design firm spoke the same language, and thus were able to discuss ideas together with ease. Ideas that otherwise might scare all but the most visually literate client—abstract design concepts like appropriation and recontextualization, and visual ideas such as repetition, irregularity, texture, layering, asymmetry, and juxtaposition. As a result of such a discussion, Nina began thinking about using materials that brought a sense of past life, materials that were previously used or evocative in some way—all characteristics of the materials and treatments V Pliant uses for their clothing.

The production challenges were, for the most part, due to budget. But out of such restrictions, resourcefulness is born. The client was hesitant to spend too much money on printing sew-in labels for the garments and bags. So Wishnok suggested using rubber stamps, which saved on printing costs and also suited the industrial, funky, V Pliant aesthetic. This brought flexibility and variability to the materials, which turned out to be one of the most interesting aspects of the system.

The response to the materials has been very positive. The client loves it because it's flexible and variable but still coherent. Vendors and customers say it really fits the V Pliant personality and products.

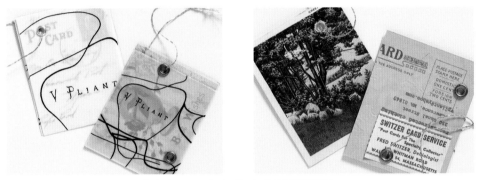

The hangtags were made using old postcards together with vellum, grommets, metallic thread, and rubber stamping.

The letterhead was created by rubber stamping the logo on vellum, then folding it into various found materials such as wrapping paper and magazine pages.

Design Firm **Elfen**
Client **Wales Arts International**
Project **Identity and Stationery Materials**

The brief from the client was simple. Wales Arts International didn't have much money, but wanted to "create an interesting identity that would inspire." The identity needed to promote the council as an organization that cares about the image of contemporary Wales and is interested in the benefits that international collaboration can bring. And the client had one mandate: "We like strong, bold, confident colors."

Small Budget, Big Look

So Elfen, a design firm in Wales, started the project with gusto. Most of their clients have small budgets, so they were no strangers to limited funds.

The new identity for Wales Arts International needed to include letterheads, compliment slips, business cards, folders, and moving announcements. The target audience is the international arts scene, which includes artists and arts organizations in Wales.

Wales Arts International is a partnership between the Arts Council of Wales and British Council of Wales that works to promote knowledge about contemporary culture from Wales. Both organizations encourage international exchange and collaboration and help build a dynamic international context for the local arts. Established in 1997, the organization undertakes project work that promotes and develops contemporary art form practice and supports individual artists and arts organizations to explore international partnerships.

The goal of re-branding Wales Arts International was to portray an organization that cares about the image of contemporary Wales and is interested in the benefits that international collaboration can bring.

Elfen sent the materials to arts organizations all over the world. They also sent it to funding bodies and individual artists in Wales and abroad.

Marking a Location

So the birth of the idea occurred from the original client brief—it contained a list of all the British embassies around the world with which Wales Arts International is connected. The identity uses a strikingly simple graphic of location markers, showing Wales Arts International's position geographically and connecting it graphically to the points where the British embassies are. This created an underlying theme for Elfen's work for the client, and each time they approach a new project, the theme gave inspiration to create something new within the same idea. To generate interest in and knowledge of the organization, Elfen established a design and logo that would withstand time, was effective, and was understood internationally.

Elfen also devised a creative production process for printing materials that looked very high-end on a limited budget. The printwork uses cyan, magenta, yellow and black (CMYK) inks but is set up as specials so that they can create three-color print using, say, the yellow, magenta, and black or any other three color combinations. This process keeps the customer print cost low, as most presses are set up for CMYK, and Elfen only ends up using three plates. Or if the job requires full-color image printing, the full CMYK achieves the same result for the logo. The identity has four versions of the logo in different colors. Color calibration had to be noted for consistency from project to project, as all the colors depended on two of the CMYK range and were printed at a high density.

The end result? Bold, strong, confident colors, just like the client ordered.

Guto Evans explains Elfen's philosophy: "We are driven by ideas, even if we are just working on a letterhead! The best projects always have ideas behind them; if people read into them, they decide for themselves what that may be. But if anyone asks, 'So how did you come to this design?' we always have an answer."

The Wales Arts International promotional materials were received with much interest. The design style met positive comments from existing and potential clients and partners.

Design Firm **Evolve Design**
Client **Evolve**
Project **Self-Promotional Book**

An eight-month labor of love that leads to an incredible return on investment. That's the long and short of *Sixty-four Printed Leaves*, a lovely 128-page, case-bound, self-promotional book that highlights the portfolio of London-based design firm Evolve.

The book is "used to accompany tender documents, or in presentations where supporting credentials are required," explains designer Jonathon Hawkes. Its uncoated plain brown cover is embossed with an intricate leaf pattern. Inside, the smooth white pages carry glossy, colorful examples of Evolve's work.

A Soft Sell

Evolve is a small partnership of designers with no sales team and no business developers. They are often too immersed in design work to develop new contacts and search for the next big project, and as a result they have quiet periods. *Sixty-four Printed Leaves* was produced to do the soft sell on the design firm's behalf.

This little pocket book is deliberately understated, reflecting the size and philosophy of Evolve. It is small and accessible, yet substantial. As Hawkes notes, "I'm always suspicious of companies that shout about themselves. If a product is good, it should speak for itself. This book lets our work do the talking."

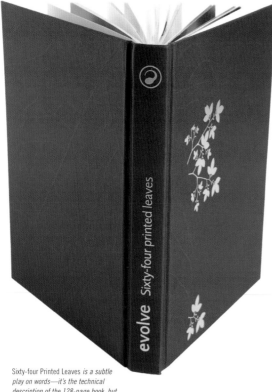

Sixty-four Printed Leaves *is a subtle play on words—it's the technical description of the 128-page book, but also refers to the environment that Evolve loves so much.*

The book sets the stage for an environmentally focused design firm that is housed in the woods. "Highgate. A tranquil place with room to think. This Hilltop village surrounded by dense woods and open parkland overlooks the urban buzz of London. Evolve lives here."

The remaining 50 pages showcase Evolve's work, which includes identity systems, stationery, brochures, sales promotions, and magazine advertisements.

Inspiration Was Right Outside the Window

The genesis of the idea stemmed from the desire to separate Evolve from dozens of similar-sized competitors by projecting a unique and memorable image. Evolve operates from a large treetop studio, in the beautiful leafy village of Highgate, North London. This alone helps paint a mental picture. Combined with the fact that a large proportion of the work the firm produces is environmental literature, it made sense to use the natural surroundings as a selling point. The embossed structure on the cover is taken from one of the branches that presses up against the studio windows.

Although Hawkes readily admits he's no copywriter, the words are as equally well crafted as the design. He insists, "It's just sheer luck. I guess all those late nights writing design proposals have rubbed off."

Attention to Detail

The production process speaks to the design firm's attention to detail. Once the color had dried, the gloss varnish and metallic silver were run through the press in a second pass to maximize their shine. The metallic silver text adds brightness throughout the book and works equally well on both white pages and dark photos. The only real problem encountered was with the cover emboss, which started out as much deeper. Unfortunately, air bubbles developed at the gluing stage, so the emboss die was altered. This gave a more subtle result.

Also of note is that committing to print, rather than merely updating an ever-changing website, means Evolve is now treated with more maturity. Their projects are becoming more substantial. The success of their book speaks to the power of print, in an age where electronic communication is the norm.

Although the immediate cost was sizable (GBP £8,000 to print 1,000 copies), the return on investment was immediate and gratifying. The first commission it helped generate was worth GBP £60,000. More importantly, it's bringing in the right kind of work—greener projects. Since the promotion has been put in place, Evolve has been commissioned to produce an environmental training program, a series of documents on historic architecture, and an environmental report for the Ford Motor Company.

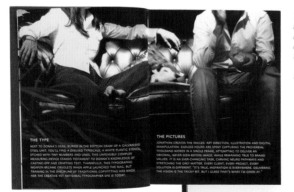

The first few pages speak of the design firm and the people who work there. The text describes Donna: "Training in the discipline of traditional copyfitting has made her the creative yet artisanal typographer she is today." And Jonathan, for whom "endless hours are spent capturing the proverbial thousand words in a single frame."

The promotion has generated more of the kinds of projects that Evolve loves the most—environmental ones. They already had good experience in the field, which deserved to be showcased. Here are some spreads from a book the design firm did for the Henry Ford European Conservation Awards.

Design Firm Dinnick + Howells
Client The Water Drop
Project Graphic and Retail Design Program

Water. Needed by all, yet largely taken for granted.

A Store That Sells Water

For example, when asked what 75 percent of our brain is made of, water does not usually come to mind. We complain when it rains and complain about the prices of bottled water. Even the color of water is, well, invisible. Therefore, Dinnick + Howells had a challenging task in front of them when they took on the retail client The Water Drop. This is because The Water Drop isn't any store; it's a store dedicated to selling only water. How could Dinnick + Howell create a design out of the element that is so largely ignored and can barely be seen?

Enter into the store called The Water Drop. You will feel like you are entering a place that is part museum, part artsy boutique.

Water
75% of the
human brain
is water and
75% of a living
tree is water

The strategy was to create a visual language that celebrated water—its importance to human health, its beauty, and its relationship to the natural world.

The Message Is in the Mascots

What they came up with was the idea of water mascots. These mascots came in the form of Water Drop, Cloud, and Sun, and convey the message of simplicity, cleanness, and life. Decorating the walls of The Water Drop with bold facts about water, these mascots transform a space into a boutique. They act in the same way water itself does—they bring life to what otherwise could be dark, bland, and bleak.

Dinnick + Howells wanted to figure out a way to create a visual language that celebrated water, and the result was the mascots. This idea came to them because in The Water Drop, "water is the star." With a store dedicated entirely to water, what would make more sense than a design also dedicated entirely to water?

As it turns out, photographing something that is nearly invisible is a bit difficult. For one thing, under the camera the mascots would "act as mirrors to a certain degree and therefore catch lights and flare." Additionally, water seems to have a mind of its own. "Pure water is just too watery and wouldn't sit still for the camera," Jonathon Howell, creative director on the project, says. This was solved by adding sugar to the water, which helped it sit in place long enough to be photographed.

The Facts of the Matter

Once photographed, the mascots were placed on bottle labels and blown up to huge proportions on posters around the store. The personality-filled mascots are complemented by cold, hard facts about water. You know that 75 percent of one's brain is water, but did you know that even 22 percent of our bones are made up of water? You would find such facts in the store tucked around corners, behind doors, inside the filtration room, and in the washroom. Next in the works was a wonderful, encyclopedialike diagram that will explain the "path to purity" on the glass of the filtration room.

The end result is that the promotional graphics are so captivating that the store has been getting "compliments on the space and [finding] that the design of The Water Drop is very closely linked to people's return visits." Maybe the 75 percent of our brain filled with water is finally doing the thinking.

The store also wanted to be presented as the authority on clean water, a place where you can ask anything about it and get the answers. They sell bottled water, of course, but also coolers, home water filters, and other accessories. But it's all about water and nothing more.

Dinnick + Howells of Toronto, Canada, wanted to make this feel like a very different kind of boutique—sophisticated, smart, natural, but also friendly for the whole family.

How do you give a bottle of water personality? The design team created mascots in the form of Water Drop, Cloud, and Sun.

Design Firm   stilradar
Client   stilradar
Project   *910* (a magazine for Stuttgart by stilradar)

A Brief History Lesson

Stuttgart, Germany—it's well known as a tourist center as well as a manufacturing center of electrical and photographic equipment, machinery, optical and precision instruments, textiles, clothing, chemicals, beer and wine, pianos, and motor vehicles. It's also known for having the highest per capita income of any German city. And it's also known for a funky little beautifully designed magazine known as *910*, produced courtesy of stilradar, a design firm.

The name *910* relates to the geographical coordinates of Stuttgart with 910 being the short term for 9°10' (9 degrees 10 minutes). The magazine is 60 pages long, each page measures 11" x 8½" (28 cm x 22 cm) and is produced in a limited edition run of 1,000. Anyone who is interested in the music, arts, lifestyle, fashion, architecture, and other happenings of Stuttgart can buy it at select shops throughout the town.

Featured here is the second edition of the magazine. The release is sporadic because it depends on the design firm's budget and time. But as with any self-promotion, the design firm tries to create time for the magazine because it showcases the designers' skills and gets the stilradar name known throughout the city.

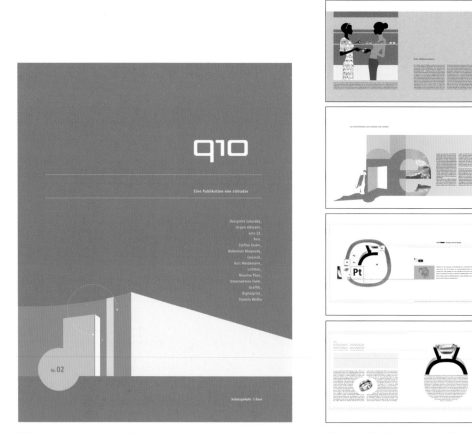

910 is a promotional magazine designed by stilradar for Stuttgart, a German city with a significant design scene.

Photography, illustration, and typography interact in surprising ways throughout the magazine, giving it a truly fresh feel and showing off the designers' capabilities.

Challenge Yourself

The *910* concept was the brainchild of Raphael Pohland and Simone Winter. They simply wanted to see if it was possible to push themselves to design and write an entire magazine. Each topic was different—they picked what was interesting to them personally, and so the topics include artists, musicians, and architects from Stuttgart. As Raphael explains it: "There was a wide range of not very well-known people but the articles in the magazine displayed them in a light that was exciting in contrast."

So *910* is a self-promotional magazine for the design firm, but it is also more than that. Raphael Pohland says: "It is our surroundings. People here are interested in these fields. The choice of the themes is subjective. For each edition we try to draw in a local photographer. They have full artist control and no restrictions. They can offer themes they are interested in and incorporate it into the magazine."

The second edition, shown here, was photographed by Jürgen Altmann. Raphael and Simone wrote nearly the whole magazine, from the first contact to the interviews to the articles. Besides the editorial work, they also did the design.

Visual Architecture

And the design is stunning. Type forms cityscapes. Photos and type interact in surprising ways. In the table of contents, for example, columns take the form of a cityscape. It is reminiscent of the way that Stuttgart as a city evolved. The center of the city, which formed its oldest part, was almost totally destroyed in World War II. After 1945, many old buildings were restored, and striking modern structures, such as the city hall and the concert hall, were erected.

As in the best of design, the design approach, the target audience, the content, and the surroundings all interact to form a whole that is greater than the sum of its parts.

The people gracing the pages of the magazine include a wide range of not very well-known people who are featured in unique ways.

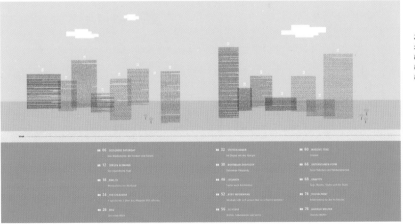

Stuttgart is the capital of the state Baden-Württemberg on the Neckar River. Here the typography treatment echoes the cityscape.

Tactile

Some promotions are designed to be touched. Some are made with unusual materials. Others are rendered in three dimensions when one would expect only two. Still others actively call out to the recipient to pick the piece up and interact with it. Whatever the method, the outcome is the same: these pieces say, "Please touch!"

Design Firm **Kinetic Singapore**
Client **SingleTrek**
Project **Cannondale Headshok Bikes Poster Series**

When Two Dimensions Aren't Enough

What better way to show the rugged terrain you might encounter on a mountain bike than with a series of posters that are actually three-dimensional? SingleTrek, a bike shop in Singapore, wanted to promote their Cannondale Headshok suspension mountain bikes. The strategy given to the design firm was single minded: find a unique and engaging way of demonstrating the capability of the new range of bike. So Kinetic, a local design firm, came up with a clever and unusual solution: to create a series of posters that each had its own 3-D paper sculpture depicting rugged terrain. According to Roy Poh, creative director, this let the audience "feel the action and show the true potential of the Headshok suspension mountain bikes"—a pretty impressive feat for something that doesn't use a word of copy.

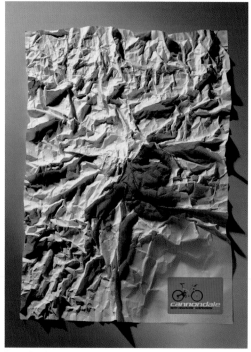

No copy here. Just paper sculptures.

According to creative director Roy Poh, these posters let the audience "feel the action and see the true potential of the Headshok suspension mountain bikes."

ℛ Roads Ahead

The client immediately gravitated to the concept, which created a classic case of *be careful what you wish for*. Roy and his creative partner, Pann Lim, then had to figure out a way to get it done. And because they had never created 3-D paper sculptures to be used on posters before, they didn't realize the numerous obstacles that would come up. There were problems with the thickness of the paper. First, it was too thick to create the perfect textures for the poster. Then, it was too thin to hold the poster together. After they finally determined the perfect thickness for the sculpture itself, they were chagrined to note that the poster kept becoming an odd shape after the textures were done. After much experimenting, the creative team arrived at the perfect solution. The trick, they discovered, was to use a much bigger piece of paper for the sculpture, create the texture, and then cut it down to size. The end result was 80 posters, each handmade and unique.

After much painstaking work, the response was all the creative team and client could have hoped for. The posters attracted a lot of attention, got people talking about the bikes, and the bike shop noted that the posters actually made people want to ride and feel the bikes on rough terrains.

Eighty of these posters were produced, and each one was handmade and unique.

Design Firm Iridium, a design agency

Client Genome Canada

Project Promotion to Mark the Discovery of DNA

A Celebration of Science

A three-dimensional model of DNA pinned like a butterfly specimen to a poster. What better way to promote the fiftieth anniversary of the discovery of the DNA structure by Watson and Crick!

Genome Canada, a corporation funding genomics and proteomics research in Canada, wanted to mark the DNA anniversary in a notable way. They turned to Iridium of Ottawa, and asked them to get the attention of a target audience of federal government parliamentarians, health research–related agencies, scientific researchers, and academics.

A Touch of Creativity

The idea (reminiscent of scientists mounting exotic butterflies with pins) was certainly novel: no one had ever seen a poster that showcased the double helix as a natural specimen. Not to mention a poster in which the double helix has rivets holding it in place, as if the helix actually existed physically. It was an idea that immediately resonated with the target audience, who admired the innovation and understood what it was all about. In their eyes, the DNA molecule was treated as a true precious specimen from nature by mounting it on the poster. As in scientific research and laboratory protocol, the full scientific name was then applied to the poster on a simple white label. The poster was sent in a transparent

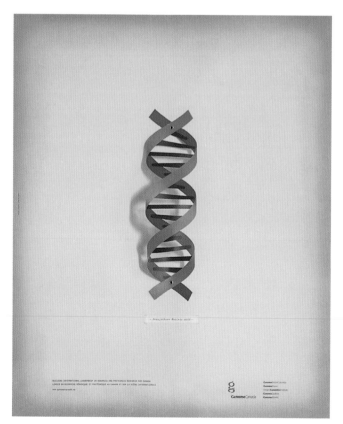

The double helix is actually a three-dimensional model, which is pinned to the poster like a butterfly specimen with metal rivets.

mailing tube echoing a test tube. Also included in the promotional package were a numbered, limited edition card, a book-mark, and a commemorative booklet that touches on the past, present, and future potential of the groundbreaking research being done by Genome Canada.

Finding clear plastic mailing tubes that resembled giant test tubes was no easy feat. Iridium finally was able to track them down from a California supplier. In another painstaking feat in honor of the DNA anniversary, the metal rivets on the poster had to be hand-applied because of the oversized sheet and required special handling and care. In total, 750 promotional packages were created.

The Crowd Cheers

Feedback was marvelous. People were pleased to receive a personalized package with a numbered limited edition card, a bookmark, and a commemorative booklet. This booklet was rather small in size as it had to be inserted into the mailing tube. All the pictures were printed on translucent paper stock, with the article by Watson and Crick published by the journal *Nature* in April 1953 serving as a colorful backdrop. On the cover of the booklet, on the tube, and on the bookmark, there is one simple word—extraordinary—where the letters d, n, and a are highlighted. This simple but effective play on words quickly resonated with the audience. Special box-framed versions of the poster were presented at a Genome Canada commemorative ceremony honoring their chairman and an academic head researcher. The overwhelming positive response from the enthusiastic audience created a rush for the posters from those in attendance. In fact, several requested that their posters be framed in the same display-style box frames as those presented.

All the promotional materials were packaged in clear plastic mailing tubes reminiscent of scientific test tubes.

On the cover of the booklet, on the tube, and on the bookmark, there is one simple word—extraordinary—where the letters d, n, and a are highlighted. According to art director Mario L'Écuyer, "This simple but effective play on words quickly found resonance with the audience."

Wake up and smell the coffee. Slow down, you're moving too fast. Relax, enjoy yourself. Go ahead, indulge. You're worth it.

As you age, you gain perspective. Certain things become easier than they ever were. Perhaps you're more secure in your job, or your children have grown. You seem to be more aware of how life works. You appreciate indulgences, feeling you've worked hard for them. Yet at the same time, there are definite physical signs of aging that need to be confronted. Your knees give out in bad weather, you don't sleep like you used to, you need to give in and get a pair of reading glasses. It's by no means impossible to keep up with life. But it does require a little extra effort.

First and foremost, marketing to the midlife group follows the rule of marketing to anyone: Talk to them as people. These are folks who have come into their own as individuals and who are reflecting on their life. If they are not content with the choices they've made thus far, they're in trouble.

For some purchase decisions, this is a group for whom brand loyalty may be firmly established, and there may be resistance to change. In fact, this is a group of people that often re-adopts brands from childhood. At the same time, they don't see themselves as totally inflexible either. They will try new things if the cues are in place that tell them, "This is something worthy of my time and energy, it is well made, well designed; this is something that's unique to me."

Design Firm **Iridium, a design agency**
Client **Iridium, a design agency**
Project **Self-Promotional Giveaways**

To talk to the target audience in the 46- to 60-year-old age range, Iridium came up with the concept of a Power Nap Pillow.

What better product to give a hard-working older generation than their own custom-created blend of coffee?

Iridium, of Ottawa, Canada, wanted to send out promotional packages to people who had followed their career path and had entered the midlife age range. The people in this target group had successful jobs as group marketing and communications managers of high-tech and government agencies and were still very active with tight deadlines and hectic daily work schedules.

To talk to this group in a way that would feel unique to them, Iridium came up with the concept of a "Power Nap Pillow." This innovative product lets the target resuscitate their energy or reflect on personal burnout—not to mention that it offers the chance to take a discreet nap at their desks. The end result looks less like a promo item than a high-end product—and it comes complete with a 12-page guide on how to take time to rest.

Next, Iridium came out with their own brand of designer coffee, also to be given away to this target. Branded Big Dripper, it was delicious, custom-blended coffee, presented in its own custom-designed bags.

Iridium soon discovered that it wasn't talking to this group of people that was extraordinarily difficult, it was creating a custom coffee blend that people would actually like to drink that was challenging. Iridium studio staff became taste testers of various bean combinations for two weeks before the final Big Dripper blend (a mix of four different coffee beans) was settled upon.

Their target responded with widespread positive response to the fictitious coffee product. Many remarked: "I never heard of this coffee brand before, where can I get some?" Little did they know it was their first and last taste of Big Dripper.

While the design is detail-oriented and sophisticated, copy on the product itself takes a decidedly tongue-in-cheek approach. The coffee was called "radical designer coffee" that was "wind tunnel tested" and "DNA modified for ultimate caffeine wake-up power."

After all, although this group may be a bit older, they still have a sense of humor.

While the design is detail-oriented and sophisticated, copy on the product itself takes a decidedly tongue-in-cheek approach. After all, although this group may be a bit older, they still have a sense of humor.

Design Firm   Iron Design
Client   Iron Design
Project   Self-Promotion

Safety Precautions

When designing a promotion involving flammable materials, please keep the following in mind:

1) Fireworks cannot be sent through the mail unless a designer doesn't mind designing from a jail cell.

2) Matches must always say "close cover before striking"—it's the law.

3) Regulators will not allow you to use coated two-sided stock for the cover, as they feel the matches might ignite coated stock on the inside of the matchbook, but not uncoated stock.

When Iron Design was founded 10 years ago, they got their start designing fun and irreverent packaging for the entertainment industry. Over the years, they've become more focused on branding and identity design, disciplines that demand a more sensitive aesthetic and maturity. Yet they've made an effort to hang on to their original directive to think outside the box and create design solutions that are charged with energy.

In the Event of Industry Stagnation . . .

On the other hand, the past several years have been depressing for the design business. So when it came time to do a much-needed self-promotional piece, Iron Design really wanted to wake up their audience up with a powerful, "let's start something" kind of a message. They definitely did not want this promo to be a static representation of their projects.

From concept to mailing the project took approximately 12 weeks to complete. As usual, self-promo pieces always get pushed to the back burner.

According to Todd Edmonds, creative director on the project, "The promotion gets great reactions from everyone who sees it. And the matches are a great leave-behind at restaurants, bars, clients, bowling alleys, police stations, mechanics shops, brothels, etc."

. . . Think Creatively

What they did want was a vehicle that would allow the design firm to show off work to potential clients who have never heard of them, while making the promotional piece interactive, clever, and unique. Also, a 10-year anniversary was approaching, but Iron wasn't sure the message of "10 years old'" and "hire us" made sense in the same piece. So the idea evolved into custom matches. New contacts get the matchbooks with a mini portfolio inside. Existing clients receive the promo with the ten candles to remind them of Iron's history. The first thought was to send firecrackers along with the matches (see above for why they decided not to), but they settled on candles as a safer bet.

Boxes are recycled paper board jewelry boxes, insert cards are 1-color (metallic silver) on 100-pound dull-coated stock with die-cut slots for candles and matchbooks, 10 black candles are bundled together with red string (giving it that dynamite look), and matchbooks are custom designed.

Meeting Federal Regulations

Finding a vendor for the matchbooks took some research. Iron Design found a couple of vendors on the Web, requested samples, and finally chose Wagner Match in Colorado to produce the matches, based on the variety and quality of their work. Most of the high-end matches they produce are manufactured in Japan, where they can circumvent U.S. federal regulations—but it takes a month longer to complete them. Because Iron needed them in four weeks, they had to settle for U.S.–made matches. In the United States, all matches have to say "close cover before striking" and the matches must be made of cardstock with white tips. In Japan, a wide variety of match colors and tips are available and there's more latitude with matchbook cover text.

The match company assured Iron they could replace the "close cover before striking" line with "keep cover open—live dangerously," but the proof contained the standard saying. Iron decided to go with it for this round, and plans to produce future matches in Japan to allow more control. Live and learn. Next time they might try to live a little more dangerously. But hopefully they'll still stay out of jail.

Matches cost approximately $.16 each, boxes $.75, and cards and vellum about $1.50. An estimate of 600 matchbooks was sent out. Interns, as well as a staff assembly line, helped put them together.

Ten years in business: To celebrate, the recipient gets 10 black candles and a custom-designed matchbook complete with a mini portfolio.

The Flaming Iron: The latest representation of Iron Design—a "simple, colorful, hard-line graphic of a hot iron shooting off like a rocket [that's] easy to work with, representative of [Iron's] house style, and exciting."

The Assignment

"The brief is on your desk. You need to design a holiday greeting card."

Two little sentences that are sure to strike fear into the heart of almost any designer.

The simple Christmas greeting can be one of the most challenging and tension-inducing briefs for a designer. You know it's coming at the same time, year after year, but finding yet another original, special, and festive idea seems almost impossible in the face of what's been done before.

The brief for this particular fear-inducing project was given to Bisqit Design for Hill & Knowlton UK, part of a global PR consultancy with a broad industry sector base. The brief said that the card needed to be able to be sent from both corporate and consumer divisions, and it should be multinational with no distinct religious or cultural bias. It was being sent out to clients worldwide—about 3,500 total.

As it happened, Bisqit Design had three briefs for Christmas cards going at the time and had been experimenting with stand-up trees and folds and die-cuts. The design firm went through two concept stages for this card, without any ideas catching the imagination or fully meeting the brief. So they returned to the simplicity of the materials, print processes, and die-cuts. Reconsidering how a tree could be realized as a die-cut from a different perspective produced an impressive result. The finishing touches of the gloss one-side "white Christmas" and uncoated one-side "green Christmas" flowed immediately. Like many solutions, it looks a lot simpler than the process from which it evolved.

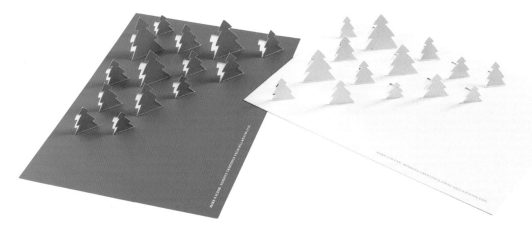

The client originally asked for their logo to be printed on the card, but when it came time to consider the type and text greeting, it was obvious that the full-color logo would detract from the simple effect of the tree scenes. Bisqit recommended the understated typography and spelled out the company name as a more sympathetic approach to the overall design.

Card Specifications

The resulting card is 8¼" x 6" (21 cm x 15 cm), printed on Chromolux 700 (coated one side), matched green one side, silver print both sides, and was mailed in an Exposé pearlescent envelope.

Because of the very short lead time for production, Bisqit knew they wouldn't be able to laser-cut the trees, making the less forgiving die-cutting technique the only option. They wanted to maintain a simple elegance and curvaceous quality in the tree outlines, so they worked closely with the finishing company to make sure the small turns and curves of the trees could be achieved in the metal cutter. A few back-and-forths with PDF die-cut outlines and folds that wouldn't crack when creased, and they hit upon the final design solution.

Now Everyone Wants One

The card was designed and produced for the United Kingdom office of Hill & Knowlton, but when other offices saw the card, they wanted it, too, including the worldwide CEO of Hill & Knowlton based in New York City. The print run of 3,500 was quickly depleted as people scrambled to get their hands on some. Bisqit was asked to a do a reprint, but it would not have been delivered by Christmas. Many recipients called and expressed their delight at being able to send out such a surprising, elegant card to their clients.

Now the question arises: "What in the world are we going to do for *next* year?"

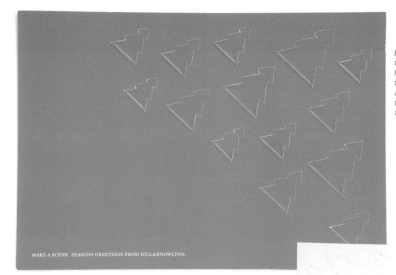

Bisqit designed this holiday card for PR firm Hill & Knowlton UK. From the agreed design route through testing to delivery took about two weeks; design and tests took five days; and printing and finishing took five days.

Bisqit Design's philosophy: "We start with the expectation that something great is what we will achieve. Brave clients, forgiving deadlines and budgets, unexpected moments of inspiration, paper, and the desire to always try again if it isn't quite working are just a few of the potential contributors to success."

Interactive

Although most of the promotions in this category are Web-based, we really mean "interactive" in every sense of the word. Each promotion in this category is designed to require some sort of involvement with the target audience. Not always an easy task, but the best interactive promotions do this to a tee.

Design Firm **Origin**
Client **Claire Monaghan**
Project **Business Card**

Okay, tough guy. You want your own personal fitness instructor? First you'll have to pass the all-important test—being strong enough to open the business card.

That's right. No need to read that sentence again. This is a business card that is actually designed so that it takes sheer physical strength to get at the information.

A "Tough" Client

Self-employed personal fitness instructor Claire Monaghan was looking for a business card and letterhead that would make her memorable among all the other fitness instructors around the Cheshire-area gyms in the United Kingdom. The plain white cards that you could do yourself at a copy shop just weren't for her. She knew that she might be the expert on personal fitness training, but she was no design guru.

Enter Origin.

It looks like an ordinary business card, albeit in a bright, contemporary color scheme. But, wait, there's no information on the outside . . .

. . . and it takes brute strength to open it up to get the information. Perhaps because you need a personal fitness trainer?

A small design firm in the United Kingdom, Origin jumped at the chance to do something that would solve a unique problem. Origin has on its roster big names like Bentley Motors, Rolls-Royce, and Coca-Cola, but there's nothing like a unique design challenge to get the creative juices flowing. In fact, the design firm states as part of their credo on their website: "If you're looking for design with an agency house style, ideas initiated by computer, the latest marketing jargon, then maybe you shouldn't stop here. That's not what Origin is about. If on the other hand you want designers who you can talk to intelligently about strategy and brief, who are talented and commercial enough to create work that excites them, excites you, and impacts your brand then please continue."

So when a client who wants something exciting meets with a design firm who wants to make it exciting, guess what the results are? Monaghan came to the design firm knowing she wanted a card with an overall look that was contemporary as well as unique. The clientele she was going after were young professionals who were active and hip. The rest she left to Adam Lee, designer at Origin.

By Design, a Card That's Hard to Open

From the very start of the project, Lee felt it would be appropriate for the stationery to be physically difficult to open; it was just a question of how. All the creative challenges in this case were mental, not physical. The solution was simple and elegant. By doubling the pages of a four-page card and folding them inside itself, the elastic band could be hidden from the viewer until they tried to open it. A similar method of thinking was applied to the letterhead. A perforated strip was added to the bottom and then stuck into the base of an A4 envelope. The result is that the recipient of the letterhead would have to apply quite an effort to separate the letterhead from the glued strip when pulling it out of the envelope. For both pieces, a contemporary look was achieved by using cool colors and large text in a clean sans serif font.

The Claire Monaghan stationery won a Commendation at the 2002 Roses Design Awards and was also nominated for a Cream Award in the same year. And people all around the health clubs of the United Kingdom are stronger from it.

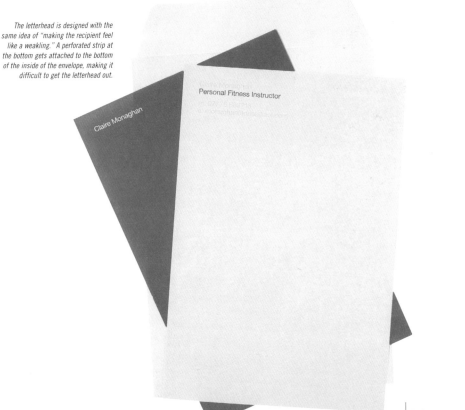

The letterhead is designed with the same idea of "making the recipient feel like a weakling." A perforated strip at the bottom gets attached to the bottom of the inside of the envelope, making it difficult to get the letterhead out.

Personal Fitness Instructor

Claire Monaghan

Instructions for Destruction

Imagine a promotion where you are told you had to smash your keyboard in order to participate. That's exactly what visitors to the online promotion for Diesel International were told to do.

The site was designed by Double You, in Barcelona, Spain. It's all part of Diesel International's campaign "Action for Successful Living." And how does one live more successfully? As copy on the website states, "If you want to live a successful life, you have to fight for it. Shout. This is a wake-up call for the rebel inside you." The Diesel advertising campaign was telling people to stand up, join together, and clamor for those things that could help them to get to more successful living—write more love letters, kiss your neighbors, free every goldfish, help create a world with more green traffic lights, and four-day weekends, for starters.

Double You, of Barcelona, Spain, was charged with creating a microsite under the brand of Diesel International's "Action for Successful Living."

Diesel's interactive website is all about rebellion and the fight for life. In fact, it encourages users to break their keyboards—something Double You actually admitted to doing during site testing.

A visitor to the site soon discovers that smashing the keyboard or shouting at the computer's microphone is the only way to navigate around the site.

Leading an Interactive Rebellion . . .

So Double You was charged with creating a microsite within Diesel's main site, one that would provide a type of interactive training for trendy demonstrators who wanted to voice their rebellion. The aim was to involve people in an unexpected and "out of the box" Diesel interactive experience built around the concept of "Action for Successful Living." Double You knew that what they wanted most was to provoke a strong physical interaction between the users and the microsite. The birth of the idea came during a passionate group brainstorming session where the designers were discussing how to make that happen. Suddenly someone said, "In riots people shout and smash things." Bingo! Let's smash the keyboard! As a user soon discovers, smashing the keyboard or shouting at the computer's microphone is the only way to navigate around the site. And it's certainly one way to "experience successful living," especially for the core target audience of boys and girls ages 17 and 30. This is a group that likes to be surprised. And the site does that by providing a new way of experiencing a website.

. . . Can Be Rewarding

Although it might usually be difficult to sell a promotional idea that incites people to smash their keyboards, in this case, Diesel expected the agency to come back with something like that. The end result is a site that has been one of the most-awarded Diesel advertising action sites in 2002 and 2003. The agency credits the success of the campaign with its guiding philosophy of keeping it simple, creating a dialogue with users, and improving the power of interactivity. And they also admit that they broke two keyboards during the first testing of the site.

The Diesel advertising campaign was telling people to stand up, join together, and take action for successful living—write more love letters, kiss your neighbors, free every goldfish, help create a world with more green traffic lights, and four-day weekends, for starters.

According to Diesel International, "If you want to live a successful life, you have to fight for it. Shout. This is a wake-up call for the rebel inside you."

The target audience is boys and girls ages 17 and 30, a group that likes to be surprised.

Design Firm   Double You

Client   Seat

Project   León Cupra R Promotional Campaign

A Speedy Call to Action

Step on the accelerator. With those simple words, an online promotion for León Cupra R, the fastest and most powerful car ever made by Seat, was born.

The idea came from Double You, a design firm in Barcelona, Spain. Double You has an agency philosophy that vows to "keep improving the power of interactivity." They certainly seem to be succeeding, as indicated by this bit of press: "For the first time in the history of the San Sebastian Festival an interactive agency is awarded as Agency of the Year." And that recognition was at least in part due to their work for Seat's León Cupra R automobile.

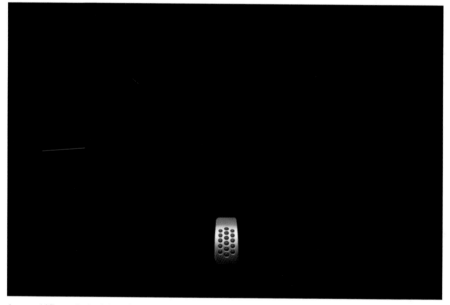

Are you ready? Then go ahead and step on the accelerator.

You'll immediately experience a dizzying rush of type as it flies at you. Blink, and you'll miss what's being said. But no matter. Words just can't equal the feeling of acceleration.

Talk Is Cheap

Double You knew they wanted to make the online experience for potential car buyers a visceral one. They wanted to make the user experience the power and speed of the sports car, rather than just tell them about it.

As Fredo puts it, "We were obsessed with the idea of a site that could make users feel the sensation of speed and power without any kind of blah-blah. We wanted something they could easily experience by themselves. When the team was talking about the first thing you want to do when you test a real sports car everybody agrees on one thing: step on the accelerator."

So take a client who was enthusiastic from the get-go, and combine it with a target audience of middle-class men between the ages of 20 and 30 who enjoy sporty cars. The result is a *The Fast and the Furious*–type experience on the web. A simple iconic accelerator pedal soon turns into a dizzying rush of type flying at the viewer. Blink, and you'll miss what's being said. But no matter. Words just can't equal the feeling of acceleration. The experience is equal to the feeling of pressing the gas pedal of a 210-horsepower Seat Cupra R, with its power and head-spinning speed. Only at the end of the journey is a picture of the car and readable information actually revealed.

The Finish Line

Not only does the target audience enjoy the online experience, but the Cupra R, Sport FR, and Sports Limited models have become the bestsellers of Seat's Leónrange. The promotion has won many awards, and even though it was designed only for the website in Spain, Seat Mexico bought the site for the Mexican market.

Are you ready? Then go ahead and step on the accelerator.

Only at the end of the journey is a picture of the car and readable information actually revealed.

New SEAT León Cupra R

more information at www.seat.es

SEAT
auto emocion

Design Firm deepend
Client bluecashew
Project Website

Fun with Words

First of all, you've got to love the name. Bluecashew is a PR and event production agency, and its name is a play on the name of the founder, Sean Nutley. And with a name so cool and sophisticated, they needed a way of promoting themselves online that would do the name justice.

Design firm deepend was called in to establish bluecashew as a premier player in the world of public relations and event production. An online presence was needed to create a coherent and seamless identity program that elevates the company a notch above their competitors. And yes, deepend helped with the name generation as well.

The conceptual idea of the site was to show how bluecashew works hard for you "behind the scenes." One of the most graphic ways of showcasing that idea is through the sliding doors, which open and close to reveal layers of type, information, and illustrations. The illustrations—with a charming whimsy that's part fashion, part art—add to the behind the scenes concept by allowing the people depicted to remain faceless yet somehow imbued with personality. The combined result is a format that allows the dynamic events and promotions organized by bluecashew to be showcased without needing to be overly specific.

The sophistication and elegance of the execution speaks volumes in a marketplace where the competition can come across as being too corporate or not trendy. It seems particularly appropriate for a target audience composed of higher level decision-making executives in the industries of fashion, media and communications, marketing, art and design, publishing, and benefits.

Bluecashew is a PR and event production agency, and its name is a play on the name of the founder, Sean Nutley. And with a name so cool and sophisticated, they needed a way of promoting themselves online that would do the name justice.

The conceptual idea of the site was to show how bluecashew works hard for you behind the scenes. One of the most graphic ways of showcasing that idea is through the sliding doors, which open and close to reveal layers of type, information, and illustrations.

Everything's Symbolic

Because details are everything in design, one small one seems worth pointing out. Deepend chose to make an icon out of the letters ec—the bridge between the word *blue* and the word *cashew*. This ec icon was designed to function similarly to the © or ® symbol, in which it could be placed after a client's name. This device helps to reinforce the behind the scenes aspect of the brand concept.

The illustrations were created by one of the in-house designers, and they came about from the notion that the company needed to create a stylized way to portray what bluecashew does without getting too specific. It helps that the illustrations give it a unique look, a look that communicates the brand's essence in an elegant and sophisticated manner.

And it is certainly befitting a company with the name of bluecashew.

It helps that the illustrations give it a unique look, a look that communicates the brand's essence in an elegant and sophisticated manner.

Memo to self: Lose weight. Stop smoking. Save money. Every year around this time that little voice enters our head. We may not give it much regard, but it's in there. The voice that tells us to face our future this year with resolve.

And so starts this lovely little booklet of New Year's resolutions, sent out as a promo piece by IE Design. But it's New Year's resolutions with a twist, or should we say a flip? The piece is actually a miniature flip book with which readers interact to form their own New Year's resolutions, which are surprising and inspiring.

Trust Your Wardrobe

Every year, IE Design produces an extravagant holiday mailing for friends, clients, and contacts. The piece serves not only as a promotion for the studio, but as a creative release for the design team—a showcase of the design firm's talents. For this year in particular, they wanted the mailing to be "poignant and thoughtful, but still depict a bit of wit and playfulness," according to Marcie Carson, project designer.

Question the Government

The small format (3½" x 4¾" [9 cm x 12 cm]) and die-cut pages allow the reader to flip through the book to create an array of New Year's resolution combinations. These permutations cover the spectrum, from "Stop—Fingernail Biting" to "Love—The Neighbor's Dog" to "Celebrate—Your Family." The best thing about it is that the reader gets to create messages that are uniquely personal.

IE Design's promotional holiday booklet titled "Re:Solutions" successfully addresses the many emotions associated with the holiday season.

Forgive Your Car

The target audience is particularly diverse, so it was important that the language and image selection appealed to most anyone. The word choices and corresponding photos took a long time to select, especially since the designers were working on a very tight budget and only wanted to use images from their existing royalty-free library.

Focus on Your Family

In the end, this elegant concept complemented the format. As Carson puts it, "It's one of those times that form and function meld together perfectly."

Celebrate the Neighbor's Dog

Each year IE Design receives numerous phone calls and email messages regarding their holiday mailings. Although it's not clear if an awarded project is a direct result of the holiday mailing, it's still a great way to keep creativity in front of clients.

Memo to self: Do what you are able. And always, always remember to take time out to enjoy. Happy holidays from the friendly folks at IE Design.

It's New Year's resolutions with a twist—a flip of the hand and an almost infinite number of funny, poignant, and quirky resolutions can be created.

Design Firm · Dotzero Design
Client · Dotzero Design
Project · Invitation and T-Shirt

"Come one, come all! Gather 'round and see the Dotzero crew with your own eyes—prepare to be amazed and astonished! Anyone with a ticket is guaranteed to walk away with a prize!"

Sounds like something a sleazy carnival guy would say, right? Well, don't worry, this promotion has nothing to do with circuses or carnivals—although there is a giant fish involved, but we'll get to that later. For now, let's talk about parties.

Time to Celebrate

Dotzero, a Portland, Oregon–based graphic design outfit, had just relocated to a new office, and it was time for a party. To promote the open house, they wanted to design a piece that could serve as both an invitation and an announcement, as well as create T-shirts to hand out on the night of the event. Their target audience included friends and family members of the Dotzero community and other designers in the field. Of course, the design firm called upon their own creative team for this project; why hire someone else when the most qualified people for the job are in house?

Announcing the Open House

The front of the invitation was heavy on earth tones—it was composed mainly of browns and tans—and featured a sequence of shots that showed the location of the office. Each frame brought the viewer progressively closer to Dotzero's headquarters; the first shot was a distant view of the building, the next one was of the lobby entrance, and so on.

The flip side read, "Our mothers have always said, why don't you move out of the house? So, we did. Announcing our new office right above Mother's (Bistro)." Jon Wippich, the creative director at Dotzero, explains that Mother's Bistro is a sort of landmark in the area, so they decided to work it into the copy in a creative and humorous way.

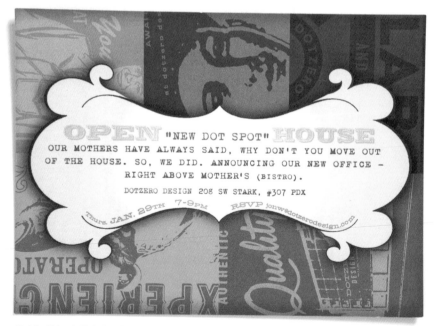

The folks at Dotzero had just relocated to a new office and
set out to design an invitation promoting their open house.

The final component of the invitation was a ticket to the open house. It was attached to the actual invitation, adding an element of tactility and interactivity. The ticket resembled an old-fashioned movie pass and carried more humorous copy: "Come topless if you want. Or not. We'll give you a free T-shirt to wear home. Bring this ticket and select from five different designs."

Something to Take Home

The second half of Dotzero's open house preparations involved churning out five T-shirt designs for the event. One of those T-shirts showed a man riding on the back of a giant fish. Its copy read, "Experienced operators." Another T-shirt announced, "Authentic quality design since several years ago!" And although each of the T-shirts was different, they all had a vintage, retro feel about them, with slogans reminiscent of old print advertisements.

A Challenging Business

Dotzero encountered some slight pratfalls, er, obstacles and challenges in the production stage. Wippich recalls they had to determine which ink palettes were best suited for which fabric colors—and, as an added complication, women's shirts came in different colors than the men's. As for the invite, the creative team originally wanted the ticket to resemble a postage stamp, with a rough, staggered edge—but that was too pricey. Wippich explains, "We changed the design to be more like a movie ticket, with the quarter circles cut on the corners."

Phew! Life under the creative big top can certainly be unpredictable. Thankfully, there were no reported cases of elephant tramplings.

The old-fashioned movie tickets added
an element of tactility and interactivity
to the open house invitations.

The creative team designed several T-shirts for
the open house to hand out as giveaways—
and although each one showed off a unique
graphic, all the designs had a
vintage, retro feel.

Design Firm   Wasserman & Partners Advertising Inc.
Client   Whistler Blackcomb Mountain
Project   Poster/Web Ad

How do you come up with a great design concept when there's simply no time to do so? Kai Clemen of Wasserman & Partners explains how they did it: "We came up with the idea somewhere between ummmm and errr."

Whistler Blackcomb Mountain (WB) was experiencing a shortfall in holiday bookings at many of the major hotel and accommodation destinations. To kickstart bookings, WB asked Wasserman to create an online viral campaign to drive people to book online.

There's No Time Like the Present

The request was simple: come up with something clever, funny, and simple, something people would forward to their friends. There was only one snag; the project had to be completed immediately. The Web ad needed to be up and running within the week.

With such little notice the folks at Wasserman quickly realized they would need to talk to a local market—people who could take advantage of the deal now. And those people, they found, tended to avoid Whistler Blackcomb because they perceived it to be overcrowded and way too expensive. So Wasserman had to adjust that perception and tell people there was plenty of room available at a great price.

"Hello, hello, can you hear me? You just got knocked out. Next time, wear a helmet."

Wasserman & Partners in Vancouver, Canada, wanted to illustrate how much kick-ass air time you can get at Whistler Blackcomb.

The limited time frame meant the production had to be very simple. With little time and money, the design firm decided to illustrate the piece, which helped give it a young and comic feel. They wanted it to be irreverent to appeal to the local markets' cynical perception of tourists cluttering around their mountain. Plus, Clemen adds, "it made us laugh, and that's always a good sign."

With the clock ticking, they had a local Flash artist record his voice to create some hilarious, low-budget sound effects for the cursor icons. It gave the piece that extra kick for talk value and encouraged users to pass the URL along to one friend, and then another, and another.

A Rush Project Has Benefits All Its Own

The good thing about such a speedy turnaround time is that things just have to happen to stay on schedule. There were no production issues, no time for client revisions, and no time to overthink it. All in all, it took about two days to conceptualize, two days to execute, and one day to approve.

To tell people that helmet rentals were available, we get the view from someone just recovering consciousness. The second was designed to promote how "kick ass" Whistler Blackcomb's terrain park is, how much air time you can get, and basically how cool it is. The promo shows a snowboarder doing a trick in the air—and the view is from inside an airplane cockpit. "Young kids like that sort of stuff," says Clemen nonchalantly. Two stock images from Getty pictures were combined to create the simple effects. The ad is just a neat and simple idea, which is what most ads should be.

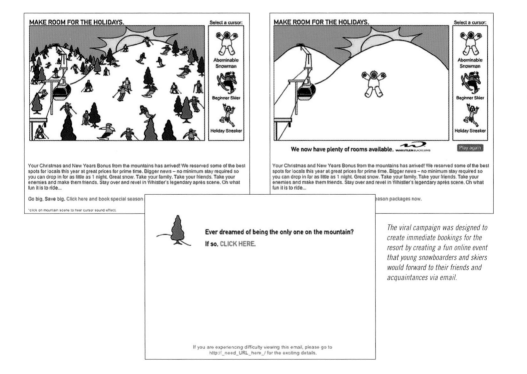

The viral campaign was designed to create immediate bookings for the resort by creating a fun online event that young snowboarders and skiers would forward to their friends and acquaintances via email.

Design Firm   Nesnadny + Schwartz
Client   International Spy Museum
Project   Website

Spies Like Us

Espionage is a funny thing. Its fantasy and reality are so blurred that we don't even know where to draw the line. There are so many spy movies, so many tall tales about spies from all over the world, and so many spy jokes and gadgets and clichés, but what do we really know about the profession?

The International Spy Museum tries to crack some of these codes (no pun intended). The Museum is impressive not only for what it contains but also because it is "the first museum in the United States solely dedicated to espionage" and the only one in the world that provides a global perspective of this secretive profession, a profession that has shaped history and continues to influence world events. As the website proudly proclaims, "The International Spy Museum features the largest collection of international spy-related artifacts ever placed on public display. The stories of individual spies, told through film, interactives, and state-of-the-art exhibits provide a dynamic context to foster an understanding of espionage and its impact." Founder and chairman Milton Maltz adds, "The International Spy Museum is more than history—more than information or entertainment—its mission is to reflect the significance of intelligence as a critical component of national security."

Wow! Heavy stuff. But it's also . . . well . . . fun.

The problem with designing a website for something that's so monumental is that you have a lot to live up to. That was the challenge faced by design firm Nesnadny + Schwartz when they were hired by the International Spy Museum to create their website.

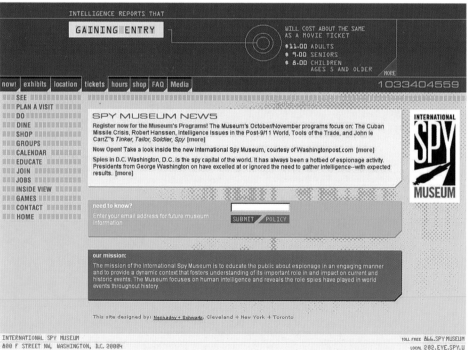

The mission: To educate the public about espionage in an engaging manner and to foster an understanding on the importance of espionage on current and historic events.

Mission, Accomplished

To start this mission, Nesnadny + Schwartz determined what they wanted the website to accomplish. These goals included: create a valuable tool for multiple audiences; create awareness; give attendees and the media a visual hook; introduce the new logo and brand efficiently; and provide users with up-to-date news, games, and a countdown clock for the grand opening of the museum. They also posed the challenge to themselves to make the website "historical, yet contemporary; simple, yet iconographic, as well as memorable." As the process began, Nesnadny + Schwartz made sure to keep the design for the Spy Museum's logos, brochures, and website all the same to create a unity between all forms of design for the museum. The project took six months to complete.

As you sign on to the website, you feel excited immediately, as you are told that your mission is to "gather information and discover secrets." If you answer "yes" to the question "Do you accept?" then you are let past the introductory page. When users visit the site, they can "cover, break codes, identify disguised spies, and become subjects of covert surveillance throughout their visit."

So sit yourself down, pour yourself a martini—shaken, not stirred—and become a spy for a day from the safety of your own home.

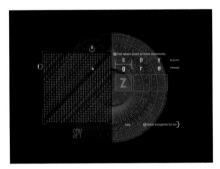

An elaborate secret code allows visitors to the site a way to compose encrypted messages and send them to a friend.

This engaging, important, and, well, secretive-looking website that Nesnadny + Schwartz designed for the International Spy Museum encourages viewers to "gather information and discover secrets." Its no-nonsense technical feel is the perfect look for this fascinating new museum.

Design Firm Jack Morton Worldwide

Client ScanSoft

Project Speechify Challenge

"You are the weakest link. Got it? And wait, there's more—you don't know Jack!"

A New Technology, A New Kind of Promotion

Tune in to a modern game show, and you're guaranteed to sharpen your tongue by picking up a handy new phrase or two for your arsenal of verbal insults. But just how sharp are your listening skills? Well, there's a game for that, too—you can test out your aural acuity by playing ScanSoft's Speechify Challenge.

Jack Morton Worldwide, a New York City marketing firm, created the interactive Flash-based game as a promotion for Speechify, a product of ScanSoft. In brief, it was a new text-to-speech (TTS) technology that converted strings of text into natural-sounding human voices. Although Speechify wasn't the first computerized speech engine to hit the market, it was able to simulate inflections more accurately and convincingly than its predecessors.

Getting Down to Business

However, ScanSoft's new TTS engine wasn't developed merely for entertainment purposes; it was, in fact, designed specifically for professional use. Anya Beaupre, the producer of brand marketing at Jack Morton, explains, "The target audience consisted of clients that ScanSoft believed would have the greatest need for text-to-speech technology—virtually any business with a large portion of its customer base calling in for automated information, such as airlines, banks, and credit card companies."

The Speechify Challenge is an interactive, Flash-based game that Jack Morton Worldwide created to promote ScanSoft's new text-to-speech technology.

Jack Morton adopted a game show format for their promotion as a way to engage users while educating them on the capabilities of Speechify.

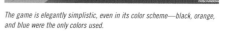

The game is elegantly simplistic, even in its color scheme—black, orange, and blue were the only colors used.

Take a Game Break

Jack Morton decided to adopt a game show format for ScanSoft's interactive promotion as a way to engage clients while educating them on the capabilities of Speechify. Potential clients were encouraged to visit the site and play the game: for each of six multiple-choice questions, players would first hear a sound bite, then decide whether it was a text-to-speech voice or a real human voice. As a bonus feature, users could sample a clip demonstrating Speechify's capabilities at work in their specific business or industry, but they had to finish the game first!

From a graphic standpoint, the game's design was elegantly simple; the only colors used were black, orange, and blue. And instead of live photography, Jack Morton used all digital artwork. Incidentally, this project was their first in which all the digital video they shot would later be converted into Macromedia Flash. The host of the Speechify Challenge, although a mere silhouette, was realistically rendered. That unique visual element, in combination with the modest use of color, resulted in a somewhat mysterious, yet alluring, user interface.

The Good News First

Because all game scores were recorded into a database, ScanSoft was able to track players' success in distinguishing real voices from digitized ones. On average, they found, people only responded correctly to about three or four of the six questions. As Beaupre concludes, "Most people still couldn't tell the difference between a text-to-speech voice and a human one—good news for ScanSoft."

It's a shame the Speechify Challenge wasn't a certified hearing test—then, it would have been great news for ear doctors, too.

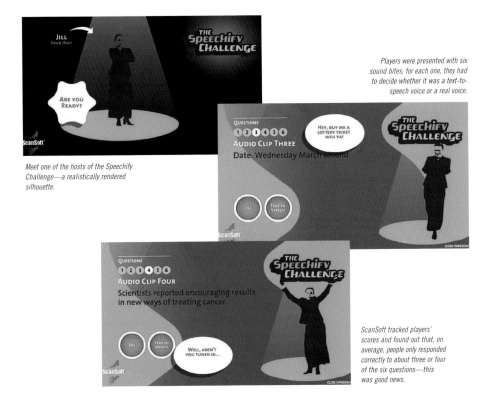

Players were presented with six sound bites; for each one, they had to decide whether it was a text-to-speech voice or a real voice.

Meet one of the hosts of the Speechify Challenge—a realistically rendered silhouette.

ScanSoft tracked players' scores and found out that, on average, people only responded correctly to about three or four of the six questions—this was good news.

Design Firm   **Kolegram Design**
Client   **Kolegram Headlight**
Project   **360 Circle Promo**

A Perfect Circle

The perfect circle. Throughout the ages, the circle has been a highly symbolic and almost mystical shape. And it's also the perfect symbol for an innovative promotional piece designed to show off a 360-degree virtual tour.

Kolegram is a design firm in Canada. Headlight is a photography studio. Together, they wanted to send out a promotional piece that would tell people they were partnering up to provide 360-degree motion photography to those who wanted it. The package was sent to potential clients—those most likely to have a need for the sophisticated photography and those that would benefit from 3-D Web display of their product or service. Organizations such as museums, tourist attractions, parks, and clients in the automobile, retail, and technology industries were the target market.

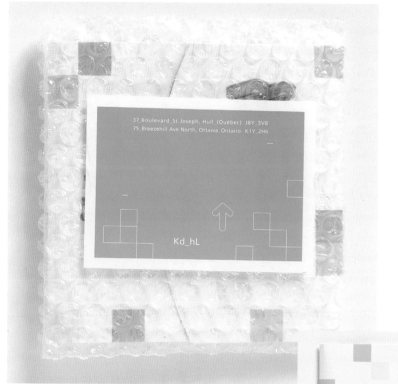

The bubble-wrap envelope is just the beginning
of this intriguing package.

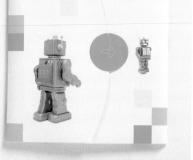

The piece is a self-promotion for
Kolegram (a design firm) and
Headlight (a photography studio).
Headlight produces the virtual tours
for clients and Kolegram produces
all the design elements.

Interesting Even Before It's Opened

The piece is interesting from the moment it arrives in the mail because it is packed in a bubble-wrap envelope that allows the design to peek through. Bubble wrap, as you may know, is inherently funny. The designers had immediately made a choice that was part design, part functional—the bubble wrap protected the actual CD-ROM enclosed in the mailing process, but it also looked intriguing. Upon opening up the envelope, the recipient sees a cute 1950s-style robot and green pixels. The pixel is a nice design element, but according to Mike Teixeira, creative director on the project, it also signified the birth of the original idea. They wanted to show that it all starts with a pixel and then ultimately a 360-degree virtual tour is born. The idea comes to life as the recipient continues the unfolding process and the piece ends with a perfect circle. A flat, panoramic view of 360 photography graces the outer edge, with an actual CD-ROM sitting snugly in the middle. The CD gives a demo of the actual tour. As the copy states, "Visitors are immersed in authenticity; the result, a genuine comprehension of your environment or product."

A Few Small Headaches

Producing the piece had its share of headaches. First, a glitch occurred in the folding process. The designers found that the thickness of the paper combined with the unusual task of folding something that's final flat shape would be a circle meant that it was difficult to get a nice, neat, flat folded piece. A double line score fixed it.

Another interesting thing about the production process is that once the round shaped die cut was done, there were left-over bits of paper along the edges. The only way to clean the edges was by paper sanding it.

Not so easy to form a perfect circle after all. No wonder it's so symbolic.

This piece is appealing because of its unusual die cut. It forms a perfect circle, which is a visual way to show the three-dimensional environment on a two-dimensional piece of paper.

The reaction to the promotion was very good but due to virtual tour production costs, the market wasn't ready to jump in yet.

Universal Wisdom

"Form follows function—that has been misunderstood. Form and function should be one, joined in a spiritual union."

Those were the wise words of Frank Lloyd Wright, master architect of the late nineteenth and early twentieth centuries. Although it's safe to assume he was describing his technique as an architect, his philosophy is an important one to consider even outside the realm of blueprinting. And it's not just a coincidence that some of the best promotional tools employ this exact methodology.

How to Promote a Restoration Effort

Which brings us to Minneapolis, Minnesota—home of the Design Guys and the Willey House. The former is a design firm that provides its clients with a wide range of services, including branding, advertising, product development, and website design. The latter is Wright's 1934 creation for a client by the name of Malcolm Willey.

But what do the two have in common? Design Guys purchased Wright's creation in 2002 with plans to restore it. Shortly afterward, the Minneapolis design firm put their own architectural expertise to use and created a website detailing their recent acquisition.

Potential visitors to the website include Wright enthusiasts, historians, architects, and students. Art director Steve Sikora explains, "The purpose of the site is to inform to almost any degree the visitor is willing to go." And, as there had been both local and national concern surrounding the preservation of the house, the site effectively assured visitors that the house would be properly rescued. To invite traffic, the site was linked to numerous other Frank Lloyd Wright websites, and its URL was included with stories published on the Willey House.

Visitors to the website include Wright enthusiasts, historians, architects, and students.

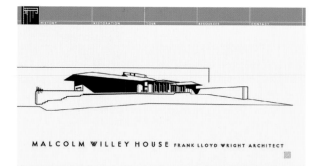

The site's elegance and simplicity make it unmistakable to users that they have stumbled across Frank Lloyd Wright in cyberspace.

Site Architecture

One of the most effective design elements at work on the website is the use of colors and typeface; they make it unmistakable to the user that he or she has stumbled across Frank Lloyd Wright in cyberspace. Graphically, the site is also very geometric; linear and rectangular forms serve as the main building blocks for each page, resulting in a layout that complements Wright's architectural style.

But aesthetics aren't the website's only strong suit. Want to read up on the history of the Willey House? Just click the History tab from the main menu and gain access to a timeline, a historical archive, and even recollections from previous owners of the house. Under the Restoration link, users will find a journal tracking the progress of the project. There, they can also view the various restoration plans in store for the house, in order of priority.

Still, the most unique feature on the site is the massing model—a three-dimensional blueprint engine that shows, in more than 30 stages, how the house was laid out and later constructed. This section of the site is extremely memory intensive, so low-bandwidth users may not be able to view it properly. But, as Sikora explains, it was a sacrifice they had to make: "We made a decision early on that we wanted the site to do things others have not. On a phone line, most of the site is viewable, but the highlights would [require] very long load times. Nevertheless, we decided to be forward looking rather than backward compatible."

Continuing the Tradition

Sikora says that they have received some praise, though more often it is for the restoration of the house than for the website itself. Nonetheless, he explains, "Guests frequently see the house through the lens of the site without being distracted by the site," which establishes that perfect union between form and function. Wright would have been proud of these Design Guys.

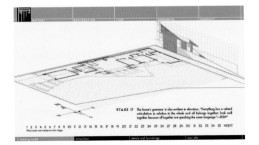

The Tour section includes a virtual tour, which takes users through the interior of the Willey House.

Aesthetics aren't the site's only strong suit, and this informative restoration journal is evidence of that.

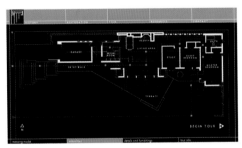

Arguably the most unique feature on the site, the massing model is an interactive blueprint that shows the various stages of Wright's creation.

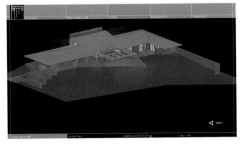

Some portions of the site are extremely memory intensive, but as Sikora explains, "We decided to be forward looking rather than backward compatible."

An optimistic future. Surrounding ourselves with people we love. A roof over our heads. A garden. Food. Clothing. Shelter. Having your basic needs met is important at any age, but perhaps even more so as we grow older. We all want to retain as much self-sufficiency as we can, yet we realize that as we get older, we simply need some help in some areas. How do we strike that balance? And how do we keep from worrying about a future that we know is growing shorter? How do we maintain our peace of mind that we've struggled so hard to achieve all our lives?

Camden provides housing for people. With more than 50,000 apartment homes in 145 communities across the United States, Camden has long been the leader in apartment home living. Many of these are apartment complexes are designed to fill the needs of those 60 years of age and up. However, Camden's image and name had not changed in more than two decades. As the multifamily residential real estate leader, the brand needed to evolve to stay on top.

Design Firm **Metal**
Client **Camden**
Project **Camden Brochure**

To create a lifestyle brand that would appeal to seniors, Metal created an optimistic, light, and airy feel that would bring peace of mind to the target audience. There is a certain comfort in still being able to ask "Why?" and "Why not?"

Working with a marketing team from Camden, Metal came up with a positioning for apartment living that creates a bright, inviting, and new lifestyle brand. Building a new corporate soul for the Camden brand involves everything from a new corporate paper system, a website, a massive intranet and extranet system design and development, a multitude of collateral/marketing materials, an interactive CD, the annual report, and an advertising campaign. The quantity of brochures produced is quite sizable, at times numbering up to 100,000 for a single print run. The brochures target residents as well as investors and employees. The design uniqueness and the materials used in the pieces is what makes the brochures so appealing.

Targeting seniors as a group means finding ways to make things that could be cliché not so cliché. As a lifestyle brand, it was important to show people within the Camden environment—for example, a woman is shown interacting with her grandson and his Gameboy. No fear of staying current for the older set here! Yet the surroundings are soft, warm, comforting, and the expression on the boy's face is a little poignant. The photo works so well because it could be a real moment. There is also a sense of peacefulness about the garden photo. It's lovely and quiet and rich, and the copy explains how Camden will perform all the maintenance, leaving you with peace of mind.

Peace of mind. Such a nice thing to have at any time, but especially as we grow older.

the yard

go ahead

what maintenance?
we do it for you

maintenance?

forget about mowing the yard too

Rich, inviting—and very, very peaceful.

the convenience

micky

loves his gameboy
and taking naps after
playing hard on the game

The attention to detail in this photo makes it seem very real and thus appealing. Everything feels comfortable — from the softness of the couch to the textured shirt, to the way that grandmother and grandson are interacting.

phyllis

can do laundry anytime
her grandson wants to nap

Design Firm **IE Design**

Client **IE Design**

Project **Creative Solutions Self-Promotion**

Involve the Reader

In this day and age, when "interactive" immediately calls to mind the latest new website with bells and whistles, is it possible for a regular, printed-on-paper brochure to be "interactive"?

IE Design proves that it is.

"Creative Solutions" is the name given to the design firm's corporate capabilities brochure, and it certainly is an apt name. Everything about it is a little unexpected, starting with the size. IE wanted the piece to be slightly oversized, but still able to fit in a file cabinet, so they chose to make it 9½" x 12" (24 cm x 30.5 cm). The brochure gets mailed to client contacts or anyone inquiring about IE Design. They also use it as a leave-behind at new client pitches or meetings.

Tell a Story

First and foremost, IE wanted the piece to captivate the reader, a task deemed even more important than conveying a bit of the design firm's personality and talents. The decision was made to have a "story" run horizontally through the book with interesting anecdotes and print techniques. It was a successful way to not only visually showcase their portfolio, but the format of the piece displayed IE's creativity.

With die cuts, short sheets, unusual printing techniques, and varied paper stock throughout, the piece feels truly "interactive" in the best possible sense of the word. Marcie Carson of IE Design explains, "The interactive quality speaks to our personality as well as our creativity. We like to have fun with what we do. I think the playful format conveyed this."

What makes you tick? What makes you laugh? What makes you inspired? Although most design firms speak only about themselves, this brochure uses clever ideas like this small, three-page insert to talk to the reader directly about what they like.

In the End

There was a slight glitch in getting the logo on the cover to be dark enough, but that was nothing compared to the timing. Even when the design firm *is* the client—or possibly *because* the design firm is the client—there is often a problem meeting the deadline. The brochure ended up not being printed and sent out until a couple of months after they hoped it would.

When asked how long it took to produce, Marcie responds with the sigh of a true creative: "I was totally absorbed by this brochure. It was all I thought about night and day for weeks. It's a huge challenge to design for yourself. Without making it sound overly dramatic, it really becomes a process of self-awareness and soul searching. It felt like a year, but it was probably only about two months."

The piece ended up being quite costly, especially for such a small studio. But here too, "creative solutions" ended up being important. The printer gave them a great deal. And they also cooked up a little cost-saving juggling, as all the short sheets were printed at a small mom-and-pop printer and shipped to the larger printer for binding.

Although Marcie is ready to embark upon the process again by designing a new promotional piece, IE's director of business development is screaming, "No!" He says it's the best tool he has.

Even on the cover, the small arrow-like die cut speaks of the various design surprises to be found within.

The arrow theme continues as silver graphic design elements over a sepia tone photo. This spread highlights client testimonials.

A functional yet innovative way to always be able to keep the piece updated—the case studies are printed separately and put in a pocket so they can be adapted as needed without redoing the entire brochure.

Design Firm **Blue River Design**
Client **MetroMail**
Project **We Love Mail Campaign**

Everyone Loves a Good Game

Anyone who has ever played Spin the Bottle—a game popularized by kiss-hungry kids and drunken students—might think that it would be difficult to sell a promotion based on that game to a direct mail client.

Luckily, even direct mail marketers have a sense of humor.

Blue River Design, in Newcastle, England, had gotten a brief from their client, MetroMail. The brief was to attract the attention of targeted direct mail marketers and to introduce them to MetroMail in a lighthearted and unusual way so they would be receptive to a follow-up telephone call. They wanted to do something that would stand out in the mailing industry (which usually promotes themselves in a dry, straightforward way) and show that MetroMail was passionate about the work they do.

It was that idea of being passionate that sparked the idea behind the promotions. The first, the Engagement Ring mailer, consists of a red ring box, a toy engagement ring, and a small leaflet inside the box. It was mailed out in a small white box that was sealed with a MetroMail branded sticker. A booklet inside offered the receiver a "proposal" to form a meaningful relationship with MetroMail.

MetroMail's We Love Mail campaign has featured a range of different pieces since it was implemented by Blue River, including press advertising, exhibition stands, a calendar, interactive flash games, and multiple printed and three-dimensional mailers. These two provocative mailers demonstrate the company's passion for direct mail.

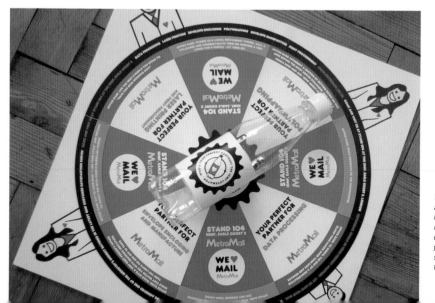

To keep the humor of the piece amid the sales benefits of MetroMail, the game featured a number of Office Dares. An example: "Say to your boss 'like your style' and pretend to shoot him with double-barreled fingers."

Game Time

The Spin the Bottle game mailer was sent to targeted direct mail marketers as an invitation to MetroMail's booth at a large direct marketing trade fair in the UK.

It was mailed out in a large, bright red tube that contained a branded bottle, a game board with playing instructions, and a reply mechanism. The aim of the MetroMail version of the game was to spin the bottle to find your perfect partner at the trade fair. The perfect partner, of course, was none other than MetroMail. The information on the game board outlined different benefits and services of choosing MetroMail and also featured office dares (such as "Ask the next eight people you work with 'Have you been working out?'") to make the mailer a bit provocative.

Blue River had no qualms about presenting such a provocative concept to the client. In fact, they were confident that both the Engagement Ring mailer and the Spin the Bottle mailer would be received well and were reluctant to submit a more toned-down version. MetroMail, the client, appreciated the humor and felt that it fit well with the overall campaign concept of "We Love Mail." They understood that the humor in this case is simply a vehicle to make MetroMail stand out from the crowd before the receiver is immediately presented with the attractive benefits of using MetroMail's services.

Addicted to Gaming

Blue River received immediate feedback from MetroMail that one of the UK's leading media companies called to say that office staff had been playing Spin the Bottle for an entire morning. It was the only direct mail invite that didn't end up in the bin. See what a little passion can do!

Although humor is often a hard sell (with some people simply not getting the joke), the mailers and the campaign as a whole have a great deal of serious sales messages and customer benefits.

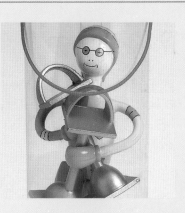

PART III

IMAGERY CAMPAIGN
(visual puns)
TELEGRAPHS CLIENT INTO THE NEW CENTURY

The Client

HGV Design Consultants was given the job of creating an identity that would take the Telegraph Colour Library into the next century. The company's image needed a substantial facelift, having inherited its logotype from the *Telegraph* newspaper, which used an old-fashioned gothic script. The Library, which banks photographic images for sale to the media, graphic designers, and art buyers, needed a mark that would rejuvenate its appeal and assert its independence from the newspaper of the same name.

ABOVE: **Images change as do their letter positions wherever the *Telegraph* logotype appears.**

The Brief

Designers conducted a visual audit of the competition searching for commonalties, differences, and inspiration, and in doing so, discovered that despite the arsenal of imagery at their disposal, none of the other photo libraries in the United Kingdom used graphics in their identity. If HGV designers could craft an identity from the Library's photographic imagery, they would not only differentiate their client from its competitors, but showcase the variety and quality of its products as well.

LEFT: **Proofs are sent in this yellow envelope where a loupe replaces the second *e* in Telegraph.**

BELOW: **No detail was overlooked as demonstrated by this mailing envelope with the copy "urgent photographic submissions enclosed," which is reinforced by an image of a rocket replacing the *R* in Telegraph.**

NT:
Telegraph Colour Library

DESIGN FIRM:
HGV Design Consultants

ART DIRECTORS:
Pierre Vermeir, Jim Sutherland

DESIGNERS:
Dominic Edmunds, Mark Weathcroft, Pierre Vermeir, Jim Sutherland

PHOTOGRAPHER:
John Edwards

CAMPAIGN RUN:
1998 through 1999

TARGET MARKET:
Media, designers, art buyers

new year, same
staff, new identity,
same service,
new images, same
day delivery, new
catalogues, same
quality, new cds,
same sweets...

telegraph colour library
the innovation centre
225 marsh wall
london e14 9fx
sales direct line 0171 293 2929
fax 0171 538 3309

Selling to Designers

What would catch the eye and appeal to discriminating, visually literate media, design, and advertising agencies? That was the question at hand when HGV took on the assignment. The Library's target market is regularly assaulted with all kinds of gimmicky mailers and graphics that not only seize your attention, but refuse to let go. What could designers possibly dream up that would have the ability to compete visually in such a competitive market?

Designers grappled with the problem before finding their solution in taking a fresh approach based on using the library's own products as photographic puns to express its innovation and creativity. The idea was a winner. Not only did it look fresh and innovative, but with each successive incarnation of the logo, another image from the Telegraph Colour Library's bank of photos was advertised—successfully demonstrating just how varied the collection is.

Creating Visual Puns

Designers tackled the job with a mix of design savvy and humor. The result: a logotype that uses cutout photographic images as visual puns to replace letters within the word *telegraph*. Only the letters *t* and *h* would remain as static sentinels to give consistency to the campaign, the other letters in the word would be interchanged with images as deemed appropriate.

"The new identity had to communicate the experience of dealing with the Telegraph account handlers all of whom are extremely helpful, friendly, and interested in the creative services sector. Ideally, the identity also had to express the size of the image bank, a staggering 300,000 images to choose from," says Pierre Vermeir, who worked on the project along with other creatives. "Using cut-out images communicated fun and friendliness and was flexible enough to demonstrate the versatility and breadth of the library."

ABOVE AND RIGHT: **A post-card mailing rings in the New Year and proclaims a new identity and new images, but with the same staff and the same quality. Surprisingly, the logotype on the front of the card replaces all but two letters with photographic images.**

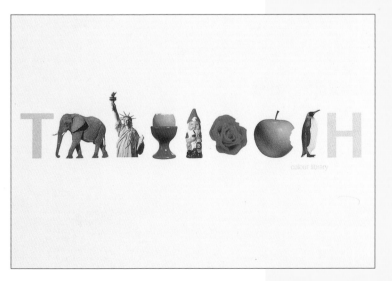

Cut-Outs That Cut Up

The team individually designed each item of stationery and promotional marketing materials and fully exploited the new identity, capitalizing on the fun aspect of the identity and tying in the copy, images, and visual puns to the logotype. Equally important, the library's friendly service and immense range is suggested through the photographic puns used throughout the campaign.

All of the marketing materials were targeted to the creative services industry, business-to-business, and publishing sectors, and included product catalogs, direct mail pieces, print advertising, calendars, and gift items.

Designers didn't randomly pull images for the identity but took care to match the right visual pun with its relevant application. For instance, the logotype shown on an invoice uses a cutout image of an abacus while mailing envelopes showcase either a mailbox or a pigeon.

The print advertising demonstrates designers' wit by using existing images, which interact with the logotype, such as a child reaching for the udders of a cow.

The library's Elvis mailer uses existing *Telegraph* images of Las Vegas combined with related copy and photographs of an Elvis impersonator to promote a competition where the winner receives a trip to the gaming capital.

The dog and bone mailer also uses existing *Telegraph* images and relevant copy to promote the launch of a new catalog. The sports image catalog relies upon a pool game's eight ball set within the logotype; the piece was launched at a party held at a sports bar where Telegraph Colour Library clients received a magic eight ball as a gift.

RIGHT AND BELOW: Designers packed plenty of wit into the library's holiday greeting card by creating doodles on photographs of staffers and including their personal signatures inside. Here, a reindeer injects some holiday spirit into the logotype.

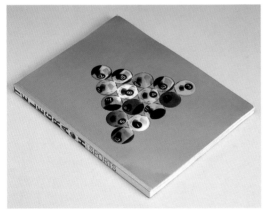

ABOVE: A catalog of sports images relies upon a pool game's eight ball set within the logotype; the piece was launched at a party held at a sports restaurant where Telegraph Colour Library clients received a magic eight ball as a gift.

Integration

The identity, promotional materials, and the launch of new catalogs were all related. Designers ensured that the identity always used a relevant visual pun in the logotype, and where possible, the copy, imagery and format were designed to communicate the client's key messages: fun, friendly service and a broad range of photographic images to choose from.

Designers applied the logotype consistently across all applications, while demonstrating flexibility by taking different approaches, using unexpected imagery, and applying them to different promotional items. "The promotional materials were targeted to creatives, very sophisticated judges of graphic design, so they had to appear fresh, fun, and highly creative whilst championing the new logotype," says Vermier.

The Budget

The overall budget for the new identity, application to catalogs, and promotional items was in excess of £65,000 or approximately $93,000. For designers, the budget was very workable given the scope of the job. "The initial budget was set out in the design proposal submitted to the client before any work was commissioned. In this way, HGV was able to design and implement all items within the scope of the budget across two years of launching the new identity," says Vermier.

The results

When the new identity with its vibrant yellow signature debuted, it received an overwhelmingly positive response from 90 percent of existing library users, while telephone inquiries climbed by 40 percent as the result of the campaign. Likewise, clients responded positively as evidenced by the fact that image searches increased 30 percent and responses to direct mail also climbed—as a direct result of the campaign.

"It is interesting to note that each time a promotional mailer or a calendar was distributed to the client database of 20,000 people, sales of the *Telegraph* images shown increased," says Vermier.

What Worked

Quite simply, the promotion worked because the target market responded to the wit and humor inherent in the new identity, especially in light of the fact that previous marketing pieces had long since become staid, dull, and predictable—especially to an audience consisting of creative-service industry professionals who are accustomed to being enticed by exciting, creative mailers.

ABSTRACT GRAPHICS (pattern graphics)
IDENTIFY DIVERSE PRODUCTS AS A COLLECTION

The Client

One company came from France and the other from England to form Arjo Wiggins, the second largest paper company in the world. One of the company's brands, Argo Wiggins Fine Papers, is widely recognized throughout Europe where it enjoys high visibility and name recognition in the design community. So when the company decided to bring six of its most unique papers to North America, they thought they could follow the same marketing strategy that served them so well in Europe all these years.

Not so fast, cautioned Frank Viva, creative director, Viva Dolan, who recommended against marketing their products to North America by following the same tact that worked in Europe. Why? While the company was widely known throughout Europe, few designers in North America were familiar with its name, let alone its products.

CLIENT:
Curious Paper Corporation/
Arjo Wiggins Fine Papers

DESIGN FIRM:
Viva Dolan Communications
and Design Inc.

ART DIRECTOR:
Frank Viva

DESIGNERS:
Frank Viva, Dominic Ayre,
Natalie Cusson, Pam Lostracco

ILLUSTRATOR/PHOTOGRAPHER:
Photonica

COPYWRITER:
Doug Dolan

CAMPAIGN RUN:
1999 through 2000

TARGET MARKET:
Graphic designers

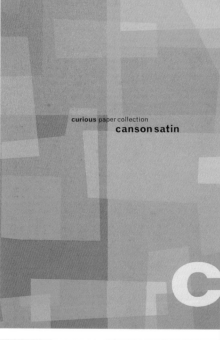

TOP AND BOTTOM: The pattern created by Viva Dolan for Canson Satin, a translucent sheet, highlights the paper's transparent overlaying squares of color.

The Brief

Arjo Wiggins wanted to launch six new products on a very lean budget, which would be nearly impossible to accomplish successfully. Instead of launching six individual products, Viva Dolan counseled the company to package all six products under one new name. More important, the budget could support one brand adequately; if it was used for six individual launches, the budget would be spread too thin.

The idea didn't fly the way designers hoped it would. "We had one champion here who believed in our strategy, but others in England and France were very reticent because they were aware of the whole brand history. Some of these papers have a history dating back over a hundred years, Conqueror, in particular," says Viva. "It was hard for them to get out of that mindset of understanding the paper so intimately and its quirky history and the quirky history that lead to its current day branding. There was a bit of a fight, but they really didn't have the budget to launch and build equity in six new brands new to the North American market. They really only had the budget to, at the very best, build equity in one brand."

Viva Dolan suggested one overarching brand that would include all six grades of paper—Popset, Keaykolour Metallics, Canson Satin, Sensation, Conqueror, and LightSpeck—and proposed launching them to the design community as elements of the Curious Paper Collection. "We invented the Curious Paper name because it was a very diverse collection of papers. The grades are very unusual and very unique," says Viva, citing a shimmery letterhead paper that seemingly flips back and forth between colors. "There is nothing else available in North America like that."

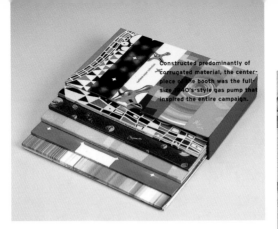

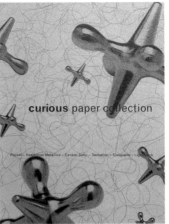

ABOVE: Swatch books for each of six grades of paper are presented in a slipcase as the Curious Paper Collection.

Creating an Umbrella Brand

By placing all the grades under one umbrella collection, new, unusual papers could be added easily. Moreover, Viva wanted the single brand to draw attention to the fact that Arjo Wiggins is an innovator in paper technology. "We wanted whatever brand we came up with to speak to that issue, be memorable, and have positive associations in the North American design community," Viva adds.

ABOVE, RIGHT, AND TOP RIGHT: Viva Dolan would have liked to blanket every issue of every design magazine, but the budget didn't allow for many media buys. Instead, they created ad inserts that ran seven times during a twelve-month period in targeted magazines.

The team at Viva Dolan developed a strategy to introduce the six grades of paper. Their recommendation: Organize the swatch books in such a way that designers only have to remember one name. From a design point of view, they also knew they had to craft a graphic element that tied the diverse stocks together. They found that if they could create a series of patterns for each paper, the six individual sheets would appear to be a system of papers. The patterns bring into focus the papers' unique characteristics. For example, Canson Translucent has transparent overlaying squares of color, which the pattern only accents. The same is true of Sensation, a sheet that reproduces full color very well even though it is uncoated and Keaykolour Metallics, which is distinguished by metallic flecks throughout the pattern.

While the graphic elements were paramount, Viva says that the use of humor throughout was equally important. The pieces don't take themselves too seriously and include sly reference to the curious aspect of the promotion including taglines on ads like, "Printed on one of the five colors of Popset Cover (we're curious to know which one)."

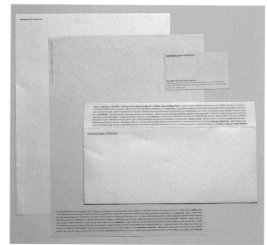

Presenting a Collection

When rolled out, The Curious Paper Collection included a collection of individual sales items. The six swatch books were presented in an elegant slipcase—giving the impression of a paper resource. Other items included a stationery system, an advertising campaign consisting of full-page color ad inserts printed on Curious Paper grades, a detailed Web site that works for printers and designers at www.curiouspapers.com, and the Curious Designer Awards booklet, which perhaps is the best example of Viva Dolan's injection of humor into the project.

The Budget

Even though they were gearing up for one launch, not six, the budget was still lean. Each grade still needed its own swatch book, which is among the most expensive items to produce because of its complexity including tricky folds, tiered waterfalls, and in this case, a slipcase that housed the books as a collection. Costs also escalate when special printing techniques are included that that show the paper performing at its best.

Designers recognized that some items would be costly. Yet, the team contained costs where they could without compromising the overall effort. Careful planning was key to their wise spending. They chose their media buys after reviewing the editorial content of targeted magazines. They strategically chose the best issues based on the most widely read and those that tied into paper concerns or color issues. "We would have liked to blanket every issue, but the funds didn't exist," says Viva. All totaled, they ran seven ads during a twelve-month period in major design magazines such as *Communication Arts* and *How*.

With plenty of forethought, they optimized the swatch books to make them exciting and interesting stand-alone paper promotions, reducing the need for additional collateral pieces before and after their debut. "We hope that the swatch books, besides being a tool, will ignite the imagination and build the Curious brand. We tried to make the swatch book work a little harder on the promotional side," Viva says.

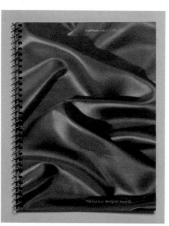

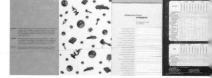

curious paper collection

click if you're curious

ABOVE AND RIGHT TOP, MIDDLE, AND BOTTOM: The Curious Paper Collection's Web site, www.curiouspapers.com, is geared to designers and printers alike.

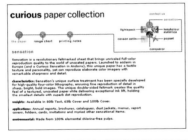

Finding a Common Thread

Selling the European company on the new direction—consolidating six papers into a single brand—was difficult. Anticipating this, Viva Dolan had strong arguments to support their stand. "They wanted to launch all these brands simultaneously. It just wouldn't be memorable. I can't believe that any designer in North America could be expected to remember all six of those names, so we tried to make it easy for the design community by housing the books in one slipcase and giving them only one name to remember," says Viva.

Once they had their okay to proceed, the next problem was how best to organize a collection of fine papers, all with existing brands into a cohesive memorable unit. "Each paper had a brand legacy in Europe that the client wanted to carry forward in North America. We convinced them to start fresh because there was no equity here," Viva explains.

"It seemed on the face of it to be a huge, insurmountable problem because there were all these existing brands and they all did have their own unique identities," he says. Some stocks came from France and some came from Britain, while others were cutting-edge-of-the-minute fashion papers and some were more traditional content, letterhead papers. Designers grappled at finding a common thread that would hold all these diverse papers together.

"We knew the strategy of launching one brand instead of six was right, but what's the glue that holds them all together?" asks Viva. "We couldn't hang our hat on an historic aesthetic because of the high fashion, of-the-moment papers, and we couldn't go that way because of the historical aspect." With no clear-cut solution, designers chose to use abstract graphics—a pattern—as the graphic middle ground that visually holds the diverse collection of papers together as a system. "There was nothing else—culturally or emotionally—that would work."

LEFT AND BELOW: Popset is a unique pearlescent sheet that appears to alternate between different colors in shifting light.

RIGHT AND BELOW: Sensation reproduces full color very well even though it is an uncoated sheet, so a vivid color pattern was used as its identifying graphic.

ABOVE AND LEFT: Keaykolour Metallics is distinguished by metallic flecks throughout the stock, so a metallic pattern was chosen for its identity.

ABOVE AND RIGHT: LightSpeck, one of the six Curious Papers, is the "original white-flecked" paper, according to company literature.

The results

Designers are certainly curious about the Curious Paper Collection. Tonnage sold has exceeded the year-end target by a margin of 45 percent. Paper merchant specification reps say it is memorable, and it has won industry awards. Operators logged in an average of 200 calls per day to the company's toll-free 800 number in the weeks after an ad runs.

Not surprisingly, the president of Arjo Wiggins Fine Papers likes the strategy so much, he introduced the Curious Paper Collection into South America and Mexico; local firms in Brazil and Mexico have adapted the Curious Paper name and artwork to their markets and have translated the materials into Portuguese and Spanish. There is unconfirmed talk about rolling it out in Asia and Europe as well.

"It would be an incredible feather in our cap...if this whole strategy that was designed just for North America with so much resistance was...introduced back in the Mother Country, if you will. The president is toying with the idea, but there may be resistance because they do have equity there," says Viva.

What Worked

"When the thinking is really good up front...you have the buy-in from client, you roll out the strategy without shifting sands and changing direction midway through, and you roll it out with confidence, it has a better chance of working," says Viva. "It works because all the thinking was straight up front and it got rolled out without being undermined or compromised."

REVITALIZING CAMPAIGN
SPARKS SALES FOR WIDMER BROTHERS BREWERY

(graphics that redefine a category

The Brief

Specifically, Widmer Brothers asked HADW to create a strong brand architecture for a proprietary bottle to packaging for four of its core lines—packaging that would revitalize the brewery within the craft beer category. The team at HADW went to work, and the concept they presented to the client so redefined the craft or micro beer category that the project literally exploded when Widmer Brothers awarded the firm with more than three hundred of its other promotional components, including point-of-purchase displays, cooler stickers, metal signs, coasters, and much more.

LEFT: Widmer Brother 3'
x 3' (.9 m x .9 m) banner
and corro-wrap that
dresses up the bottom
of grocery store pallets.

BELOW: Richly designed
tap handles heighten
brand visibility.

CLIENT:
Widmer Brothers

DESIGN FIRM:
Hornall Anderson Design Works, Inc.

ART DIRECTORS:
Jack Anderson, Larry Anderson

DESIGNERS:
Jack Anderson, Larry Anderson,
Bruce Stigler, Bruce Branson-Meyer,
Mary Chin Hutchinson, Michael Brugman,
Kaye Farmer, Ed Lee

ILLUSTRATORS:
John Fretz, Susy Pilgrim Waters,
Jeff Yeomans, Steve Hepburn,
Michael Sternagle, Tom Reis

COPYWRITER:
Pamela Mason Davey

CAMPAIGN RUN:
February 2000 to Present

TARGET MARKET:
Consumers 22 to 38 years old

The Client

"Widmer Brothers came to us to not so much for rebranding as to make their brand stronger and they wanted us to revitalize their look, not from an identity standpoint, but from a packaging standpoint," says Larry Anderson, senior designer/project manager, of the challenge presented to Hornall Anderson Design Works, Inc. by Widmer Brothers, a brewery and beer distributor. "When we looked at the packaging, it didn't have a lot of punch," he admits.

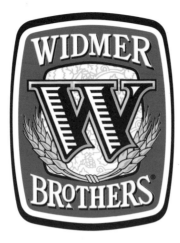

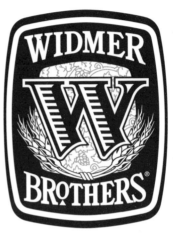

The Problem: Art on a Box

Everyone agreed that the current packaging wasn't as strong as it should be. The company's core brand, Hefeweizen, featured tone-on-tone imagery of a wheat field on its six-packs, while the seasonal flavors featured scenes designed to remind consumers of pleasant times growing up or enjoyable experiences—a feeling that Widmer Brothers wanted HADW to retain to some degree, but, hopefully, execute more effectively.

"Jack Anderson coined a phrase, 'You've got art on a box, just like everyone else,'" says Hornall Anderson of the dilemma. The team mulled the situation over and finally concluded that if you want someone to remember something, why not go a step further and try to create the moment rather than just a memory. It was this lightening bolt moment that inspired the idea of freezing a moment in time from which, they would develop the look and feel for the revitalized identity.

The Concept

Once polished, the concept HADW dreamed up, which so enthused Widmer Brothers and won the firm more than three hundred additional components, was replacing the original scenes with stories that tell of a moment in time and reflect the inherent characteristics of each of the blends—a seemingly endless tale told in text and graphics that would wrap around the packaging. The "moment in time" wouldn't appear on one panel, but would continue around the entire package.

A New Logo

Yet, there was one more hurdle to overcome; designers felt that the current mark didn't fit the new concept. "If we're redesigning everything else, why aren't we freshening up the look of their mark? It seemed a bit dated and inappropriate for where we were going with the design," says Anderson. The team convinced Widmer to allow them to also review the mark, reenergize it, and give it a sense of heritage by emphasizing the history of beer, including wheat, hops, and the client's filigree. Heritage and craftsmanship were emphasized to give it a back-to-basics look and feel.

Using Illustration to Hone the Message

Unique to this promotion is the attention to detail devoted to each six-pack carrier design. The illustrations that freeze various moments in time allow each six-pack to tell a story and generate a feeling associated with the beer's characteristics. The illustration on the box becomes more than just packaging graphics, but communicates a lifestyle brand that makes the beer memorable to the consumer. The rich illustrations lend a personality to each blend that extends beyond its taste to the packaging's visually stimulating graphics.

Hefeweizen, the brewery's best-known core brand, is a wheat beer usually served with lemon. The tale told in its graphic packaging is the transcript of a phone call between the two Widmer brothers, where one invites some friends over for an impromptu gathering on a summer afternoon. The illustration shows an open house with an inviting deck and umbrella table, a dock stretching out onto a lake, lemon wedges, cheese and crackers—all layered over a written message transcribing the conversation taking place. The combination of atypical beer packaging graphics, combined with an interesting story, are the factors that will motivate consumers to pick-up the package and look at it, according to HADW.

Hop Jack, another core brand, is treated in the same manner. The graphics on the six-pack reference the twenty-three to thirty-year-old crowd, potential buyers of the brand. Background photos show active, young adults having a good time. Being the computer-oriented market that they are, the story includes snippets of an e-mail message from one brother to his coworkers inviting them to a local nightclub after work to wind down. The e-mail message about the get-together is the story behind this hip blend.

The Sweet Betty brand gets the same graphic treatment, but the story takes a different approach. Here, sepia-tinged illustrations conjure up scenes one might envision while listening to an old-time radio broadcast of a baseball game in the 1940s. Graphic elements included in the wraparound pictorial are baseball cards, ballpark tickets, baseball equipment, banners, peanuts and popcorn, and the announcer. Sweet Betty, herself, is given a persona; she is portrayed as a wholesome, postwar housewife, similar in style and appearance to Doris Day or the fictional June Cleaver in the 1950s. The background includes copy similar to that used in scripts read by radio announcers.

Widberry, a black raspberry–flavored beer, appeals to a demographic more populated by women. The intent of this six-pack design was to portray a café scene where the background copy reads like the specials of the day with suggested beverage choices to complement the menu. Wrought-iron bars and checkered tablecloths are layered with the copy over a rich burgundy background to emphasize the berry flavor blend.

LEFT: The six-pack wrap-around artwork is displayed on three of Widmer Brothers' seasonal beers, Springfest, Sommerbrau, and Oktoberfest.

LEFT: Winternacht features traditional winterscapes that remind buyers of the heart-warming occasions of the season, including horse-drawn sleigh rides and building snowmen, while boasting a cool color palette.

THE CHALLENGES

A Cohesive Look for Many Items

As one might suspect, integrating graphics onto more than three hundred items that keep each brand distinct yet part of a cohesive whole, is not an easy feat, but was accomplished with strategic planning. "[When] we developed this vocabulary of creating a moment in time for the core brands and had this freshened up identity, we ended up with a kit of parts. We had the belt buckle with the lockup of the logo. We've got the product descriptor in there; and we've got some imagery that pertains to that individual product. With these components, you can create guidelines that give a cohesive look and feel to all the pieces, which can also be passed onto the client, who can extend them further," says Anderson.

The Belt Buckle

The "belt buckle" that was among the designers' kit of parts, also helped the team establish a hierarchy of the first, second, and third read when first looking at the bottle or package. Designers felt that the original packaging failed in this area; consumers saw the Hefeweizen name, but the Widmer logo didn't stand out. To give each element equal visual footing, designers created a "belt buckle" layout with a strong banding system at the top of the design that locks up or houses the Widmer logo along with the type of beer it is. As a result, there is a very strong read behind the two elements—What kind of beer is this and who makes this?—from a branding and a product standpoint.

The theme for Springfest, one of the seasonal brands, plays on the oft-repeated forecaster of March weather—comes in like a lion; goes out like a lamb. The lamb and lion are illustrated as cloud shapes on either sides of the carton. The graphics take advantage of the seasons by using scenes and colors congruent with spring, such as a woman holding an umbrella in the wind and rain.

Summerbrau, another seasonal brand, showcases a swimming hole on a late-summer afternoon where friends have gathered to cool off. The package gets its punch from an image of the sun.

Oktoberfest, too, takes advantage of the season and its imagery, using traditional autumn visuals such as Halloween images, including a pumpkin-head character with personality, as well as harvest time. Its color palette employs a combination of blue/gray, gold, and orange.

Winternacht features traditional winterscapes that remind buyers of the heartwarming occasions of the season, including horse-drawn sleigh rides and building snowmen, while boasting a cool color palette.

ABOVE: The only time a rabbit appears on the Hop Jack materials is on this Hop Jack enameled metal sign, shown here alongside a metal sign for the Sweet Betty brand.

TOP AND BOTTOM LEFT: Artwork on product half-cases and full cases carry through the moment in time theme.

Continuity throughout

The newly revised logo and illustrations were applied to hundreds of program elements, including everything from a comprehensive stationery system, bottle labels, six-pack packaging, case and half-case packaging, the corporate brochure, six-pack stuffers, data sheets, gift promotions, tap handles, T-shirts, coasters, posters, cooler labels, metal signage to ancillary materials such as blank reply cards, banners, and corro-wraps that dress-up grocery store pallets, among other items.

The Budget

Initially the project entailed creating a packaging structure for four of Widmer Brothers' six-packs, including labels, bottle design, and mother cartons within a budget of $90,000. Once the project took off, however, Widmer added additional seasonal brands, plus branding for the new Widberry and Sweet Betty lines, along with more than three hundred other promotional and collateral pieces—all of which more than doubled the budget. The budget for the initial scope of the project was adequate and as the campaign expanded, the budget remained sufficient to cover work and expenses, but it didn't afford a lot of cushion. To maintain quality, HADW credits its skilled and talented staff that delivered quality work without exceeding budget limitations. "A competent team that follows through can make all the difference," says Anderson.

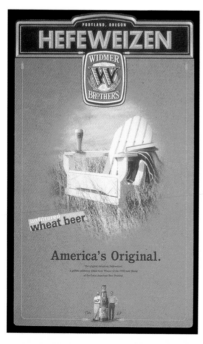

The results

The imagery for the campaign is undeniably eye-catching, but the promotion does more than provide visual stimulation. It actually works—something not all pretty campaigns do. This campaign is strong because of its unique combination of branding presence, coupled with the prominence of the brand. These things, combined with the product descriptors that create a moment in time, differentiate the Widmer brand from other products on beer shelves. "I don't see anyone out there doing that. This was the brand difference we thought would make them stand apart," says Anderson.

It appears that the work accomplished just that. When Widmer was founded in 1984, it was a keg only brewery; bottles were not introduced until 1996 and while sales were good, the goal was to have bottles and kegs each account for 50 percent of sales. Through October 2000, bottles had climbed to 45 percent of sales. "The packaging redesign really helped us increase our bottle business," says Tim McFall, vice president of marketing, Widmer Brothers. "It helped us gain more distribution and it helped us increase sales in our existing distribution," he adds, citing a total increase of bottles sales of 30 percent, well over Widmer's projections in its distribution areas including Oregon, Washington, California, New York, Michigan, and several midwestern states.

What Worked

"To make a campaign of this scope work, you have to surround yourself with talent," says Anderson. "When I remember where we started and where we ended up, [I realize that] this really elevated the brand, raised the bar for the client, and redefined the craft beer category for them and for the people out there. They're making waves, and that's the satisfying part about it. When you hear word on the street that the competition is a little worried about Widmer, then you know you've done a good job."

PHOTOGRAPHY REINVIGORATES (photo graphics)
MATURE BRAND WITH SENSUAL, YOUTHFUL GRAPHICS

channel surf, the future in swimwear

jantzen

CLIENT:
Jantzen, Inc.

DESIGN FIRM:
Plazm Media

ART DIRECTOR:
Joshua Berger

DESIGNERS:
Joshua Berger, Niko Courtelis, Enrique Mosqueda, Pete McCracken

COPYWRITER:
Kristi Klainer

PHOTOGRAPHER:
Nicola Majocchi

MODELS:
Tilly, Shkara, Christine, Jolijn

MAKEUP:
Jamie Melbourne

HAIR:
Azuma

STYLIST:
Sabina Kurz

CAMPAIGN RUN:
July 2000 through July 2001

TARGET MARKET:
Women 15 to 25 years old

jantzen .01

ABOVE AND LEFT: "Channel Surf the Future," a direct-mail piece announcing Jantzen's new line, invited industry insiders and the media to Jantzen's 2001 season premier and featured extreme close-ups of fabric swatches.

The Client

Does this swimsuit look like one your grandmother has worn for years? Jantzen, Inc., the company who pioneered the development of commercial swimwear for women back in 1910, is betting the answer is no. However, to strengthen its hand, Jantzen tapped Portland, Oregon–based Plazm Media to reinvigorate and reposition the mature brand.

The Brief

Jantzen supplied Plazm with plenty of market research, which helped narrow down the objectives. Plazm was to redirect the marketing to a younger demographic, develop the next generation of Jantzen customers, nurture downstream business, and build future advocacy. In short, Jantzen retained Plazm Media to transform the company's matronly image into one that represents the forces that shape and define today's fashion—all in time for the company to reemerge in the marketplace.

The Concept

The Jantzen brand has existed for nearly one hundred years and was in need of a facelift, yet it possessed a very deep and unique heritage. "Jantzen is responsible for the prevalence of swimming in this country in the same way that Nike is responsible for jogging," says Joshua Berger, art director. "In the last fifteen years or so, the perception of the brand has really stagnated. Most of the research that we did and the client did indicated that people perceive it as an older brand."

To combat its aging persona, designers opted to retain the company's heritage—which lent itself to Jantzen's Riviera line, swimwear inspired by vintage styling—while communicating that Jantzen is about fashion. Designers crafted the relaunch to address the overlap between fashion and culture, while paying attention to style and fabric. Fabric was deemed integral to this campaign, as it was part of the product offering. To illustrate its importance, fabric swatches were scanned in and rendered in extreme close-up in the direct-mail piece as well as other campaign components.

ABOVE: An invitation to a personal viewing of Jantzen's Riviera line, a fourteen-style collection that brings back the classic lines and handcrafted fashion from the 1940s and 1950s in modern fabrics.

LEFT: A limited-edition poster was silk-screened and letterpressed to announce Riviera line, a line of swimwear that interprets fashion patterns of the 1940s and 1950s with modern fabrics. Designers wrapped it in a silvery art paper for an elegant appearance.

THE CHALLENGES

Perception vs. Reality

Designers had to fight hard to overcome the perception that the Jantzen brand had grown old and musty, but most importantly, they had to fight the battle amid budget constraints on the creative end, as well as limited resources for media buys.

"We pursued a grass roots marketing plan, including guerilla marketing, and reached out to a list of popular figures and industry influencers. We showed the suits in a new way that speaks to a younger demographic, focusing on the confluence of fashion and culture."

Limited Funds

Working with a limited budget and trying to have impact for a global brand was tough. "Other companies have a big enough budget to do brand advertising all year around on a global level, including TV and print advertising," says Berger. "Jantzen doesn't have this kind of budget. We don't have enough money to run ads all year round...let alone get items produced for retail needs, sales needs, trades needs, and on a consumer level. We're doing it at reduced rates because we're excited about the product. The photographer, the models, the stylist, everyone gave 110 percent to make it happen."

"Creatively, if we're excited about something, that's the best you can have."

Influencing the Media

When a client has a limited budget, the only alternative is to find a creative way to optimize funds. Plazm did just that by including an influencer program in the mix. This effort reached out to people designers determined were key influencers within the world of contemporary culture and fashion including filmmakers, musicians, actresses, and models. These people were sent a copy of the look book and a catalog of suits accompanied by a personal letter inviting them to sample the products. In addition, Plazm targeted costumers of television and motion pictures to include the suits in their wardrobe departments.

Using Voyeuristic Photography

Photography is the primary communicator in this campaign where the copy is kept to minimalist subheads. At first glance, the shots are just about beautiful women sporting Jantzen suits, but there's more. The idea was "to capture a moment before an action takes place and make it really intimate, almost voyeuristic," says Berger. "The person you're looking at in these shots is engaged. It's unexpected. There's something about to happen. This differs from other photography in the swimwear category that is styled to the point it is hyper-real. It's not attainable. It is beyond reality. On the other side, there are lifestyle shots...people on the beach playing. These are created moments that attempt authenticity. Jantzen's ads fall somewhere between these two."

THIS PAGE: Suits featured in Jantzen's oversized look book, *Jantzen .01,* sport such names such as Me Jane, Eclipse, Hooked on You, Concentricity, Traffic Jam, Rangoon, Tattoo You, and Rubberband Man—all of which are skewed to appeal to a younger consumer.

The Youth Movement

The project includes trade and consumer print advertising, marketing collateral, internal sales promotions, trade show design, retail point-of-purchase, and a runway show, as well as related guerilla marketing. *Jantzen .01,* Jantzen's oversized look book, and related collateral demonstrate an awareness of fashion sensibilities: style, color, fabric, cut, and line drawn together by young, modern photography, which combined with an aggressive, youth-oriented presentation capitalizes on the element of surprise.

Copy is regulated to punchy taglines. "Preview the future," the tag that appears on all the ads, coupled with the headline "Life begins at 80°," which appears inside the *Jantzen .01* look book, reinforce the theme of a newer and younger Jantzen. Names given to each swimsuit follow along the same lines—Me Jane, Eclipse, Hooked on You, Concentricity, Traffic Jam, Rangoon, Tattoo You, and Rubberband Man—are not the names of swimsuits of old.

Not only does Jantzen's campaign show-off its new styles, new colors, new fabrics, new cuts, and new lines, but the campaign is notable for its modern imagery, which is sensual, fashion-forward, and, designers hope, engaging enough to draw people in on multiple levels.

Build from the Product

Designers created all the components to build out from
the product. Each image in the series of six trade
advertisements has a different color tone. For instance,
an ad titled Pre-Modern has a greenish hue to the
background. Working with the photographer, designers
filtered the background and reverse filtered the model
so that she appears in a normal light without the background hue. The result creates contrast and mood. "It's
all understated, but the effect builds off the product,"
says Berger.

"[The ads] ... aren't product advertisements, they are
product driven, which bridges a gap between strict
product advertising and brand advertising. The client
doesn't have a big enough budget to have those different levels, so it all has to be one thing," says Berger.

The results

Both Jantzen and Plazm Media are pleased with the success of the promotion, which effectively spread the word that Jantzen was back—stronger and more youthful than ever. Plazm points to the media blitz that resulted from the campaign—as well as interest among Hollywood types who suddenly are seeing Jantzen suits in a new and sexy light.

PR Hits

The new campaign created a stir among the fashion-conscious media, netting numerous editorial mentions with headlines that garnered publicity that couldn't be bought and further stretched the budget. *W* talked about the new "Jantzen," while *Women's Wear Daily* opined "Jantzen Revamp: Young and Sexy" and *Fashion Market* proclaimed, "Jantzen to Strengthen Brand." The company also benefited from plenty of ink and photos in the *Swim Journal's* Cruise Preview issue, *California Apparel News*, and *Jane* magazine where the fashion market editor was first introduced to the Riviera line at the Miami Market. After reviewing the video of the fashion show, the editor decided to feature Jantzen's Arabesque, The Vina del Mar, and Fatale styles in the magazine.

Since then, the media has revisited the story with editorial following up the initial launch. One such example is *Women's Wear Daily*, which had an editor on-site at Jantzen for two days of interviews and photo opportunities.

Going Hollywood

The media isn't the only group talking up Jantzen's merits; it appears Jantzen has gone Hollywood, too. The annual "Marketplace" gala for the Set Decorator's Society, a group of television and motion picture professionals in Los Angeles, clothed their models/hostesses in Jantzen suits and cover-ups. In addition, each Marketplace attendee took home a copy of Plazm's *Jantzen .01* brand book.

Major Film and TV Product Placements

Jantzen suits have been placed into a variety of motion pictures including Columbia Pictures' *The Glass House* starring Lee Sobieski, Diane Lane, and Rita Wilson; *Inferno*, an independent film featuring two young, up-and-coming actresses; MGM Studio's *Bandits* starring Bruce Willis, Cate Blanchett, and Billy Bob Thornton; *Zoolander*, a Ben Stiller comedy about male models, as well as television series such as *Baywatch Hawaii* and *Freakylinks*.

"Overall, the reaction has been really strong. People are definitely talking within the industry. Editors are calling the client to find out what's going on." exclaims Berger.

What Worked

"The element of surprise has a lot to do with its success. The promotion took an aggressive stance and it stands out as unique in a really difficult marketplace. For a brand with the perception of being older, more established, not young and hip, to come out and print a 17" x 22" (43 cm x 56 cm) huge book with this kind of content in it is pretty aggressive and makes a bold statement for Jantzen," says Berger.

"Also, we had the element of surprise on our side. We completely changed the visuals and the attitude that the brand has been putting forward, so the element of surprise is really important," adds Berger. "We told Jantzen, 'This is what we think will achieve your objectives.' They gave us a problem and we solved it."

NICKELODEON QUIETLY BREAKS (minimalist graphics) THROUGH THE CLUTTER OF KIDS' TV PROGRAMMING

The Client

When Nickelodeon debuted in 1984, it was a one of a kind—the only television network for kids. It was different, irreverent, fresh, and very successful. Since then the market has grown and there are plenty of new kid networks on the block. Nickelodeon, while still on top, had lost some of its irreverence and wanted a strategy to recapture its edge before it was too late.

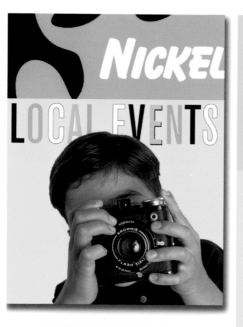

CLIENT:
Nickelodeon

DESIGN FIRM:
AdamsMorioka

ART DIRECTORS:
Lisa Judson, Niels Schuurmans, Matthew Duntemann, Sean Adams, Noreen Morioka

DESIGNERS:
Sean Adams, Noreen Morioka, Volker Durre

ILLUSTRATORS:
Various

PHOTOGRAPHER:
Blake Little Photography

PRODUCTION:
Nick Digital

COPYWRITERS:
Sharon Lesser, McPaul Smith

AUDIO:
Voodoo Productions

CAMPAIGN RUN:
March 1999 through September 4, 2000

TARGET MARKET:
Children 4 to 12 years of age

The Brief

The network retained Los Angeles–based AdamsMorioka. The assignment: reevaluate, reposition, and restructure the Nickelodeon global brand. "The objective was to evolve the Nickelodeon brand visually and maintain its leadership position in an increasingly crowded competitive marketplace for kids' programming and entertainment. A primary objective was to remain true to the Nickelodeon attitude of flexibility and creativity, while increasing its visual presence," says Sean Adams, partner, AdamsMorioka.

"As opposed to many corporations that address issues of branding strategy after things stop succeeding, Nickelodeon was, and is, the leading network for children's programming. It has maintained a high level of expansion and success in new arenas such as movies, themed environments, on-line presence, consumer products and sister brands Nick at Nite and TVLand. The problem lay in the future. The need was to refocus and reclarify the Nickelodeon message during this extreme growth and expansion," he adds.

ABOVE: A press kit was created to highlight local events.

LEFT: The new identity was applied to a variety of promotional items including hats, bags, and mouse pads.

Nine Months of Research

The final concept was born out of nine long months of painstaking research before designers started putting anything on paper. They conducted scores of interviews with Nickelodeon staff from people in the mailroom to the president of the network to determine where the brand was and where it should go, all the while keeping Nickelodeon's overall brand strategy and positioning top-of-mind. Most important, the brand had to become more focused and more proprietary now that there are other competitors on the market who weren't there ten years ago like the Disney Channel, Fox Kids, or Cartoon Network.

Designers watched hours of Nickelodeon's on-air programs such as CatDog, SpongeBob, and Rugrats —shows that have become network icons—as well as new programming still in development to try and get to the heart of Nickelodeon's identity. In addition, they audited hours of competing programming to get a sense of where they were going and to ascertain what messages were borrowed from Nickelodeon. "Nickelodeon once had ownership of kids' programming. We had to pull it back and re-own it and get to the heart of the story Nickelodeon is telling," says Adams.

Minimalist Graphics

What they found was chaos. According to their research findings, the current marketplace of children's entertainment is literally exploding with opposing patterns, colors, and text layered together as often as possible. Designers queried, "What if we take the opposite tact?" Would a system composed of a very reductive color palette, simple typographic palette, minimal shape choices, and overall minimalist compositional vocabulary appeal to kids?

ABOVE: Designers created this ad to raise awareness for new programs premiering on Nickelodeon.

Maintaining the Spirit

"The idea of creating a system for a brand built on irreverence, surprise, freedom, and creativity is challenging," says Adams, claiming that their biggest problem was trying to maintain the spirit of irreverence and flexibility that is inherent in the Nickelodeon system. "From the 1980s on, Nickelodeon always had amazingly fresh, innovative work. We wanted to keep that and make sure that the designers in-house didn't feel stifled by the system. When Nickelodeon was just a television network, it could get away with doing everything under the sun. That's part of the corporate culture—take risks, do new things, surprise us."

Pulling the Design Back to Center

"We didn't want to lose that, but at the same time, Nickelodeon had grown beyond being simply a television network to a global brand, and that lack of focus was starting to dilute the brand. We had to figure out a way to refocus and pull it all back to center without losing that sense of irreverence and creativity."

Adams wanted to build a system that he could turn over to Nickelodeon's in-house design teams (consisting of about 300 designers in the off-air and on-air design departments, as well an advertising agency among others) that inspired creativity as opposed to stifling it. Rather than giving them a system that is very regimented, the idea was to give them a kit of parts. "The final system was, in fact, not a system, but a set of parts, a foundation for ideas rather than a collage, to be brought to life," he says.

In the end, AdamsMorioka turned the standards over to Nickelodeon's designers and said, "Here are all the parts, make something of them."

"I hoped I would see things that I would never expect...that we would be surprised all the time...that people would push it [the system] to its limits. We give them just the bones. We want them to breathe life into it," says Adams. "The graphic language is so strong in this, you can't screw it up. As long as you stay within the specific vernacular, everything is going to tie together. At the same time, everything should be different. It's television. It should be entertaining. It's not supposed to be hard-edged. We don't want to whitewash the network. We want to make sure there is variety."

AdamsMorioka thought so and established a strong set of criteria for the brand's growth, recommending several action steps, including refacing the on-air environment utilizing a strong proprietary system. The system was designed with the entire brand and all of its parts in mind. The first phase was the on-air environment, followed by implementation and planning for the system off-air (print media), consumer products, and international on-air components.

Keeping it Simple

The basic concept came down to simplifying the color palette to make orange a more prominent color and simplifying the shape system so that the Nickelodeon logo, which changes shape all the time, doesn't have to compete with the background, and to push forward the product, which for Nickelodeon is its program characters, like CatDog and Rugrats. "These things together make the basic visual system hold together," says Adams.

BELOW: The do's and don'ts of Nickelodeon's visual system point to its simplicity in everything from the flexible logo to the use of simple typography and shapes.

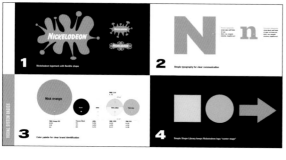

Clutter-Free Graphics

AdamsMorioka began the project in March 1999, but the result of their work did not hit the airwaves until September 4, 2000. The system as designed by the firm includes the identity positioning, identity usage refinement, on-air identity usage guidelines, five-second on-air bumpers, on-air promotions, on-air credit crunch, printed promotional collateral usage, and printed collateral.

In all instances, these items were created as prototypes for the new visual system. Some were used as is, while others work as primary examples for additional pieces to be created in-house. One such example is a poster featuring the character of Spongebob Squarepants, which was created as a prototype for an ad system intended to run in *Nickelodeon* magazine, a publication by and for the network. The basic ad format lent itself to most messaging and required only minor tweaking when Nickelodeon designers tailored the ad to include an announcement of a sweepstakes promotion targeted to people in the advertising sales department to generate regional ad revenue. The ad appeared in flyer form in Nick's internal magazine and communications.

Cleaning up the Digital Clutter

Within the system, there are many unique aspects including the motion-free on-air promotions. Only still frames are used. The audio was also pared down from "big music" to sounds from a kid's life like ringing bells and barking dogs. "Slowing television down to a quieter place amidst the chaos that is utilized by most children's marketing was a brave choice on Nickelodeon's part," says Adams. "This reductive attitude in print also elevated Nickelodeon's overall visual equity amongst the thousands of patterns, different typefaces, and digital clutter.

"Kids are smart. I don't buy this thing that kids are idiots who will respond to flying shapes and lots of colors. They, like everyone else, want to be talked to intelligently and with respect," adds Adams.

ABOVE: Billboard advertising promotes Nickelodeon's evening programming lineup.

RIGHT: This ad promotes
Nickelodeon's program,
Brothers Garcia and its
new timeslot on Tuesdays.

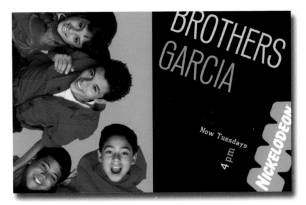

Similarly, AdamsMorioka created billboard advertising promoting Nickelodeon's evening programming lineup. Nickelodeon is no stranger to billboard advertising, having previously placed outdoor advertising in high-profile markets including Los Angeles, New York, and Orlando to promote new programming, special events, and environments like Blast Zone at Universal Studios, Florida.

Print advertising was also part of the mix. Adams Morioka created a variety of advertising prototypes for execution by Nickelodeon's in-house designers including one to promote the premiere of new programming and another variation to promote an existing program's new timeslot.

AdamsMorioka's press kit design provided the framework for a grassroots public relations spin-off campaign that was used to highlight local Nickelodeon events "coming soon to a town near you." "Local events are part of Nick's larger initiatives that promote and celebrate kids' power and ability to make change. The Big Help is a good example, serving as a catalyst for change; cleaning up the neighborhood, collecting canned food for the homeless. These initiatives were generated and made successful by real kids across the country," says Adams.

Finally, designers provided examples of how the new imagery would play on promotional items that Nickelodeon relies upon—including calendars, T-shirts, hats, bags, and mouse pads—which are regularly distributed to advertisers, affiliate networks, such as CBS and MTV, as well as Nick's creative partners.

Every element in the campaign—whether created as a prototype or used as is—features a reductive minimalist palette and shape library versus lots of flying things for a much more focused appeal. This graphic treatment not only marks a departure from competing children's networks, but also is a clear delineation from commercials, which are chaotic, too.

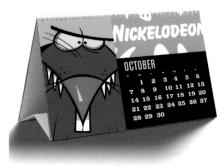

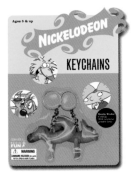

LEFT AND RIGHT:
A calendar, keychain,
and a T-shirt are among
Nickelodeon's many promotional items.

On-air promotions consist of still frames only; there is absolutely no motion. Five-second on-air bumpers play like a slide show, all of which sets Nickelodeon apart from its competitors because it presents an abrupt calm. When channel surfing, one can't help but stop on Nickelodeon because it is paced so differently. "We could have made it louder and faster, but then, where would that stop?" asks Adams.

Reaction—Inside and Out

The system has received critical praise from the business community and increased advertising revenue. Among Nickelodeon's in-house designers reaction has been varied. "There are those who embrace it wholly —and those that are more resistant," says Adams. "You can't design a system and allow more than three hundred designers to have input, but it seems that those who were not aware of the project, the marketing strategy, and brand issues behind it are a little more resistant to it.

"For someone to come in and say, 'Be creative, but you only get to work with five colors and this minimal typeface collection,' particularly when the previous dictate had been do anything you want, can frustrate designers who want free creative reign," Adams acknowledges. "Now it is getting a pretty good response. Those who were frustrated at the outset are finding that it has made their lives easier. It has stopped being a matter of 'I don't like that' and has become an issue of 'Are we communicating the things that the system should be communicating at all times?' It has taken some of the subjectivity out of the hands of the people who are handing out the assignments.

Inspiring Creativity

"We found that by giving designers who are working on it fewer choices, it forces them to actually start thinking more about ideas as opposed to simply relying on a collage. This system was meant to be turned over to hundreds of people to implement, and we wanted to make sure that they were forced to think through a narrative storyline or come up with a funny punch line or interesting point of view as opposed to 'I'll take this pattern and this pattern and throw them all together.' The concept of ideas—not collage—seems to be working very well."

RIGHT: Nickelodeon's on-air system including sample frames from a five-second bumper that play like a slide show, all of which sets Nickelodeon apart from its competitors because it presents an abrupt calm

BELOW: Nickelodeon identity applied to the corporate system.

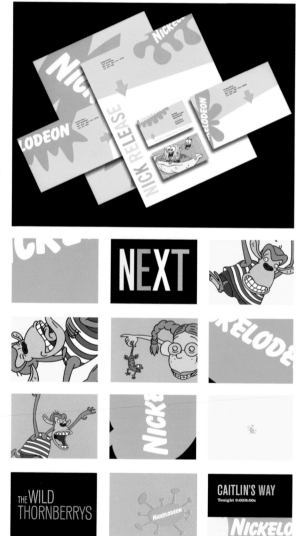

The results

"Typically, it is difficult to point to higher ratings and increased revenue and claim that the redesign and focus of the brand is responsible. In the end, Nickelodeon's high quality of programming and product is responsible for this success," explains Adams.

The strategy and visual system added to this success in several ways. Primarily, clarifying the message internally promoted all decisions ranging from programming choices to the design of an ad to follow the Nickelodeon promises. The visual system increased brand recognition and ownership of properties on-air dramatically.

What Worked

"[The system] works well because it addresses the bigger strategy issues versus just being nice graphics that decorate something. All of the elements are born out of a specific marketing need and are coming from a long-term goal," says Adams. "Television networks can fall into the trap of trying to look cool, so you just get this cake decoration on everything. We're happy that the system cuts to core of who Nickelodeon was and what it wanted to become and started a foundation to build on.

"This isn't the last iteration [of the system]. It is only the beginning of the project."

CHILDREN'S TELEVISION WORKSHOP (equity graphics) GETS A NEW NAME AND IMAGE IN IDENTITY CAMPAIGN

CTW
SESAME STREET ®
CHILDREN'S TELEVISION WORKSHOP

CLIENT:
Sesame Workshop

DESIGN FIRM:
Carbone Smolan Agency

ART DIRECTOR:
Justin Peters

DESIGNERS:
Tom Sopkovitch, Christa Bianchi

CAMPAIGN RUN:
June 5, 2000 to Present

TARGET MARKET:
Media, partners, and licensees

The Client

The Children's Television Workshop, a respected entity in children's television programming, enjoyed the equity it had built in its name, but at the same time, the name that had become so widely recognized for quality television programming, had also become limiting—leading the marketplace to think of the organization in terms of television only, while ignoring its other successful endeavors. It needed a brand identity that spoke to a larger audience and a short list of new names was developed. But, Children's Television Workshop knew this was not a project it could manage on its own; it needed help and turned to New York's Carbone Smolan Agency to craft a new name and launch an entirely new identity

ABOVE: **Children's Television Workshop was a good name with a great deal of built-in equity.**

OPPOSITE: **Carbone Smolan's early work showed the graphic possibilities of using just the words *Sesame Workshop*, all of which was positively received.**

The Brief

When faced with the challenge of developing a new name and brand identity for Children's Television Workshop, designers at Carbone Smolan Agency faced the facts, and the truth was Children's Television Workshop was a good name with a great deal of built-in equity. In 1969, CTW made a significant impact on television that changed children's viewing forever by packaging educational programming in such a way that it appealed to children's natural attraction to a new electronic world.

Since then, children's media choices have expanded well beyond television, and once again, CTW is leading the way by seeking new ways to make the world of media more valuable to children. "Children's Television Workshop had been effective for three decades as an institutional descriptor, but its institutional nature had become a liability," says Ken Carbone, cofounder and executive creative director, Carbone Smolan Agency. "Additionally, CTW recognized the need to function as a brand with a name and identity that has clear and specific meaning to audiences and opinion leaders."

Weighing the Value of Feedback

"Consumer testing was one of the obstacles when our very simple house started to take on characteristics that made it look like a chateau," jokes Carbone. Comments received in early testing suggested changes to make the house appear more global, more fun. "You have to know how to sift through all that and there were some bumps in the road, but in some cases we were trying to translate, too literally, the requests, which compromised the simplicity [and] the clarity that the logo needed to have. The design team delivered a revised house based on all the recommendations set forth in the testing, presented it alongside the original house, and asked "Which feels more vibrant and warm?" It was unanimous—stick with the original concept. "I think of it [feedback] for reference, not direction," advises Carbone.

Navigating Tight Deadlines

Also complicating the project was its urgency. CTW wanted to launch the new image by June 5, leaving only about six weeks of production time. Then, there was the International Film and Programme Market for Television, Video, Cable, and Satellite (MIPCOM) exposition in Cannes, France, where Sesame Workshop's trade show booth made its debut—in record time as well—marking the first three-dimensional expression of the brand.

Establishing a New Identity

"Research showed that for those who recognize CTW at all, it is virtually interchangeable with public television and other brands that produce children's programming. In these fast-paced times, parents (and kids) need brands that signal quality and trust. With a powerful global brand in their portfolio —Sesame Street—that represents a cultural touchstone synonymous with a dedication to children, education, and fun, CTW sought to capitalize on this shorthand equivalent for excellence in children's media," says Carbone.

The short list of alternative names included Sesame & Co., Sesame Unlimited, and Sesame Workshop. CTW felt each one worked because each borrowed upon CTW's equity in Sesame Street while suggesting an entity that was more than television programming, but devoted to multimedia. Carbone Smolan's proposal cover captured this and was instrumental in helping them win the business. But when the list had to be narrowed, representatives of Carbone Smolan felt that neither Sesame & Co. or Sesame Unlimited were distinctive in any way, but neither did they advise starting over with an entirely blank slate. Instead, they suggested CTW build on the equity of Sesame, known internationally, plus Workshop, which connotes energy and a place where new things are created, invented, experimented with, and built. The name provided a good foundation by which to imbue it with all kinds of character and visual cues that would suggest what the new mission was—to become a new multimedia enterprise.

Research also revealed that the word *workshop* was rich with meaning. It connotes a creative, stimulating, and active environment. The new name, Sesame Workshop, fuses the best of CTW's past while providing a branding platform for the future.

Moreover, it included part of the original name—Children's Television Workshop—that gave the new name even more value. Carbone Smolan's early work showed the graphic possibilities of using just the words Sesame Workshop, all of which was positively received. But then, designers started rethinking using only letterforms for the mark and wondered what else they could do creatively to bring brand essence or some kind distinctive character to the name. When the team looked at the competitive landscape, they found a lot of icons, symbols, and characters. "So we said, 'Let's try to develop a mark or symbol that is more embraceable by this particular audience, which is kids and parents, than just a name,'" says Carbone.

SESAMEWORKSHOP SESAMEWORKSHOP SESAME WORKSHOP

sesameworkshop sesame workshop SESAME WORKSHOP

Giving Voice to the New Identity

The word *workshop* suggested a place, a shelter, a safe haven, but what kind of place should it be, designers wondered, a spaceship or some other vehicle that can take you places, or a house? They ultimately decided on a house so full of energy and creative activity that it is literally exploding through the roof. A shooting star soars past the roof to suggest a source of ideas and inspiration. "The new logo symbolized the visceral and intellectual benefits of CTW's work in the lives of children," says Carbone. "It really defined the brand. It has a luminescence about it. It has its lights turned on. There's also a graphic innocence that appeals to this audience; it is bold and bright. It is also unadorned, but rich. It's not complex and dense. The voice, meaning the editorial voice, is all about being witty and clever."

Play by the Rules. Have Fun. Love Sesame Workshop.

It is that kind of direct language that is found throughout this brand, so the voice of the brand is very much embedded in the voice behind the workshop. "We also made it lean, in that a lot of its properties are character-based, very fluffy, kid focused, so that when it has to be used with Big Bird or Elmo or other character-based brands it isn't too cute or saccharine, but kid friendly," says Carbone.

sesame workshop™

The Creative Process

With the basic logo in hand, designers developed the brand architecture, an analytical process that included finalizing the color palette, typography, and testing how it worked with other partners such as Sony and Nickelodeon. In addition, designers looked at how the mark would work in one-color, against a background and test how it would work in print, on air, and digitally. We have a primary palette, secondary, and tertiary palette that allow people to work with the brand, depending upon the environment. As a result, a palette of primary colors was chosen for the identity that included both the constant elements and those that would evolve in response to different contexts in which the mark is used. The new mark was then applied to identity materials, advertising, press kits, signage, a new home page, among dozens of other pieces.

The Internal Launch

The identity program was launched internally to 500 in-house staff, board, and partners—totaling a 2500-unit mailing to introduce people to Sesame Workshop. The team focused as much on the internal launch as the external one because both are equally important to building a brand. Overnight the change took place. One day employees walked out of Children's Television Workshop and the following work-day they showed up for work at Sesame Workshop. Everything from business cards to memo pads had changed. Employees received new materials and everything they needed to do business, as well as a handsomely designed "thank you" brand book from the president and CEO that recognized how difficult change can be while reassuring employees that CTW's original mission was still intact.

ABOVE, RIGHT, AND FAR RIGHT: The Sesame Workshop logo is simple, which allowed it to be placed on a variety of items from letterhead to program literature and T-shirts.

Why the focus on the internal audience? "You want to change naysayers into cheerleaders," says Carbone. "I work with corporations who have all kinds of money to throw at their brand launches; all kinds of resources to make sure things happen efficiently, on time, and in a way that the whole culture of the company embraces. It isn't easy. Change is difficult. You have to manage that change very carefully so that everyone from the receptionist to the CEO can embrace it and get behind it and, essentially, become ambassadors of the new brand. I see many companies who don't do this very well. This organization is nonprofit with limited resources. They are always strapped for staff to do these kinds of things, yet with all these obstacles, they launched this brand 100 percent on the day they made the announcement. When people came to their offices June 5, they already had the new letterhead and business cards…it was a wonderful moment because the

momentum that's built with that and the goodwill that's built was invaluable. As an organization, they were terrific in getting behind this and understanding the value in not letting it trickle out.

"This wasn't about dropping a pebble in the pond and watching the gentle ripples emerge from it. This was about throwing something substantial in the pond and making a big splash and having the ripple effect be controlled the way you want it to be. Over a weekend, the culture changed, the brand essence changed. The only thing that was missing at the launch was the redesign of their home page, which wasn't launched until November 2000."

RIGHT: A "thank you" brochure was designed as a special item for employees.

LEFT AND BELOW: A media launch kit including a box with a T-shirt and set of markers for coloring in the logo line art, press kit, and folded card announcing the name change from Children's Television Workshop to Sesame Workshop was distributed to media and partners while an announcement card spread the word of Children's Television Workshop's name and identity change.

The External Launch

The logo itself is deceptively simple. On paper, it is reproduced in simple four-color process, but Carbone says that it is its simple, unadorned nature that makes it successful. Which is a plus, because the mark was applied to a range of paper elements from the new corporate identity to program literature, as well as T-shirts that were distributed to Sesame Workshop's external audiences.

A media launch kit including a box with a T-shirt and set of markers for coloring in the logo line art, press kit, and folded card announcing the name change from Children's Television Workshop to Sesame Workshop was distributed to media, partners, the Board of Directors, various potential sponsors and sponsors including the Corporation for Public Broadcasting. An announcement card spread the word of Children's Television Workshop's name and identity change. Similarly, print advertising was placed in a diverse collection of media ranging from *Parents* magazine to *Variety*, and the *New York Times* announcing the new Sesame Workshop name and identity.

The debut of Sesame Workshop's trade show booth at the International Film and Programme Market for Television, Video, Cable and Satellite (MIPCOM) show in Cannes, France, marked the first three-dimensional expression of the brand. There, a custom branded pair of binoculars was gift packaged and distributed by the hotel staff and left as a surprise gift for potential partners to find upon returning to their hotel rooms. The gift was packaged in a custom pouch with Sesame Workshop's URL emblazoned on it along with the tagline, "For more than bird watching" to encourage prospects to think of Sesame Workshop as more than Big Bird, particularly in light of its three new programs being launched at the show.

Throughout the creative process, designers had to ensure that the brand would work in myriad applications from two-dimensional art to a digital, animated version used at the end of the shows, in broadcast, as well as in three-dimensional environments. To ensure accuracy in all its forms, Carbone Smolan laid out the do's and don'ts for the new Sesame Workshop logo and identity in its *Standards Manual*.

BELOW: Print advertising announced the new Sesame Workshop name and identity.

TOP, MIDDLE LEFT AND RIGHT, AND LEFT: **The debut of Sesame Workshop's trade show booth marked the first three-dimensional expression of the brand.**

The Budget

As for the budget, "It's never enough, but for this organization, they put in the proper investment," says Carbone. "[It was a] careful balancing act of giving them a 200 percent solution while being careful of the time. The brand was not built to be extravagant. I'd like them to put their money into their programming. I have two-year-old twins so I'm immersed in this. I like the fact that we've given them a brand that doesn't require eight-color printing. It doesn't require elaborate packaging and promotion, it can be done simply and effectively."

The results

Throughout the process and after the launch, the client was so happy with the work that it has continually awarded Carbone Smolan more work, which is always an indication of satisfaction.

What Worked

Without digging too deep, one would be inclined to cite the obvious factors to explain why this promotion worked so well: A strong belief in the concept that was not swayed to its detriment by focus-group feedback; a client who backed a launch 100 percent instead of letting it dribble out; an adequately funded budget; and an agency that was willing to give a 200 percent solution. But there are other reasons why the promotion worked, according to Carbone.

"[The promotion] helped what we call legacy brand. It helped navigate a complex maze where we have 100 percent buy-in across the organization. The materials that we gave them—from the overall brand essence to the way the trade show was built—on a tactical level, everything we did was on brand and showed anyone who worked with the brand in the future that this is the way it should be done. This is the vocabulary," says Carbone.

"We've given them the right tools to make this campaign work on a continuing basis. That's why I think it really works. The brand platform that we developed is something that can grow organically over time without losing its basic foundation. They work with a lot of different companies, so it's important that they have a viewpoint that can be embraced by others and work. If this brand had been more designer-ly with bells and whistles, it would be bound to fall apart. In its simplicity, it has a great chance of succeeding for a long time."

A UNIVERSAL SYMBOL (symbol graphics)
PROPELS THE GRAPHICS FOR ANNUAL GLOBAL CAMPAIGN

The Client

Like many graphic design firms, Pepe Gimeno—Proyecto Gráfico inherited a problem when, in 1998, it was awarded the job of promoting the 36th annual Valencia International Furniture Fair scheduled for September 1999. The fair, the third biggest trade fair in Europe and one of the biggest in the world in its sector, annually attracts exhibitors and visitors from around the globe. That was the good news.

The Brief

On the downside, designers quickly realized that one of the greatest problems they were up against was the weak and vague image of the fair due to the lack of consistency in the communication and approaches used in previous years. Given the situation, they focused their attention on three primary goals: Creating an image that could be maintained and transformed to get consistent and continuous communication over several years; creating an image that would reflect the variety of styles and trends in furniture exhibited at the fair and the international nature of its visitors and exhibitions; and creating a style of its own to differentiate the Valencia Fair from its competitors.

LEFT AND BELOW: The designers' interpretation of the chair symbol that identifies promotional materials for the 2001 fair as applied to a poster and a direct-mail postcard.

CLIENT:
Valencia International Furniture Fair

DESIGN FIRM:
Pepe Gimeno—Proyecto Gráfico

DESIGNERS:
Suso Pérez, José P. Gil, Didac Ballester

CAMPAIGN RUN:
September 1998 to Present

TARGET MARKET:
Furniture manufacturers and industry professionals, the general public

LEFT: Designed fashioned the symbol of the chair from wide black, blue, and pink brush strokes to represent the 36th annual Valencia International Furniture Fair in September 1999.

Creating a Campaign That Translates

One of the biggest problems facing designers was the vast number of countries and variety of languages that had to be considered in the promotional materials. Designers had to translate copy into eight languages and address the corresponding semantic problems in each country that could hinder communication.

Dealing with language barriers made the use of the chair system that much more important to successful communication. The chair—a dynamic, globally recognized symbol—worked as well at communicating as any headline could do.

Crafting a Symbol to Differentiate

Designers pored over old promotions and brainstormed in an effort to find a means of achieving not just one, but all three of their goals. Surprisingly, they found a solution in a promotion created for the fair in 1991 by Mariscal—a chair. If they made the chair the standing symbol for the event and used it annually, designers reasoned, they could achieve the consistency and continuity that they wanted.

The Common Denominator

They made their recommendation and, anticipating their client's reaction, was ready with a response: To avoid the monotony of using the same symbol year after year, they would craft different interpretations of the symbol using different graphic styles and techniques. The client signed onto their proposal and the firm set to work on the 1999 event, seemingly fashioning the chair from wide black, blue, and pink brush strokes.

When the time came to get to work on the 2000 event, designers wiped the slate clean of everything but the chair, and this time, gave it an abstract interpretation, coloring it in warm shades of orange, gold, red, and rust.

LEFT: Designers interpreted the chair in abstract patterns and colored it shades of orange, gold, red, and rust for the 2000 event.

Feria Internacional del Mueble presenta en su 36 edición el certamen comercial que todos los profesionales del sector estaban esperando: una feria **pionera** en la cultura del diseño, **innovadora** por la selección y sectorización de su oferta, **coherente** con su larga trayectoria, **fascinante** como la ciudad que la acoge, **completa** por su amplia superficie de exposición, rentable por su volumen de negocio y competitiva por sus excelentes comunicaciones, servicios e instalaciones. Estos siete adjetivos perfilan un evento que ha sabido posicionarse como la mayor feria monográfica de España y la sexta del mundo.

For its 36th edition the International Furniture Fair is presenting the commercial event that all the professionals in the sector have been waiting for: a fair that is pioneering in design culture, innovative through the selection and sector-distribution of its offer, consistent with its long-standing tradition, fascinating like the city that hosts the event, complete thanks to its vast exhibition area, profitable thanks to the size of its turnover, and competitive through its excellent communications, services and facilities. These seven adjectives sum up an event which has managed to become the greatest monographic fair in Spain and sixth biggest in the world.

RIGHT AND FAR RIGHT: Designers attempted to define the fair using seven different adjective ranging from *fascinating* to *pioneering* and *profitable.* Each adjective was given its own postcard and its own interpretation of the chair icon. The seven postcards were bound in the form of a booklet and are easily separated.

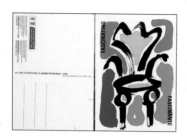

Carrying Out the Theme

Designers targeted the general public through traditional materials including a poster, display unit, and an advertising insert in the press and specialized magazines, the latter of which was limited due to budget restrictions. In addition, a parallel campaign targeted manufacturers and other professionals in the furniture sector with a direct-mail promotion. The imagery in all the supporting materials remained consistent regardless of which market was targeted as designers applied the common denominator for the whole campaign—the chair—to all supporting materials.

Regular Direct Mailings

Other mailers included the seven-adjective postcards where designers attempted to define the fair using seven different adjective ranging from *fascinating* to *pioneering* and *profitable.* Each adjective was given its own postcard and its own interpretation of the chair icon. The seven postcards were bound in the form of a booklet and, yet, could be separated easily.

Designers used a clear plastic CD-ROM jewel case as a display unit and container holding the sheets of a 2000 calendar. Once again, each month featured a different stylized illustration of the familiar chair symbol. The calendar also included a registration form for those wanting to sign up early to attend the event.

Since the designers' goal was to develop pieces with staying power, a mouse pad was included in the direct-mail mix. It was lightweight, useful, and easy to mail in quantities of 70,000 in its handy cardboard envelope.

Weighty Issues

RIGHT, FAR RIGHT, BOTTOM, AND FAR RIGHT BOTTOM: Designers used a clear plastic CD-ROM jewel case as a display unit and container holding the sheets of a 2000 calendar where each month featured a different stylized illustration of the chair symbol.

As with any direct-mail campaign, one of the greatest concerns when designing objects for mailing is their weight. The other is finding an item that will be something the recipient will use, which extends its lifecycle and keeps the promoter's name top-of-mind. Designers found that a metal page marker solved both issues—being lightweight and practical. They attached it to a large card and mailed it to the trade group—a mailing of 70,000 pieces.

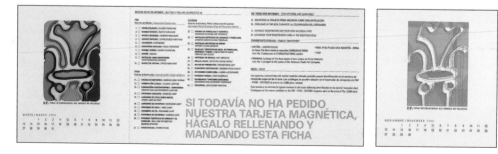

LEFT AND BELOW: A high-end book, detailing the entire history of the fair along with an overview of its current status and future goals, was created as a special promotional item for 1500 recipients. The book featured new iterations of the chair along with full-page, full-color photography.

A high-end book, detailing the entire history of the fair, its present and its future aims, was created as a special promotional item for 1500 recipients. The book featured new iterations of the chair along with full-page, full-color photography. Totaling 108 pages, the book was printed in four colors, bound with a hard cover, thermoprinted on the cover and spine, and accented with a tip-on label. A smaller version of the book, summarizing the history of the fair, was produced in a larger quantity of 70,000. It, too, was printed in four colors and featured abundant photography and included a CD-ROM with additional information.

Other items produced included a bag to carry materials picked up at the exhibition and animated graphics that opened and closed a series of advertising-report features broadcast on television.

The designers' hope was that recipients would find the materials so useful and ingenious that they would keep them around until the next year.

Consistency, Yes—Monotony, No

Designers had created a single image, which underwent successive transformations and yet still retained its visual interest with each iteration. Designers managed give the same image an entirely new look. In some examples, the image is extremely subtle and almost hard to find in the abstract treatment, in others it is bold and fresh, sometimes technological and cold; sometimes it is rendered as a whole and other times its parts are shattered into pieces. Whichever treatment it receives, the image always comes forward as something new and rejuvenated. Designers realized that apart from maintaining visual interest in all the marketing materials, the concept they hit upon accurately described the wide range of products and styles shown at the fair.

RIGHT: Ten thousand bags were printed four-color process for visitors to carry materials they picked up at the exhibition.

FAR RIGHT: A mouse pad was lightweight, useful, and easy to mail in quantities of 70,000, so it was included as part of the direct-mail campaign.

BELOW: In some cases the image of the chair was extremely subtle, in others its was daring and fresh, sometimes technological and cold, sometimes vivacious and broken up, but always coming forward as something new and rejuvenated.

The Curiosity Factor

The concept has a built-in curiosity factor as well. One can't help but wonder what form the chair will take on next. What could designers possibly dream up that will match what they've already produced? The recipient is intrigued and subconsciously looks toward the next transformation.

The designs are not selling a consumer product but are promoting a service, the potential for business. There are no points of sale; the only channel for communication with potential customers is through the media that specifically talks to the habitat and interior decorating markets. Here is a promotion with universal scope, yet the budget did not allow for a great deal of advertising placements. Consequently, advertisements appeared in a lot of media but with little intensity—perhaps only one or two times per year.

LEFT AND BELOW: A smaller version of "history" book, summarizing its past, was produced in a larger quantity of 70,000. It, too, was printed in four colors and featured abundant photography and included a CD-ROM with additional information.

The Budget

Ostensibly, the overall budget of approximately $800,000 was adequate, but because the promotion was on an international scale and there were many media outlets in several countries that had to be targeted, designers had to be vigilant about costs to ensure that the budget could be stretched to cover all the necessary advertising, as well as the direct-mail campaign, which totaled nearly 70,000. Given the size of the mailing list, the budget for the 2000 mailing campaign was increased by about $19,000 over 1999, while the advertising budget was reduced by close to $11,000 from the previous year. Given the budget restraints, designers took extra pains in researching and choosing the communication media slated for advertising insertions to ensure they were on target and further controlled the budget by keeping a tight reign on the weight of mailers so that postage costs wouldn't escalate out of control.

RIGHT: A CD-ROM, packaged in a thin tin, carries the graphics into another realm.

RIGHT AND FAR RIGHT: The *Full-Time Furniture* booklet asks the question on everyone's mind: What is the shape of the future?

The results

Exhibitors increased steadily in the years since Pepe Gimeno—Proyecto Gráfico assumed responsibility for promoting the fair—starting at 1203 in 1998 and rising to 1400 by the year 2000. Visitors also were on the rise, up from 67,200 in 1998 to 73,300 in 2000. Similarly, profits rose since the firm took control for promoting the event.

What Worked

Designers unanimously cite the use of a symbol, which they have successfully reinterpreted in numerous variations, as being the key to the campaign's success because it cleanly cuts across language barriers. They also point to the campaign's supporting graphics—color, texture line, and materials—as helping turn the promotional graphics into a universal language that conveys the diversity and international nature of the event.

"The continuous reinterpretation of the same graphic element without losing sight of the particular evolution of the market itself, the capacity for generating new concepts helping us to extend the standpoint that we have of the furniture industry, and the harmonious use of spaces and proportions in each of the different materials that we generate succeed in giving the image of the International Furniture Fair a dynamic, simple, and extremely compact message," says Didac Ballester, one of three designers on the project.

"The proper functioning of these image campaigns for the International Furniture Fair is, above all, due to the approach that has been implemented in each phase of the work," adds José Pascual Gil, designer. "A well-defined image and differentiating characteristics for the International Furniture Fair as a whole provide a central axis that can be used in all the campaigns and that marks out the boundaries for the message content in each of these.

"In each campaign, we tend to stress only one or two very basic and forceful concepts that we attribute to the International Furniture Fair and that can be understood in all the sociocultural contexts in which they are issued," he says. "Using the image as the real carrier of the message...texts and the large number of translations...lose their starring role and allow us to use a more universal language. The form of the campaign image is a synthesis of a very large number of different standpoints and techniques from which the treatment of the chair as the main element is tackled. This variety and rich depth of work help the image be expressive and specific, as well as novel, apart from extending the perspectives for the campaign for the following year."

DESIGNERS PUT A FACE (personal graphics)
ON THE AUSTRALIAN CHAMBER ORCHESTRA'S IDENTITY

The Client

The Australian Chamber Orchestra (ACO) wanted to stand out and distinguish itself from other major Australian orchestras. It needed a brand that would carry the orchestra into the future. Youthful, vibrant members characterized the ACO as a dynamic orchestra to watch.

The ACO called upon Chris Perks Design —CPd to create an image that would usher the orchestra into the millennium and beyond. Their branding choice was a fairly obvious one—play up the orchestra's primary asset: its members. CPd proposed photographing the orchestra members. "Because the orchestra is young and passionate about their work, we felt it important to convey that energy and vibrancy through both the photography, how it is used, and the typography. We still needed to portray the ACO as a classical orchestra but with a contemporary edge," says Nigel Beechey, art director.

CLIENT:
Australian Chamber Orchestra

DESIGN FIRM:
Chris Perks Design—CPd

ART DIRECTOR:
Nigel Beechey

DESIGNERS:
Nigel Beechey, Fiona Catt, Donna Taylor

PHOTOGRAPHER:
Greg Barret

COPYWRITER:
Jon Maxim

CAMPAIGN RUN:
1998 through 2001

TARGET MARKET:
Lapsed and new subscribers

ABOVE: The identity for 2000 campaign is built with plenty of white space and a palette of red and black.

The Brief

The idea arose from a previous campaign that garnered excellent feedback and was on record as the most memorable ACO campaign to date. It involved photographing the orchestra playing their instruments in a running line. "We dissected the campaign to discover why it had been so successful and decided that it was the first campaign that gave the ACO a distinct personality; one that was fun and playful, and which was a departure from the more standard, serious type imagery associated with orchestras," says Beechey.

Based on this philosophy, "We created our first ACO campaign using unusual, dynamic photography teamed with bold typography and layout. We followed this through the following campaigns, each year reinterpreting and reinventing the public face of the orchestra, keeping the language the same— interesting photography of the orchestra and clean typography, but in different ways to avoid the campaign becoming monotonous.

"The campaign's uniqueness lies in its portrayal of the orchestra as vibrant, passionate, and youthful. Many people think of orchestras as conservative, traditional, formal, and somewhat faceless. We have broken this mold and have given the Australian Chamber Orchestra a face—many faces. People are an integral part of the whole look and feature as much as music or instruments," says Beechey.

Using Type and Photography to Communicate

For the 1998 campaign, designers relied on photography that took a humorous approach, something seldom seen in promotional materials for highbrow orchestras. That is exactly why it worked so well. The sense of humor conveyed by a girl doing the splits with her cello and a woman leaping while clutching her violin all drew attention at the unexpected element of surprise proffered by the design. This approach, when teamed with clean, legible type that has bold and modern lines, allowed the players to interact with the letterforms. Seeing a woman lying on a line of type or a man leaning against a word, made the players, and ultimately, the orchestra, appear approachable, casual, and friendly.

In 1999, CPd once again created a campaign with clean, uncluttered graphics and a subtle sense of humor using only slivers of players' faces and encouraging concert-goers to "Come face to face" with ACO while merging the faces with their instruments. "The players merging with their instruments give a sense of the passion the players feel towards the music," says Beechey.

The 2000 campaign featured extreme close-ups of the members playing their instruments; the grainy photos showcase their intensity and passion. "The photography is more pensive and intense, but the sense of fun comes through the ACO mark, with figures leaping amongst the letters."

Distinctive, Yet Unified—Consistent, Yet Flexible

CPd designs for the orchestra's specific seasons, while managing to keep each loyal to the greater whole, despite the numerous elements being produced annually including brand identity, the season brochure, advertising campaign (press ads, posters), direct-mail call-to-action/teaser postcards, stationery for press releases, invitations, order forms, direct-mail acknowledgment of order/thank you pieces, folders for tickets and CDs, concert programs, and a Web site.

"By using key elements in different ways, we manage to keep each item distinctive but also unified. We design the initial concepts with the aim of keeping them flexible, knowing that it is a year-long campaign that should not become homogenized, and that the designs need to be translated into many different formats," Beechey says. "For each campaign, the photography is the most consistent element. To enhance this, we use a typographic style that will complement or contrast them. While the typeface will not change for the season, the way it is used will vary. It may be horizontal or vertical, reversed out of a background, or sit in front, concealing part of the photograph."

Similarly, color is used for consistency, yet it, too, is flexible. CPd works from a primary color palette of red and black on white with the occasional use of a third color. White space was integral to the 1998 design, yet designers added blocks of color, such as the red on the program cover. Likewise, designers added an all over flat color underneath the photographs on the invitations for the 2000 season. For a one-off concert flyer, the photograph was printed as a duotone to differentiate that concert from the rest of the season's concerts.

LEFT: The Season 2000 billboard poster, like the other elements to the 2000 campaign, features extreme close-ups of ACO members playing their instruments; the grainy photos showcase their intensity and passion.

Targeting Two Markets

For designers, the trickiest part of the job was establishing an image that would attract and hold the attention of an older, more conservative audience base while appealing to a more youthful market, in essence, the new generation of subscribers.

"The biggest design challenge was to create a campaign that appeals to the more typical orchestra subscribers who tend to be older and more conservative, as well as potential concert-goers who are interested in classical music but are perhaps intimidated by the stuffy perception of the classical concert," Beechey says. "As well as playing more traditional music by the better known composers, the ACO also includes in their repertoire more contemporary and obscure composers. The campaign needs to convey that the ACO is an innovative and experimental orchestra, while still following the traditions of good classical music.

"We solved these challenges through the way we used typography and photography together to achieve a lightheartedness but also a sense of the intensity of music playing. This way, we could make classical music feel accessible but also as something taken seriously by the orchestra."

Designers managed to blend the likes of both target audiences by crafting an identity that is contemporary but not faddish. Typography is bold, yet elegant, which gives the pieces a timelessness that doesn't lock it into a particular niche. "One campaign featured the classic, traditional typeface Bodoni, but used in a fresh and innovative way," explains Beechey. "This has been extended to the redesign of the Australian Chamber Orchestra logo, which uses Bodoni but breaks the letters with one of the long, leaping or running figures."

Season-Specific Campaigns

Each season's campaign needed to be unique in order to increase general awareness and sales from lapsed and new subscribers. As such, the annual promotion consists of many elements, targeting urban areas throughout Australia.

The first item produced for each campaign is the seasonal subscription brochure, detailing the entire season. A total of 250,000 four-color brochures are printed annually to launch the look of the new season; some are mailed while others are distributed at the venues and inserted into major newspapers and publications. The brochure includes detailed information on the concerts, dates, and guest artists. The designers' challenge is to fit all this copy onto a ten-page roll fold brochure, the size of which is determined by the publications into which it is inserted.

The paper stock used for the centerpiece brochure changes annually based on the design. In 1998, CPd's first year on the project, designers specified a satin stock to complement the fun, leaping figures and striking typography. In 1999, the imagery was more intense and moody, so designers chose an uncoated stock to give the brochure a gritty, tactile quality. The brochure included black-and-white photography, but designers printed it in four-color process to create a richer grayscale spectrum. For the 2000 campaign, a coated, glossier stock to contrast against very grainy photographs was chosen. In this instance, designers added a metallic blue-gray to the four-color process, which gave the photography a subtle shimmer and added a sense of glamour to specific typographical elements.

Immediately following the seasonal subscription brochure, designers launch the first round of advertising material, which is designed to generate an immediate response, motivating recipients to call for a brochure or visit ACO's Web site for more information. Initially, the emphasis is to get people to subscribe to the entire season. Once the concert season begins, the focus shifts to promoting the individual concerts, highlighting the guest soloists, and providing information on dates and concert venues.

Next, supporting materials are rolled out including posters, CD covers, ticket holders, and venue banners. Designers allow the printer to determine the stock and printing processes for these pieces based on the intended use. For example, banners for outdoor display are silkscreened onto waterproof fabric; indoor posters are digitally printed onto a stock that will fit through novajet printers. "Other brochures and printed material will generally use the same stock as the brochure to maintain a consistency throughout the year and often print two-colors for cost-saving purposes," explains Beechey. "Due to the great volume of items produced, we need to vary each item to avoid the designs from becoming monotonous."

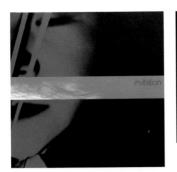

FAR LEFT: Designers added a flat color underneath the photographs in the Season 2000 invitation.

LEFT: For the 2000 campaign, a coated, glossy stock was specified to contrast against very grainy photographs. Designers added a metallic blue-gray to the four-color process, which gave the photography a subtle shimmer and added a sense of glamour to specific typographical elements.

It's All in the Details

Other, smaller promotional items are produced throughout the year to reinforce the ACO brand, including much overlooked details such as a ticket wallet. "We feel it is important, for example, that subscribers receive their tickets in a branded ticket holder. We also come up with some inexpensive novelty items such as concert reminder diary stickers," says Beechey.

The Budget

The budget arrangement is an unusual one, but one that works as well as the promotion. CPd is paid about one-quarter of the amount spent on design work, and in return, receives "the opportunity to work with a passionate and talented arts organization that appreciates the importance of good design in their promotional material. Therefore we ensure that at every step we use as many cost-saving measures as possible, without sacrificing the integrity of the design," says Beechey. Free concert tickets are an added bonus that is part of the fee arrangement.

Because of the unique budget structure, funds are limited. Typically, printing is sponsored and, consequently, designers stick to standard sizes for printed material and don't use special printing techniques, such as embossing or die-cutting. "This urges us to make the design striking with fairly limited resources, something which is exciting for anyone who works on the ACO. When designing the ACO material we are aware that we need to be budget conscious, however, we would never produce compromised work due to money constraints," says Beechey.

"We try to work as closely as possible with the printers, finding out techniques to achieve certain effects within budget. For example, when we wanted to use a metallic on a four-color process print job, we were able to cut costs by replacing the cyan plate with a metallic blue. While we tend to stick to standard paper sizes such as DL and A5, we use dynamic design techniques such as bleeding type or a figure off the edge of the page to create drama."

TOP: Taking the now famous running line image, CPd created frosted-glass panels, internal murals, and signage for the foyer of ACO's new space at Circular Quay.

BOTTOM: Photography used in the 2000 campaign is pensive and intense, but ACO's approachability comes through the ACO mark with figures leaping amongst the letters as seen in this wall graphic.

For the first two campaigns, designers used digital photography to cut the costs of processing and scanning. Due to the relative newness of the technology during the first year, the resulting images were a very low resolution. Rather than reshoot, designers converted the poor-quality images to black and white and added noise in Photoshop to give the photographs a gritty look that suited the close-up and intense nature of the shots.

The results

To date, market reaction has been positive. Subscriptions have increased steadily over the last three years. Admittedly, there were concerns that the Olympics and an increase in arts events in 2000 would provide tough competition for the ACO, but these fears were never realized as subscriptions for the 2000 season were up over 1999. Name awareness is also up, and both CPd and the ACO have received positive feedback on the campaign. "The ACO is now arguably one of the best-known arts organizations in Australia," says Beechey.

What Worked

"Working closely with the client, meeting members of the orchestra, watching them rehearse and experiencing their concerts, has given us the insight we need to create a successful promotional campaign," says Beechey. "By understanding that, as a group of young, passionate, and very talented musicians, the ACO wants to share their music with the world, not just an elite group of people, we are able to channel our passion for design to visually express the personality and vision of the orchestra."

SIMPLICITY IS KEY
TO GRAPHIC CAMPAIGN LAUNCHING DELIVERY SERVICE

(brown paper wrapper graphics)

The Client

Esprit Europe takes a novel approach to shipping parcels in Europe—it runs its delivery service on the Eurostar train. This fact alone makes the delivery service different, but how could the company communicate its uniqueness to mailroom managers, its primary target market?

The Brief

Esprit Europe tapped London-based HGV Design Consultants for help. The assignment: Create an identity and promotional items that would allow Esprit to launch its new service. HGV conducted a visual audit of the competition and discovered that no other delivery service communicated its delivery of parcels very clearly. From there, the concept fell into place. Designers tackled the identity by emulating the shape of the Eurostar train, which has a distinctive blunt nose shape, so that it appears as a "speeding parcel" to remind the public that all Esprit packages are uniquely delivered by Eurostar—a distinct advantage over the competition. To drive home the message, designers used brown paper and urgent labels to communicate parcels delivered with speed.

"Launching a new parcel service amongst severe competition on a medium-sized budget is a tough call," says Pierre Vermeir. "The strength of the promotion is its impact, the clarity of the key message: We deliver parcels to Brussels and Paris on the same day."

CLIENT:
Esprit Europe

DESIGN FIRM:
HGV Design Consultants

ART DIRECTORS:
Pierre Vermeir, Jim Sutherland, Martin Brown

DESIGNERS:
Pierre Vermeir, Jim Sutherland, Martin Brown Vermeir, Jim Sutherland

PHOTOGRAPHER:
Alan Levett

COPYWRITERS:
Pierre Vermeir, Jim Sutherland

CAMPAIGN RUN:
1995 through 1999

TARGET MARKET:
Mailroom managers

ABOVE AND RIGHT:
Designers branded watches and clocks as promotional items, blurring the numbers to communicate speed.

Standing Out in a Crowded Market

"The most difficult problem was to stand out in a crowded market, as is the case with any new identity, and to win clients for a new service. The marketing materials had to have immediate impact and hook potential clients, reinforcing speed of delivery and reassurance that parcels would arrive...the same day, a unique offer," says Vermeir, adding that Esprit Europe offers the fastest service in the sector.

To overcome this hurdle, designers gave the word *urgent* a bold, uppercase graphic type treatment and applied it to the brochure, posters, and supporting promotional materials to communicate speed and reassurance. A high-quality image was combined with minimal copy to deliver the message immediately to the target audience, not unlike how the parcels themselves are delivered. Likewise, designers integrated plain brown wrapping paper into the design, which is unique to Esprit Europe, and used it as the backdrop for the company's key message, immediately suggesting the delivery of packages.

The Launch

Esprit didn't have a name when it approached HGV for marketing assistance in launching the new service, so HGV participated with the client team to develop the name Esprit, which they chose because it lent a European sound to the company. As part of the marketing mix, the client asked HGV to design a launch brochure and supporting promotional materials.

Designers maintained consistent branding across all items but retained enough flexibility to heighten interest while differentiating the pieces. Promotional materials included a calendar made up of origami brown paper parcels, as well as clocks and watches, which were branded with blurred numbers to communicate speed. Brown paper wrapping and the urgent stickers were used to link disparate marketing items together as part of a cohesive campaign, a tactic that was used to dress up delivery trucks as well.

ABOVE: **Esprit Europe's trucks carry the promotional package motif.**

BELOW: Esprit Europe announced its new same-day parcel service between London and other cities in the United Kingdom with a mailer that features blurred scenes from the cities along the route as if seen flying by from a window of the train.

To proclaim the news, "We deliver parcels to Brussels and Paris on the same day," designers crafted a pro-motion using a French newspaper with a bellyband announcing that "News Travels Fast." As the service grew, additional promotional mailers were added. Interestingly, all feature a railway motif, characterized by train schedules, maps of train lines, and images of the cities and countryside along the route as if seen from the window of a speeding train.

Also added to the promotional mix was Esprit Europe sponsoring a competition for the fastest tennis serve and a drawing to win a pair of first-class return Eurostar tickets by simply completing the reply card built into a mailer.

ABOVE AND RIGHT: Rail lines are included in this slim mailer that informs recipients that now "your parcel can travel as fast as you can."

LEFT: Esprit Europe spon-sored a competition for the fastest tennis serves in a poster announcing the event.

Ashford to Europe, the UK and the world
Introducing the fastest parcel delivery service

esprit europe

The Budget

The total budget for developing the company name and designing the logotype, launch brochure, and promotional items was £45,000 or nearly $64,000, excluding printing. Was the budget lean? "Yes! But the client supported the design by investing in high-quality printing," says Vermier. "The initial design budget was extended over five years and we enjoyed a great relationship with the client, working on sports sponsorship deals, designing the UK rail parcels brochure, the international courier service brochure, and their Web site."

The A-B brochure creatively illustrates the morning and afternoon service available, while announcing a drawing to win a pair of first-class return Eurostar tickets by simply filling out the reply card built into the mailer.

europe

The results

As a result of the plain brown-paper promotion, the company grew from nothing to sales of £600,000 or approximately $850,000 in just five months. The direct-mail campaign generated an unprecedented 85 percent response rate. So positive were the early results that Esprit Europe extended its original promise of delivering parcels the same day to Brussels and Paris to include deliveries by rail within the United Kingdom along with an international courier service as well. If that wasn't good enough, HGV won a DBA Design Effectiveness Award for the launch brochure, supported by client sales data.

What Worked

"Targeted mail shots delivered the launch brochure to the right audience," Vermeir explains. "The logotype and brochure communicated the key messages clearly. The launch was followed-up by a personal visit from a sales representative who presented potential clients with a clearly branded, high quality promotional gift. The service was proven to be reliable, unique, and cost-effective."

PRODUCT LAUNCH FOR HAWORTH INC. DOESN'T TAKE ITSELF TOO SERIOUSLY (lighthearted graphics)

CLIENT:
Haworth Inc.

DESIGN FIRM:
Square One Design

ART DIRECTOR:
Mike Gorman

DESIGNERS:
Mike Gorman, Martin Schoenborn

PHOTOGRAPHERS:
Effective Images, Tim Parenteau

PRINTER:
Ethridge Co.

CAMPAIGN RUN:
December 1999 to Present

TARGET MARKET:
Facility managers, architectural and design community

ABOVE AND BOTTOM OF OPPOSITE PAGE: **Central to the campaign is a miniature 3" x 3" (8 cm x 8 cm) brochure that folds out to nearly 39 inches (99 cm) to tell the story of Jump Stuff. Designers created the brochure to be small and intimate to get people interested in the product, yet it had to be affordable enough to be printed in mass quantities that would allow Haworth to saturate the market.**

The Client

Cognitive artifacts—that is what the Jump Stuff campaign for Haworth Inc., a manufacturer of office furniture, is all about. Yet, you won't find the words *cognitive artifacts* anywhere in the campaign. Why? Because this campaign doesn't take itself too seriously, which just might be the single most important reason it works so well.

Jump Stuff by Haworth comprises a family of desk accessories with a difference. These work tools get everything up and off the desk, leaving a clutter-free work surface because in and out boxes, paper trays, paper sorters, and telephone, among scores of other items, are suspended above users' desks. The philosophy behind this innovative product is that desks are cluttered enough with daily paperwork; desk accessories meant to assist the user don't need to add to the commotion. The Jump Stuff system builds extra functionality into desk accessories. It works for the user by reminding them of things they can't keep in their head anymore—cognitive artifacts. The product can be purchased piece by piece or in kits, where all the desk accessories attach to a rail that is either mounted to the desk, a wall, or panel.

"Grip clips put items up there where they stay in front of you. The two-way tray and three-layer display also put things out in front of you," says Mike Gorman, creative director of Square One Design, which coordinated the campaign. "The main point is that a lot of accessory and furniture makers ascribe to workers a workstyle for them versus saying, 'Work however you want to work. This can be moved around. We're not prescribing what's right.' Jump Stuff is the ideal product for a person who has a really messy desk, but understands it and knows where everything is."

The Brief

Recognizing that the primary selling point of the product is its flexibility and ability to adapt to numerous workstyles versus dictating one way or the highway, Square One Design took a humorous approach to the project and looked around their own offices and others to find distinct office personalities with their own quirky workstyles to illustrate the product's versatility. In short, the concept, which they developed from a brainstorming session during a two-week period, was based on developing promotional pieces that focused more on the product's uses than its features and benefits. All the ideas came together at once, then designers prepared each element of the campaign in sequence.

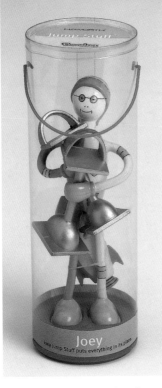

LEFT: Among the highlights in Haworth's arsenal of follow-up components was a direct-mail piece consisting of a Bendo™ doll, aptly named Joey Jump Stuff.

Reaching Two Separate Audiences

Communicating to two distinct audiences—facilities managers and the architectural and design community—was one of the design team's challenges. To that end, they created office characters that everyone could relate to. That, in combination with color, simple photography, and humor, assisted in engaging all audiences.

From a design point of view, however, the office characters that made the promotion so intriguing also presented problems executing the layout of pieces such as the spec brochure. Gorman says it was tricky to have the cut-out office workers interact with the product without it looking too trite. "We didn't want it to appear like we were doing Photoshop tricks. The trick was to avoid having them [the people] react too much in the third dimension. The guy on the rail goes the farthest," explains Gorman, citing that other characters react more with the elements of the brochure, including the edge of a page or a line on a page, and less so with the product.

Communicating Product Diversity

Central to the campaign is a miniature 3" x 3" (8 cm x 8 cm) brochure that folds out to nearly 39 inches (99 cm) to tell the story of Jump Stuff. Designers created the brochure to be small and intimate to get people very interested in the product, yet it had to be affordable enough to be printed in mass quantities that would allow Haworth to saturate the market. It tells the story of three office types that virtually everyone recognizes: Corporate Wonder Woman—a type A personality, who is very busy and probably doesn't have a whole lot of paper on her desk, but uses a lot of reminders. There's a Jump Stuff configuration for her. Then, there is Tall Guy, who oversees the human resources department and has just developed a new filing system; he works with lots of paper. There's a Jump Stuff kit for him, too. Finally, there's B.M.O.C., otherwise known as Big Man Off Campus. He works from a home office and needs help organizing and integrating his work and home lifestyles. The minibrochure was distributed with other Haworth products and includes a toll-free 800 number to call for more information and the Jump Stuff Web site where potential buyers could design their own Jump Stuff configuration on the Web.

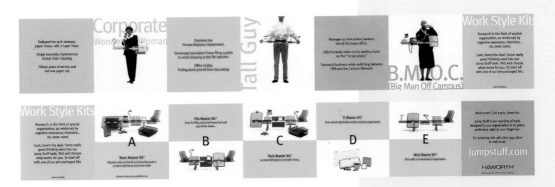

The Rollout

Those responding to the miniature brochure received
the Jump Stuff spec brochure in answer to their
request for more information. The spec brochure
continued the initial premise—only now the cut-out
office characters interact with the product and the
brochure in a clean, fresh layout that is inviting and
makes for easy reading.

Other components followed suit with various office personalities populating everything from a series of small
—approximately 7 inches (18 cm)—point-of-purchase
displays that fit into the rail of a Jump Stuff system to
full-size, 6-feet (1.8 m) tall point-of-purchase displays.

In addition, Square One created ancillary materials including gimmicky tattoos and a
"mock-up" brochure to convince office-furniture dealers to include Jump Stuff along
with their sales pitches for office furniture or panel systems. Desktop point-of-purchase displays included a plastic tray that holds the miniature Jump Stuff brochure.

Square One Design didn't overlook any details in this multipart campaign. They
created campaign complementary packing slips, package labels, and even translucent sheets, which were used as props to dress up paper trays and clip grips in Jump
Stuff displays.

Get your mock-ups to make a statement.

HAWORTH

Jump Stuff tops off a mock-up that demands to be noticed.

Bending the Message

Among the highlights in Haworth's arsenal of follow-up components was a direct-mail piece consisting of a bendable doll, aptly named Joey Jump Stuff, sent specifically to the architectural and design markets to create goodwill toward Haworth. Square One Design initiated the project by contacting Kid Galaxy, Inc., of Manchester, New Hampshire, the creators of Bendos™. The toy company was enthusiastic about working on the project, so designers downloaded blank Bendos characters and designed Joey for Jump Stuff. Designers gave Joey a pair of stilts that raised him off the ground —echoing the fact that the rail system gets everything up and off your desk—and a rocket booster to signify the fact that he boosts productivity. They dressed him in the Jump Stuff colors and sent their Freehand files to China for production. In return, they received a hand-painted proof for approval prior to mass production.

"We were looking for something to send out to 9,000 people that would be impactful, yet affordable," says Gorman. In the end, the unit price on Joey Jump Stuff was $2.50. With Joey completed, Square One Design created their own mailing label and a call for action to round out the mailing. The Bendos vendor could have handled both items, but Square One Design preferred keeping them in-house to retain more control on the project.

The three-dimensional character and his addictive playfulness promoted Haworth's Jump Stuff in a truly unique and memorable way. "People have been taken aback by getting a toy of this substance as a giveaway mailing. It's really a keeper," says Gorman, noting that it was also a big hit around the offices at Haworth where people were snatching them from the marketing department. Joey marks the first of several Bendos being used by Haworth, each representing a different product line, effectively setting the stage for several more to be created in the future to comprise a Haworth Bendos team.

Get to know Jump Stuff!

Included:
Teaser
Product Brochure
Mock-Up Flyer
Dealer Display Flyer
Handbook
USA Today Reprint
Price List
Service Parts List

jumpstuff.com

Blending Diversity with Continuity

To maintain continuity between everything from point-of-purchase standees and brochures to a bendable doll, designers worked with a color palette of three primary colors, which are used throughout the campaign, in addition to a consistent typeface. Designers used very little bold or italic type, but instead relied on type size for impact, so there's a lot of scaling. Also notable is the amount of white space that dominates each piece and the fact that there is very little black text; most text appears in green. Also maintaining continuity are the people who appear as cut-outs throughout the campaign. These standards were not set in stone from the outset, but developed from one piece to the next. "Going into the minibrochure, I don't think we knew these would be the key elements, but when we were done with it and were starting on the spec brochure, it was clear that this was what the brand would be about," says Gorman.

Work Smart
Have Fun
Get a Grip

Your Jump Stuff inside.

Jumpstuff.com

ABOVE AND LEFT: **Square One Design didn't overlook any details in this multipart campaign. They created campaign-complementary packing slips, package labels, and even translucent sheets, which were used as props to dress up paper trays and clip grips in Jump Stuff displays.**

The results

This product introduction was one of the most successful campaigns that Haworth has launched. The strong branding, use of humor, and its down-to-earth appeal all combined to generate an enormous response from their dealer network, clients, and internal staff. It marked the beginning of what has now become a much larger movement toward making the communication characteristics of the Jump Stuff launch filter into all Haworth communications.

Haworth has compiled hundreds of comments from the architectural and design community as a result of the bounce back cards included in the Joey Jump Stuff Bendo mailer. "From the 15 percent return, we have heard nothing but appreciation for the playfulness that these characters have brought to offices around the world," says Gorman.

What Worked

"The promotion worked so well because it doesn't take itself too seriously," he adds. "We just say this product works the way you do. It's fun. People don't want to read a lot of copy, so we put an incentive in there—humor. They read a little bit, enjoy what they are reading, and are inspired to read on. They have some fun. [The campaign] pulls people in and humanizes the product so everyone can relate to it in a fun and friendly way. The campaign combines a mixture of worktime and playtime and capitalizes on that."

directory of contributors ›

AdamsMorioka
370 S. Doheny, #201
Beverly Hills, CA 90211 USA
www.adamsmorioka.com

Amoeba Corp.
457 Richmond Street, West
Toronto, ON M5V 1X9 Canada
TEL 416.599.2699
FAX 416.599.2391
www.amoebacorp.com
kelar@amoebacorp.com

Angelini Design
Via del Colosso 23
00184 Rome Italy
TEL +39.06.4620.641
FAX +39.06.4360.6421
www.angelinidesign.com
roma@angelinidesign.com

Anvil Graphic Design, Inc.
2611 Broadway Street
Redwood City, CA 94063 USA
TEL 650.261.6094
FAX 650.261.6095
www.anvilpaper.com or
www.hitanvil.com
aratliff@hitanvil.com

Atom Design
47 Timber Bush
Edinburgh EH6 6QH
Scotland, UK
TEL +44.0.131.476.8044
FAX +44.0.131.476.8046
www.atomdesign.co.uk
info@atomdesign.co.uk

Barbara Lipp Illustration
313 Ringgold Street
Peekskill, NY 10566 USA
TEL/FAX 914.734.8238
www.barbaralipp.com
bl@el.net

The Bark
2810 Eighth Street
Berkeley, CA 94710 USA
TEL 510.704.0827
FAX 510.704.0933
www.thebark.com
bark@thebark.com

BBK Studio, Inc.
648 Monroe Avenue NW,
Suite 212
Grand Rapids, MI 49503 USA
TEL 616.459.4444
FAX 616.459.4477
www.bbkstudio.com
yang@bbkstudio.com

Blue River Design
The Foundry, Forth Banks
Newscastle Upon Tyne, NE1 3PA
England, UK
TEL +44.0191.261.0000
FAX +44.0191.261.0010
www.blueriver.co.uk
simon@blueriver.co.uk

Bisqit Design
5 Theobalds Road
London WC1X 8SH
England, UK
TEL +44.020.7413.3739
FAX +44.020.7413.3738
www.bisqit.co.uk
daphne@bisqit.co.uk

Bradbury Branding & Design, Inc.
11th Avenue, #300-1640
(head office)
Regina, SK S4P 0H4 Canada
TEL 800.254.7989
FAX 306.525.4068
www.bradburydesign.com
ideas@bradburydesign.com

Brown & Company Design
801 Islington Street, Suite 35
Portsmouth, NH 03801 USA
TEL 603.436.5239
FAX 603.436.1363
www.browndesign.com
davidm@browndesign.com

Bubblan Design
(Studio Bubblan AB)
Sjunde Villagatan 28
50454 Boras Sweden
TEL +46 33.414441
FAX +46 33.132968
www.bubblan.se
kari@bubblan.se

Cahan & Associates
171 2nd Street, Suite 500
San Francisco, CA 94105 USA
TEL 415.621.0915
FAX 415.621.7642
www.cahanassociates.com
info@cahanassociates.com

Capsule
10 South Fifth Street, Suite 645
Minneapolis, MA 55402 USA
TEL 612.341.4525
FAX 612.341.4577
www.capsule.us
akeller@capsule.us

Carbone Smolan Agency
22 West 19th Street, 10th Floor
New York, NY 10011 USA
www.carbonesmolan.com

Carter Wong Tomlin
29 Brook News North
London W2 38W
England, UK
TEL +44.020.7569.0000
FAX +44.020.7569.0001
www.carterwongtomlin.com
p.cater@caterwongtomlin.com

Chimera Design
6/179 Barkley Street
St. Kilda, Victoria 3182 Australia
TEL +61.03.9593.6844
FAX +61.03.9593.6855
www.chimera.com.au
design@chimera.com.au

CPd—Chris Perks Design
333 Flinders Lane, 2nd Floor
Melbourne, Victoria 3000
Australia
www.cpdtotal.com.au

deepend
813 Broadway, 2nd Floor
New York, NY 10003 USA
TEL 212.253.1974
FAX 212.253.2375
www.deepend.com
iti@deepend.com

Design Guys
119 N 4th Street, Suite 400
Minneapolis, MN 55401 USA
TEL 612.338.4462
FAX 612.338.1875
www.designguys.com
steve@designguys.com

Designation, Inc.
53 Spring Street, 5th Floor
New York, NY 10012 USA
TEL 212.226.6024
FAX 212.219.0331
www.quondesign.com
mikequon@aol.com

Dinnick + Howells
298 Markham Street, 2nd Floor
Toronto, ON M6J 2G6
Canada
TEL 416.921.5754
FAX 416.921.0719
www.dinnickandhowells.com
jonathan@dinnickandhowells.com

dossiercreative
305-611 Alexander Street
Vancouver, BC V6A 1E1 Canada
TEL 604.255.2077
FAX 604.255.2097
www.dossiercreative.com
don@dossiercreative.com

Double You
Calle Esglesia 4-10, 3-A
08024 Barcelona Spain
TEL +34.93.292.31.10
FAX +34.93.292.21.97
www.doubleyou.com
Barcelona@doubleyou.com

Douglas Joseph Partners
11812 San Vicente Boulevard,
Suite 125
Los Angeles, CA 90049 USA
TEL 304.440.3100
FAX 304.440.3103
www.djpartners.com
info@djpartners.com

Duffy Design (London)
67-69 Beak Street
London W1F 9SW
England, UK
TEL +44.0207.434.3919
FAX +44.0207.434.3923
www.duffy.com
info@duffy.com

Duffy Design (Minneapolis)
50 S. 6th Street, Suite 2800
Minneapolis, MN 55402 USA
TEL 612.758.2333
FAX 612.758.2334
www.duffy.com
info@duffy.com

DWL Incorporated
230 Richmond Street East,
Level 2
Toronto, ON M5A 1P4 Canada
TEL 416.364.2045
FAX 416.364.2422
www.dwl.com
smurenbeeld@dwl.com

Dynamo Art & Design
14 Plain Street
Natick, MA 01760 USA
TEL 617.461.8811
FAX 208.493.7895
www.dynamodesign.com
nw@dynamodesign.com

Elfen
20 Harrowby Lane
Cardiff Bay, CF10 5GN
England, UK
TEL +44.029.2048.4824
FAX +44.029.2048.4823
www.elfen.co.uk
post@elfen.co.uk

Emery Vincent Design
Level 1, 15 Foster Street
Surry Hills
Sydney NSW 2010 Australia
TEL +61.2.92850.4233
FAX +61.2.9280.4266
www.evd.com.au
sharon.nixon@evd.com.au

Evolve
Studio 6, 42 Orchard Road
Highgate, London N6 5TR
England, UK
TEL +44.0208.340.9541
FAX +44.0208.340.9634
www.evolvedesign.co.uk
jh@evolvedesign.co.uk

Frost Design London
The Gymnasium
56 Kings Way Place
Sans Walk, London EC1R 0LU
England, UK
TEL +44 020.7490.7994
FAX +44 020.7490.7995
www.frostdesign.co.uk
info@frostdesign.co.uk

Gerald & Cullen Rapp, Inc.
108 East 35th Street
New York, NY 10016 USA
TEL 212.889.3337
FAX 212.889.3341
www.rappart.com
gerald@rappart.com

Giorgia Davanzo Design
232 Belmont Avenue, E., #506
Seattle, WA 98102 USA
TEL 206.328.5031
FAX 206.324.3592
www.davanzodesign.com
info@davanzodesign.com

Good Gracious! Events
5714 West Pico Boulevard
Los Angeles, CA 90019 USA
TEL 323.954.2277
FAX 323.934.8312
ggracious@aol.com

Grafik
1199 N. Fairfax Street, Suite 700
Alexandria, VA 22314 USA
TEL 703.299.4500
FAX 703.299.5999
www.grafik.com
info@grafik.com

Hambly & Woolley, Inc.
130 Spadina Avenue, Suite 807
Toronto, Ontario M5V 2L4 Canada
TEL 416.504.2742
FAX 416.504.2745
www.hamblywoolley.com
bobh@hamblywoolley.com

Harvard Design School
48 Quincy Street
Cambridge, MA 02138 USA
TEL 617.495.4731
www.gsd.harvard.edu

Heads, Inc.
594 Broadway #1203S
New York, NY 100012 USA
TEL 212.941.5970
FAX 212.941.6087
www.headsinc.com
soso@bway.net

Hesse Design
Duesseldorfer Str. 16
40699 Erkrath
Germany
TEL +49.211.280.7200
FAX +49.211.2807.2020
www.hess-design.de
duesseldorf@hesse-design.de

HGV Design Consultants
46A Roseberry Avenue
London·EC1 4RP
England, UK
www.hgv.co.uk

Hornall Anderson Design Works
1008 Western Avenue, Suite 600
Seattle, WA 98104 USA
TEL 206.467.5800
FAX 206.467.6411
www.hadw.com
c_arbini@hadw.com

Dennis Y. Ichiyama
450 Littleton Street
West Lafayette, IN 47906-3013
USA
TEL 765.743.0440
diad@purdue.edu

Dotzero Design
208 SW Stark Street, #307
Portland, OR 97204 USA
TEL 503.892.9262
FAX 503.228.9403
www.dotzerodesign.com
jonw@dotzerodesign.com

i_d buero
Bismarckstrasse 67A
Stuttgart 70197 Germany
TEL +49.711.636.8000
FAX +49.711.636.8008
www.i-dbuero.de
mail@i-dbuero.de

IE Design
422 Pacific Coast Highway
Hermosa Beach, CA 90254 USA
TEL 310.376.9600
FAX 310.727.3515
www.iedesign.net
mail@iedesign.net

[i]e design
1600 Rosecrans Avenue
Building 6B, Suite 200
Manhattan Beach, CA 90266 USA
TEL 310.727.3500
FAX 310.727.3515
www.iedesign.net
mail@iedesign.net

Iridium, a design agency
43 Eccles Street, 2nd Floor
Ottawa, ON K1R 6S3 Canada
TEL 613.748.3336
FAX 613.748.3372
www.iridium192.com
mario@iridium192.com

Iron Design
120 North Aurora Street, Suite 5A
Ithaca, NY 14850 USA
TEL 607.275.9544
FAX 607.275.0370
www.irondesign.com
todd@irondesign.com

Jack Morton Worldwide
498 Seventh Avenue
New York, NY 10018 USA
TEL 212.401.7333
FAX 212.401.7016
www.jackmorton.com
anya_beaupre@jackmorton.com

Jason & Jason
Visual Communications
11B HaYetzira Street
Ra'anana Industrial Park 43663
Israel
TEL +972.9.7444282
FAX +972.9.744272
orily@jasonandjason.com

Kinetic Singapore
2 Leng Kee Road
Thye Hong Centre, #04-03A
Singapore 159086 Singapore
TEL +65.6379.5320
FAX +65.6472.5440
www.kinetic.com.sg
roy@kinetic.com.sg

Kolégramdesign
37 boulevard St-Joseph
Hull, QB J8Y 3V8 Canada
TEL 819.777.5538
FAX 819.777.8525
www.kolegram.com
mike@kolegram.com

Lava Graphic Designers
Van Diemenstraat 366
1013 CR Amsterdam Netherlands
TEL +31.020.6222640
FAX +31.020.6390798
www.lava.nl
design@lava.nl

Levy Creative Management
300 East 46th Street, Suite 8E
New York, NY 10017 USA
TEL 212.687.6463
FAX 212.661.4839
www.levycreative.com
sari@levycreative.com

Lewis Moberly
33 Gresse Street
London W1T 1QU
England, UK
TEL +44.020.7580.9252
FAX +44.020.7255.1671
www.lewismoberly.com
nicola.shellswell@
  lewismoberly.com

Lloyd's Graphic Design &
Communication
17 Westhaven Place
Blenheim, New Zealand
TEL/FAX 0064.3.578.6955
llyodgraphics@xtra.com

MAGMA (Büro für Gestaltung)
Bachstraße 43
D-76185 Karlsruhe Germany
TEL +721.92919.70
FAX +721.92919.80
www.magma-ka.de
harmsen@magma-ka.de

Media Consultants
461 Kingsland Avenue
Lyndhurst, NJ 07071-2707 USA
TEL 201.531.8300
FAX 201.933.6318
www.popandfoldpapers.com
hlhirsch@earthlink.net

Metal
1210 W. Clay, Suite 18
Houston, TX 77013 USA
TEL 713.523.5177
FAX 713.523.5176
www.metal.cc
info@metal.cc

Milton Glaser, Inc.
207 East 32nd Street
New York, NY 10016 USA
TEL 212.889.3161
FAX 212.213.4072
www.miltonglaser.com

Miriello Grafico
419 West G Street
San Diego, CA 92101 USA
TEL 619.234.1124
FAX 619.234.1960
www.miriellografico.com
pronto@miriellografico.com

Mirko Ilić Corporation
207 East 32nd Street
New York, NY 10016 USA
TEL 212.481.9737
FAX 212.481.7088
www.mirkoilic.com
studio@mirkoilic.com

Modern Dog
Communications, Inc.
7903 Greenwood Avenue, N
Seattle, WA 98103 USA
TEL 206.789.7667
FAX 203.789.3171
www.moderndog.com
bubbles@moderndog.com

Motive Design Research LLC
2028 Fifth Avenue, Suite 204
Seattle, WA 98121 USA
TEL 206.374.8761
FAX 206.374.8763
www.altmotive.com
info@altmotive.com

Nassar Design
11 Park Street
Brookline, MA 02446 USA
TEL 617.264.2862
FAX 617.264.2861
n.nassar@verizon.net

Nesnadny + Schwartz
10803 Magnolia Drive
Cleveland, OH 44106 USA
TEL 216.791.7721
FAX 216.791.3654
www.nsideas.com
info@nsideas.com

Nolin Branding and Design
1610 Sainte-Catherine Street West,
Bureau 500
Montreal, PQ H3H 2S2 Canada
TEL 514.846.2541
FAX 514.939.7343
or
2 Bloor Street West, 29th Floor
Toronto, ON M4W 3R6 Canada
TEL 416.413.8901
FAX 416.972.5656
www.nolin.ca
info@nolia.ca

Noon
592 Utah Street
San Francisco, CA 94110 USA
TEL 415.621.4922
FAX 415.621.4966
www.designatnoon.com
info@designatnoon.com

OrangeSeed Design
800 Washington Avenue N,
Suite 461
Minneapolis, MN 55401-1196
USA
TEL 612.252.9757
FAX 612.252.9760
www.orangeseed.com
info@orangeseed.com

Origin
Chetham House
Bird Hall Lane
Cheadie Heath
Cheshire 5K3 0ZP
England, UK
TEL +44.161.495.4808
FAX 44.161.495.4550
www.origincreativedesign.com
enquiries@origincreativedesign
.com

Pentagram
11 Needham Road
London W11 2RP
England, UK
TEL +44.20.7229.3477
FAX +44.20.7727.9932
www.pentagram.co.uk
email@pentagram.co.uk

204 Fifth Avenue
New York, NY 10010 USA
TEL 212.683.7000
FAX 212.532.0181
www.pentagram.com
info@pentagram.com

387 Tehama Street
San Francisco, CA 94103 USA
TEL 415.896.0499
FAX 415.896.0555
www.pentagram.com
info@sf.pentagram.com

1508 West Fifth Street
Austin, TX 78703 USA
TEL 512.476.5725
FAX 512.476.3076
www.pentagram.com
howdy@pentagram.com

Monbijouplatz 5
10178 Berlin Germany
TEL +49.30.27.87.61-0
FAX +49.30.27.87.61-10
info@pentagram.de

Pepe Gimeno—Proyecto Gráfico
C/ Cadirers, s/n – Pol. D'Obradors
E-46110 Godella, Valencia Spain
gimeno@ctv.es

Ph.D
1524A Cloverfield Boulevard
Santa Monica, CA 90404 USA
TEL 310.829.0900
FAX 310.829.1859
www.phdla.com
phd@phdla.com

Plainspoke
18 Sheafe Street
Portsmouth, NH 03801 USA
TEL 603.433.5969
FAX 603.433.1587
www.plainspoke.com
matt@plainspoke.com

Platform Creative Group, Inc.
80 South Jackson, Suite 308
Seattle, WA 98104 USA
TEL 206.621.1855
FAX 206.621.7146
www.platformcreative.com

Plazm Media
P.O. Box 2863
Portland, OR 97208 USA
TEL 503.528.8000
FAX 503.528.8092
www.plazm.com
josh@plazm.com

Question Design
15 Rozbern Drive
Eatontown, NJ 07724 USA
TEL 646.872.0498
FAX 212.333.2557
REP 212.333.2551
www.shannonassoicates.com
c_noruzi@hotmail.com

R2 Design
Praceta D Nuno Alvares Pereira
20 2 Box
4450 218 Matshinhos Portugal
TEL +351.229.386.865
FAX +351.229.350.838
www.rdois.com
info@rdois.com

Red Canoe
347 Clear Creek Trail
Deer Lodge, TN 37726 USA
TEL 423.965.2223
FAX 423.965.1005
www.redcanoe.com
studio@redcanoe.com

Reebok International Ltd.
1895 J. W. Foster Boulevard
Canton, MA 02021 USA
TEL 781.401.5000
FAX 781.401.4077
www.reebok.com
eleni.chronpoulos@reebok.com

Renegade Marketing Group
75 Ninth Avenue, 4th Floor
New York, NY 10016 USA
TEL 646.486.7700
FAX 646.486.7800
www.renegademarketing.com
dneisser@renegademarketing.com

The Riordon Design Group, Inc.
131 George Street
Oakville, ON L3J 3B9 Canada
TEL 905.339.0750
FAX 905.339.0753
www.riordondesign.com
greer@riordondesign.com

Sandstrom Design
808 SW Third Avenue, Suite 610
Portland, OR 97204 USA
TEL 503.248.9466
FAX 503.227.5035
www.sandstromdesign.com
rick@sandstromdesign.com

Sayles Graphic Design
3701 Beaver Avenue
Des Moines, IA 50310 USA
TEL 515.279.2922
FAX 515.279.0212
www.saylesdesign.com
sheree@saylesdesign.com

Sensus Design Factory
Sijecanjska 9
Zagreb HR-10000 Croatia
TEL +385.1.3049010
FAX +385.1.3634406
nedjeljko.spoljar@zg.tel.hr

S.L.M.doo
Kuseviceva 7
10000 Zagreb Croatia
TEL/FAX +385.1.485-222
luka.mjeda@zg.tel.hr

Square One Design
560 Fifth Street NW, Suite 301
Grand Rapids, MI 49504 USA
www.squareonedesign.com

Squires & Company
2913 Canton Street
Dallas, TX 75226 USA
TEL 214.939.9194
FAX 214.939.3464
www.squirescompany.com
murphy@squirescompnay.com

Starshot
Malsenstrasse 84
80638 München Germany
TEL +49.89.159.866.20
FAX +49.89.159.866.88
www.starshot.de
harmen@starshot.de

stilradar
Schwabstr. 10A
70197 Stuttgart
Germany
TEL +49.0711.887.5520
FAX +49.0711.882.2344
www.stilradar.de
info@stilradar.de

Strawberry Frog
Tesselschadestraat 13
1054 ET Amsterdamn
Netherlands
TEL +31.20.5300.400
FAX +31.20.5300.499
www.blueberryfrog.com
mark@blueberryfrog.com

Templin Brink Design
720 Tehama Street
San Francisco, CA 94103 USA
TEL 415.255.9295
FAX 415.255.9296
www.templinbrinkdesign.com
info@templinbrinkdesign.com

Uniform/Form
47 Tabernacle Street
London EC2A 4AA England, UK
TEL +44.020.7014.1430
www.uniform.uk.com
www.form.uk.com
studio@uniform.uk.com
studio@form.uk.com

Untitled
Nick Veasey
Radar Studio
Coldblow Lane
Thurnham, Maidstone
Kent ME14 3LR England, UK
TEL +44.0.1622.737722
FAX +44.0.1622.738644
Mobile +44.0.7976.420013
www.untitled.co.uk
info@untitled.co.uk

Viva Dolan
Communications & Design, Inc.
99 Crown's Lane, Suite 500
Toronto, ON M5R 3P4 Canada
TEL 416.923.6355
FAX 416.923.8136
www.vivadolan.com
frank@vivadolan.com

Wasserman & Partners
Advertising Inc.
Suite 160, 1020 Mainland Street
Vancouver, BC V6B 2T4 Canada
TEL 604.684.1111
FAX 604.408.7049
www.wasserman-partners.com
knishi@wasserman-partners.com

Williams and House
296 Country Club Road
Camano Island, WA 98292 USA
TEL 360.387.9336
FAX 360.387.0660
www.williamsandhouse.com
info@williamsandhouse.com

Wink
126 North 3rd Street, #100
Minneapolis, MN 55401 USA
TEL 612.630.5138
FAX 612.455.2645
www.wink-mpls.com
Richard@wink-mpls.com

WOW! A Branding Company
101-1300 Richards Street, Suite 101
Vancouver, BC V68 3G6 Canada
TEL 604.683.5655
FAX 604.683.5685
www.wowbranding.com
brittany@wowbranding.com

Zoesis, Inc.
246 Walnut Street, Suite 301
Newton, MA 02460 USA
TEL 617.969.5700
FAX 617.969.4472
www.zoesis.com
joe@zoesis.com or
laura@zoesis.com

about the authors ›

CHERYL DANGEL CULLEN is a writer and public relations consultant specializing in the graphic arts industry. She is the author of *Graphic Design Resource: Photography*, *The Best of Annual Report Design*, *The Best of Direct Response Graphics*, *Large Graphics*, *Small Graphics*, *The Best of Brochure Design 6*, *Then Is Now*, and she is a contributing writer to *Design Secrets: Products*. Cullen writes from her home near Chicago and has contributed articles to *How* magazine, *Step-by-Step Graphics*, *Graphic Arts Monthly*, *American Painter*, *Printing Impressions*, and *Packaging Printing & Converting*, among others.

Cullen Communications, a public relations firm she founded in 1992, provides public relations programs for clients in the graphic arts, paper, and ephemera industries. In addition, Cullen gives presentations and seminars on innovative ways to push the creative edge in design using a variety of substrates.

LISA L. CYR is an illustrator, designer, writer, and national lecturer. Her clients include advertising agencies, corporations, and publishers. She speaks actively at universities, professional organizations, and industry conferences across the United States about successful promotional strategies, marketing opportunities, and entrepreneurial endeavors for designers and illustrators. In addition to her speaking engagements, Cyr writes for many industry trade publications, including *Communication Arts*, *Step Inside Design*, *How*, *I.D.*, and *Applied Arts*, to name a few. Her articles range from revealing issues that face the industry to featuring top talent in the design and illustration business. Cyr is a graduate of the Massachusetts College of Art (BFA) and Syracuse University (MA). Her creative work has been exhibited both nationally and internationally and in the permanent collection of the Museum of American Illustration. Cyr is an artist member of the Society of Illustrators, New York City, and the Illustrators Partnership of America. She works in partnership with her husband, Christopher Short, a three-dimensional graphic illustrator and animator.

LISA HICKEY is founder and CEO of Velocity Inc., a Boston, Massachusetts, advertising and brand engineering firm. She has been creating innovative, memorable, and brand-defining advertising for nearly twenty years. Her work has been recognized with the industry's highest honors, including awards from Clio, Cannes, Hatch, NEBA, the London Show, *Communication Arts*, and has been included in Marquis' Who's Who in the world. She teaches at Massachusetts College of Art and Emerson College and is also a published poet.